crochet
COLLECTION

A LEISURE ARTS PUBLICATION
PRESENTED BY OXMOOR HOUSE

EDITORIAL STAFF

Editor-in-Chief: Anne Van Wagner Childs
Executive Director: Sandra Graham Case
Executive Editor: Susan Frantz Wiles
Publications Director: Carla Bentley
Creative Art Director: Gloria Bearden
Production Art Director: Melinda Stout

PRODUCTION
Managing Editor: Cathy Hardy
Senior Editor: Teri Sargent
Editorial Assistant: Sarah J. Green

EDITORIAL
Associate Editor: Linda L. Trimble
Senior Editorial Writer: Terri Leming Davidson
Editorial Writer: Darla Burdette Kelsay
Editorial Associate: Tammi Williamson Bradley
Copy Editor: Laura Lee Weland

ART
Book/Magazine Art Director: Diane M. Ghegan
Senior Production Artist: M. Katherine Yancey
Assistant Production Artists: Hubrith Esters and
    Brent Jones
Photography Stylists: Laura Bushmiaer, Sondra Daniel,
    Rhonda Hestir, and Christina Tiano

BUSINESS STAFF

Publisher: Steve Patterson
Controller: Tom Siebenmorgen
Retail Sales Director: Richard Tignor
Retail Marketing Director: Pam Stebbins
Retail Customer Services Director: Margaret Sweetin
Marketing Manager: Russ Barnett
Executive Director of Marketing and Circulation:
    Guy A. Crossley
Fulfillment Manager: Byron L. Taylor
Print Production Manager: Laura Lockhart
Print Production Coordinator: Nancy Reddick Lister

Library of Congress Catalog Number: 94-76793
Hardcover ISBN 0-942237-46-3
Softcover ISBN 0-942237-55-2

crochet
COLLECTION

Whether elegant or whimsical, hand-crocheted accessories make delightful touches for your home and your wardrobe. In Crochet Collection, we've gathered every type of project you could ever want and arranged them in seven wonderful groups, including one-of-a-kind gifts and cozy afghans.

Delicate doilies and fun kitchen magnets are just a few of the decorative accents we feature in All Through the House. To highlight special days, Hooked on Holidays provides an assortment of seasonal centerpieces and festive trims. You'll be enchanted by our selection of adorable outfits and accessories for baby in the Rock-A-Bye Collection. Peek into our Fashion Corner to find winter warmers and lacy frills, or discover the perfect present for any occasion in Gifts for All. When you're in the mood to make something fanciful, you'll love the playful patterns in Just for Fun. And no collection of crochet would be complete without the glorious assortment of throws we feature in Wrapped Up in Afghans.

Our clear instructions, helpful diagrams, and useful stitching tips make all of these designs easy to crochet for beginners and experts. And for those occasions when you're short on time, we've identified each of the "quick" projects. You're going to love having this handy treasury of crochet designs at your fingertips!

Anne Childs

LEISURE ARTS, INC.
LITTLE ROCK, ARKANSAS

table of contents

all through the house.......6

wrapped up in afghans ..26

gifts for all......................44

just for fun 60

all through the house

A touch of crochet in a room is often all it takes to create a warm, homey feeling. This delightful collection makes it easy to sprinkle handmade accessories all through your house, whether you want to add a little romance to the bedroom or spruce up the kitchen!

THE LIVING ROOM

Doilies with old-fashioned styling bring charm and grace to the living room. Crocheted with bedspread weight cotton thread, this pretty pair is made using the same pattern. The larger doily is created simply by adding a border of floral motifs to the smaller doily and then finishing it with a scalloped edging. Gathered with a satin ribbon, our lacy lampshade cover can be custom fitted to bring timeless appeal to any lamp.

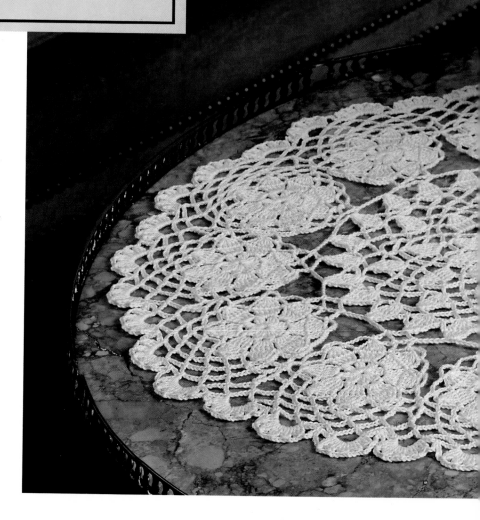

DAINTY LAMPSHADE COVER

Finished Size: The instructions are adjustable. Photographed Lampshade measures 15" around top edge, 25½" around bottom edge and 6¼" high.

MATERIALS

Bedspread Weight Cotton Thread (size 10), approximately 370 yards

Note: Thread amount given is for a Lampshade 15" x 25½" x 6¼".

Steel crochet hook, size 6 (1.80 mm) **or** size needed for gauge

¼" Ribbon - approximately 2 yards

GAUGE: (2 dc, ch 3, 2 dc) 7 times and 12 rows = 4"

TOP BORDER

Ch 6; join with slip st to form a ring.

Row 1 (Right side)**:** Slip st in ring; ch 3, (2 dc, ch 2, 3 dc) in ring.

Note: Loop a short piece of thread around any stitch to mark last row as **right** side.

Row 2: Ch 4 **(counts as first tr, now and throughout)**, turn; (3 dc, ch 2, 3 dc) in next ch-2 sp, tr in top of beginning ch-3: 6 dc.

Row 3: Ch 4, turn; (3 dc, ch 2, 3 dc) in next ch-2 sp, tr in last tr.

Repeat Row 3 until piece measures same as the distance around **top** of shade plus approximately 2", ending by working a **wrong** side row.

Joining Row: Ch 4, turn; being careful not to twist Border, slip st in third ch of beginning ch-3 on Row 1 and in next 2 chs, slip st in beginning ch-6 ring and in ch-2 sp on last row, slip st in next 3 dc and in next tr on last row, ch 4, slip st in last dc on Row 1; do **not** finish off.

BODY

Rnd 1 (Eyelet rnd)**:** With **right** side facing and working in end of rows, slip st in first row, ch 5, (dc in next row, ch 2) around; join with slip st to third ch of beginning ch-5.

Rnd 2: Ch 5, (dc in next dc, ch 2) around; join with slip st to third ch of beginning ch-5.

Rnd 3: Slip st in first ch-2 sp, ch 3 **(counts as first dc, now and throughout)**, (dc, ch 3, 2 dc) in same sp, (2 dc, ch 3, 2 dc) in next ch-2 sp and in each ch-2 sp around; join with slip st to first dc.

Rnds 4-6: Slip st in next dc and in next ch-3 sp, ch 3, (dc, ch 3, 2 dc) in same sp, (2 dc, ch 3, 2 dc) in next ch-3 sp and in each ch-3 sp around; join with slip st to first dc.

Rnd 7: Ch 8, (skip next ch-3 sp and next 2 dc, tr in sp **before** next dc, ch 4) around; join with slip st to fourth ch of beginning ch-8.

Rnd 8: Slip st in first ch-4 sp, ch 3, (dc, ch 3, 2 dc) in same sp, (2 dc, ch 3, 2 dc) in next ch-4 sp and in each ch-4 sp around; join with slip st to first dc.

Repeat Rnds 4-8 until piece measures desired length, ending by working Rnd 6.

Edging: Slip st in next dc and in next ch-3 sp, ch 3, 9 dc in same sp, ch 3, (10 dc in next ch-3 sp, ch 3) around; join with slip st to first dc, finish off.

FINISHING

See Washing and Blocking, page 140.

Weave ribbon through Eyelet rnd. Pull ribbon to gather cover around top of shade. Tie ribbon ends in a bow to secure cover to shade.

FLORAL DOILY SET

Finished Size: Large - approximately 18" in diameter
Small - approximately 10" in diameter

MATERIALS

Bedspread Weight Cotton Thread (size 10), approximately:
Large - 345 yards
Small - 100 yards
Steel crochet hook, size 6 (1. 80 mm) **or** size needed for gauge

GAUGE: Rnds 1-3 = 2¾"

PATTERN STITCHES

BEGINNING 3-TR CLUSTER

Ch 3, ★ YO twice, insert hook in sp indicated, YO and pull up a loop, (YO and draw through 2 loops on hook) twice; repeat from ★ once **more**, YO and draw through all 3 loops on hook *(Figs. 10a & b, page 134)*.

3-TR CLUSTER

★ YO twice, insert hook in sp indicated, YO and pull up a loop, (YO and draw through 2 loops on hook) twice; repeat from ★ 2 times **more**, YO and draw through all 4 loops on hook.

BEGINNING 5-TR CLUSTER (uses first 5 tr)

Ch 3, ★ YO twice, insert hook in **next** tr, YO and pull up a loop, (YO and draw through 2 loops on hook) twice; repeat from ★ 3 times **more**, YO and draw through all 5 loops on hook *(Figs. 11a & b, page 134)*.

5-TR CLUSTER (uses next 5 tr)

★ YO twice, insert hook in **next** tr, YO and pull up a loop, (YO and draw through 2 loops on hook) twice; repeat from ★ 4 times **more**, YO and draw through all 6 loops on hook.

DECREASE (uses next 2 loops)

★ YO 3 times, insert hook in **next** loop, YO and pull up a loop, (YO and draw through 2 loops on hook) 3 times; repeat from ★ once **more**, YO and draw through all 3 loops on hook.

LARGE DOILY

CENTER

Ch 7; join with slip st to form a ring.

Rnd 1 (Right side): Work beginning 3-tr Cluster in ring, ch 3, (work 3-tr Cluster in ring, ch 3) 7 times; join with slip st to top of beginning Cluster: 8 Clusters.

Note: Loop a short piece of thread around any stitch to mark last round as **right** side.

Rnd 2: Slip st in first ch-3 sp, ch 4 **(counts as first tr, now and throughout)**, 4 tr in same sp, ch 2, (5 tr in next ch-3 sp, ch 2) around; join with slip st to first tr: 40 tr.

Rnd 3: Work beginning 5-tr Cluster, ch 5, sc in next ch-2 sp, ch 5, ★ work 5-tr Cluster, ch 5, sc in next ch-2 sp, ch 5; repeat from ★ around; join with slip st to top of beginning Cluster: 8 Clusters.

Rnd 4: Slip st in first loop, ch 1, sc in same loop, ch 6, (sc in next loop, ch 6) around; join with slip st to first sc: 16 loops.

Rnd 5: Slip st in first loop, ch 4, 4 tr in same loop, ch 6, sc in next loop, ch 6, ★ 5 tr in next loop, ch 6, sc in next loop, ch 6; repeat from ★ around; join with slip st to first tr: 8 tr groups.

Rnd 6: Work beginning 5-tr Cluster, ch 6, (sc in next loop, ch 6) twice, ★ work 5-tr Cluster, ch 6, (sc in next loop, ch 6) twice; repeat from ★ around; join with slip st to top of beginning Cluster: 24 loops.

Rnd 7: Slip st in first loop, ch 1, sc in same loop, ch 7, (sc in next loop, ch 7) around; join with slip st to first sc.

Rnd 8: Slip st in first loop, ch 1, sc in same loop, ch 3, 5 tr in next sc, ch 3, sc in next loop, ★ (ch 7, sc in next loop) twice, ch 3, 5 tr in next sc, ch 3, sc in next loop; repeat from ★ around to last loop, ch 7, sc in last loop, ch 3, tr in first sc to form last loop: 16 loops and 16 ch-3 sps.

Rnd 9: Ch 1, sc in same loop, ch 9, work 5-tr Cluster, ch 9, ★ skip next ch-3 sp, (sc in next loop, ch 9) twice, work 5-tr Cluster, ch 9; repeat from ★ around to last ch-3 sp, skip last ch-3 sp, sc in next loop, ch 5, tr in first sc to form last loop: 8 Clusters.

Rnd 10: Ch 1, sc in same loop, ch 9, (sc in next loop, ch 9) around; join with slip st to first sc: 24 loops.

Rnd 11: Ch 4, 4 tr in same st, ch 3, sc in next loop, ch 3, ★ 5 tr in next sc, ch 3, sc in next loop, ch 3; repeat from ★ around; join with slip st to first tr: 24 tr groups.

Rnd 12: Work beginning 5-tr Cluster, ch 9, (work 5-tr Cluster, ch 9) around; join with slip st to top of beginning Cluster, finish off: 24 Clusters.

BORDER

First Flower

Rnds 1-3: Work same as Center.

Rnd 4: Slip st in first loop, ch 1, sc in same loop, (ch 6, sc in next loop) 14 times, ch 3; with **wrong** sides together, slip st in any loop on Rnd 12 of **Center**, ch 3, sc in next loop on **Flower**, ch 3, slip st in next loop on **Center**, ch 3; join with slip st to first sc, finish off.

Additional 11 Flowers

Rnds 1-3: Work same as Center.

Rnd 4: Slip st in first loop, ch 1, sc in same loop, (ch 6, sc in next loop) 14 times, ch 3; with **wrong** sides together, slip st in next loop on Rnd 12 of **Center**, ch 3, sc in next loop on **Flower**, ch 3, slip st in next loop on **Center**, ch 3; join with slip st to first sc, finish off.

EDGING

Rnd 1: With **right** side facing, join thread with slip st in tenth loop from joining on any Flower; ch 1, sc in same loop, ch 7, sc in next loop, ★ sc in fourth loop from joining on next Flower, (ch 7, sc in next loop) 7 times; repeat from ★ 10 times **more**, sc in fourth loop from joining on first Flower, (ch 7, sc in next loop) 5 times, ch 3, tr in first sc to form last loop: 84 loops.

Rnd 2: Ch 1, sc in same loop, ch 8, decrease, ★ ch 8, (sc in next loop, ch 8) 5 times, decrease; repeat from ★ around, (ch 8, sc in next loop) 4 times, ch 4, tr in first sc to form last loop: 72 loops.

Rnds 3 and 4: Ch 1, sc in same loop, (ch 8, sc in next loop) around, ch 4, tr in first sc to form last loop.

Rnd 5: Ch 1, sc in same loop, ch 5, work 3-tr Cluster in next loop, (ch 3, work 3-tr Cluster) 4 times in same loop, ch 5, ★ sc in next loop, ch 5, work 3-tr Cluster in next loop, (ch 3, work 3-tr Cluster) 4 times in same loop, ch 5; repeat from ★ around; join with slip st to first sc, finish off.

See Washing and Blocking, page 140.

SMALL DOILY

Rnds 1-12: Work same as Center of Large Doily; do **not** finish off.

Rnd 13: Slip st in first 2 chs, ch 1, (sc, ch 3, work 3-tr Cluster, ch 3, sc) in same loop, (ch 3, work 3-tr Cluster) 5 times in next loop, ch 3, ★ (sc, ch 3, work 3-tr Cluster, ch 3, sc) in next loop, (ch 3, work 3-tr Cluster) 5 times in next loop, ch 3; repeat from ★ around; join with slip st to first sc, finish off.

See Washing and Blocking, page 140.

FOR THE BEDROOM

*P*retty crocheted accents add feminine allure to the bedroom. (Below) Worked in motifs, the floral dresser scarf features an elegant filet border edged with picots. A pair of filet crochet potpourri holders filled with your favorite scent furnishes the room with fragrance. (Opposite) Abloom with a delicate rose motif, our filet crochet pillow makes a sweet accent piece. A plush throw rug, worked using three strands of worsted weight yarn, enhances the romantic theme.

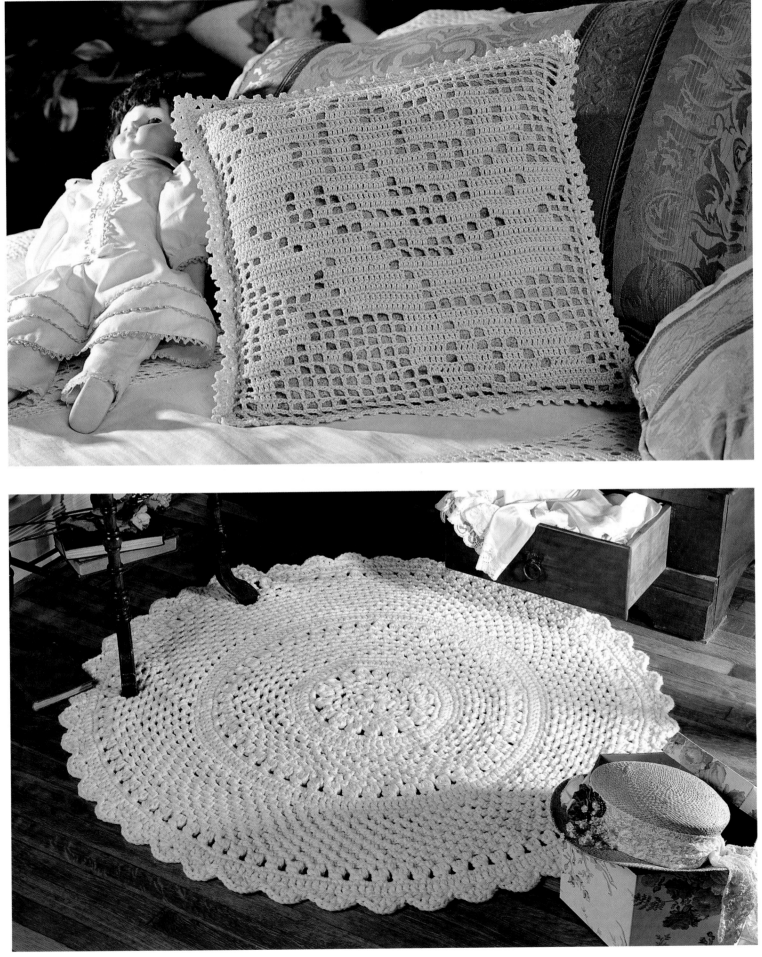

11

DELICATE DRESSER SCARF

Finished Size: Approximately 13" x 22"

MATERIALS

Bedspread Weight Cotton Thread (size 10),
 approximately 480 yards
Steel crochet hook, size 9 (1.40 mm) **or** size needed
 for gauge

GAUGE: Each Square = 4¹/₂"

PATTERN STITCHES

BEGINNING CLUSTER

Ch 4, ★ YO twice, insert hook in st indicated, YO and pull up a
loop, (YO and draw through 2 loops on hook) twice; repeat
from ★ 2 times **more**, YO and draw through all 4 loops on
hook *(Figs. 10a & b, page 134)*.

CLUSTER

★ YO twice, insert hook in ch indicated, YO and pull up a loop,
(YO and draw through 2 loops on hook) twice; repeat from ★
3 times **more**, YO and draw through all 5 loops on hook.

PICOT

Ch 4, slip st in third ch from hook.

PICOT SHELL

(2 Dc, work Picot, ch 1, 2 dc) in st indicated.

FIRST SQUARE

Ch 6; join with slip st to form a ring.

Rnd 1 (Right side)**:** Ch 1, 16 sc in ring; join with slip st to
first sc.

Note: Loop a short piece of thread around any stitch to mark
last round as **right** side.

Rnd 2: Ch 1, sc in same st, (ch 3, skip next sc, sc in next sc)
around to last sc, ch 1, skip last sc, hdc in first sc to form
last sp: 8 sps.

Rnd 3: Work beginning Cluster in same st, (ch 7, work Cluster
in center ch of next ch-3) around; ch 3, tr in top of beginning
Cluster to form last loop: 8 Clusters.

Rnd 4: Ch 1, (sc, ch 7) twice in same st and in center ch of
each loop around; join with slip st to first sc: 16 loops.

Rnd 5: Slip st in first loop, ch 3 **(counts as first dc, now
and throughout)**, (3 dc, ch 3, 4 dc) in same loop, ch 1, (sc,
ch 3, sc) in center ch of next loop, ch 1, ★ (4 dc, ch 3, 4 dc)
in next loop, ch 1, (sc, ch 3, sc) in center ch of next loop, ch 1;
repeat from ★ around; join with slip st to first dc.

Rnd 6: Slip st in next 3 dc and in next 2 chs, ch 1, sc in same
st, ch 16, skip next ch-3 sp, sc in center ch of next ch-3, ch 10,
skip next ch-3 sp, ★ sc in center ch of next ch-3, ch 16, skip
next ch-3 sp, sc in center ch of next ch-3, ch 10, skip next
ch-3 sp; repeat from ★ around; join with slip st to first sc:
8 loops.

Rnd 7: Ch 1, sc in same st, (8 sc, ch 3, 8 sc) in next loop, sc in
next sc, 11 sc in next loop, ★ sc in next sc, (8 sc, ch 3, 8 sc)
in next loop, sc in next sc, 11 sc in next loop; repeat from ★
around; join with slip st to first sc: 29 sc **each** side.

Rnd 8: Ch 5, (skip next 2 sc, dc in next sc, ch 2) twice, skip
next 2 sc, (dc, ch 6, dc) in next ch-3 sp, ch 2, ★ (skip next
2 sc, dc in next sc, ch 2) 9 times, skip next 2 sc, (dc, ch 6, dc)
in next ch-3 sp, ch 2; repeat from ★ 2 times **more**, skip next
2 sc, (dc in next sc, ch 2, skip next 2 sc) 6 times; join with
slip st to third ch of beginning ch-5: 44 sps.

Rnd 9: Ch 3, (dc, work Picot, ch 1, 2 dc) in same st, ch 1, skip
next dc, work Picot Shell in next dc, ch 1, skip next dc, dc in
next 3 chs, ch 13, dc in next 3 chs, ch 1, ★ (skip next dc, work
Picot Shell in next dc, ch 1) 5 times, skip next dc, dc in next
3 chs, ch 13, dc in next 3 chs, ch 1; repeat from ★ 2 times
more, (skip next dc, work Picot Shell in next dc, ch 1) 3 times,
skip next dc; join with slip st to first dc, finish off.

NEXT 7 SQUARES

Work same as First Square through Rnd 8.
Work One-sided or Two-sided Joining to form 2 vertical strips of
4 Squares each.

ONE-SIDED JOINING

Rnd 9: Ch 3, (dc, work Picot, ch 1, 2 dc) in same st, ch 1, skip
next dc, work Picot Shell in next dc, ch 1, skip next dc, dc in
next 3 chs, ★ ch 13, dc in next 3 chs, ch 1, (skip next dc, work
Picot Shell in next dc, ch 1) 5 times, skip next dc, dc in next
3 chs; repeat from ★ once **more**, ch 6, with **right** side of
previous Square facing, slip st in center ch of corner loop,
ch 6, dc in next 3 chs on **new Square**, ch 1, † skip next dc,
2 dc in next dc, ch 2, slip st in next Picot on **previous Square**,
ch 1, slip st in ch before slip st, ch 1, 2 dc in same dc on
new Square, ch 1 †, repeat from † to † 4 times **more**, skip
next dc, dc in next 3 chs, ch 6, slip st in center ch of corner
loop on **previous Square**, ch 6, dc in next 3 chs on
new Square, ch 1, skip next dc, (work Picot Shell in next dc,
ch 1, skip next dc) 3 times; join with slip st to first dc,
finish off.

TWO-SIDED JOINING

Rnd 9: Ch 3, (dc, work Picot, ch 1, 2 dc) in same st, ch 1, skip next dc, work Picot Shell in next dc, ch 1, skip next dc, dc in next 3 chs, ch 13, dc in next 3 chs, ch 1, (skip next dc, work Picot Shell in next dc, ch 1) 5 times, skip next dc, dc in next 3 chs, ch 6, with **right** side of **previous Square** facing, slip st in center ch of corner loop, ch 6, dc in next 3 chs on **new Square**, ch 1, ★ † skip next dc, 2 dc in next dc, ch 2, slip st in next Picot on **previous Square**, ch 1, slip st in ch before slip st, ch 1, 2 dc in same dc on **new Square**, ch 1 †, repeat from † to † 4 times **more**, skip next dc, dc in next 3 chs, ch 6, slip st in center ch of corner loop on **previous Square**, ch 6, dc in next 3 chs on **new Square**, ch 1; repeat from ★ once **more**, skip next dc, (work Picot Shell in next dc, ch 1, skip next dc) 3 times; join with slip st to first dc, finish off.

BORDER

Rnd 1: With **right** side facing, join thread with slip st in top right corner loop of long edge; ★ (sc, ch 2, sc) in corner loop, ch 10, sc in next Picot, (ch 5, sc in next Picot) 4 times, ch 10, † dc in next joining (between Squares), ch 10, sc in next Picot, (ch 5, sc in next Picot) 4 times, ch 10 †, repeat from † to † 2 times **more**, (sc, ch 2, sc) in next corner loop, ch 10, sc in next Picot, (ch 5, sc in next Picot) 4 times, ch 10, repeat from † to † once; repeat from ★ once **more**; join with slip st to first sc.
Rnd 2: Ch 3, (2 dc, ch 5, 2 dc) in next corner ch-2 sp, dc in next sc, 11 dc in next loop, dc in next sc, (5 dc in next loop, dc in next sc) 4 times, † (11 dc in next loop, dc in next st) twice, (5 dc in next loop, dc in next sc) 4 times †, repeat from † to † 2 times **more**, 11 dc in next loop, ★ dc in next sc, (2 dc, ch 5, 2 dc) in next corner ch-2 sp, dc in next sc, 11 dc in next loop, dc in next sc, (5 dc in next loop, dc in next sc) 4 times, repeat from † to † across to last loop before corner, 11 dc in next loop; repeat from ★ around; join with slip st to first dc: 596 dc.
Rnd 3: Ch 5, skip next 2 dc, ★ † dc in next corner loop, ch 2, (dc, ch 5, dc) in center ch of same loop, ch 2, dc in same loop, ch 2, skip next 2 dc †, (dc in next dc, ch 2, skip next 2 dc) across to next corner loop; repeat from ★ 2 times **more**, then repeat from † to † once, (dc in next dc, ch 2, skip next 2 dc) across; join with slip st to third ch of beginning ch-5: 212 sps.
Rnds 4-8: Ch 5, ★ (dc in next dc, ch 2) across to next corner loop, (dc, ch 5, dc) in corner loop, ch 2; repeat from ★ 3 times **more**, (dc in next dc, ch 2) across; join with slip st to third ch of beginning ch-5.

Rnd 9: Ch 6, (sc, ch 3, sc) in next dc, ch 3, ★ † dc in next dc, ch 3, (sc, ch 3, sc) in next dc, ch 3 †, repeat from † to † across to next corner loop, (dc, ch 5, dc) in next corner loop, ch 3, (sc, ch 3, sc) in next dc, ch 3; repeat from ★ 3 times **more**, then repeat from † to † across; join with slip st to third ch of beginning ch-6.
Rnd 10: Ch 3, (dc, work Picot, ch 1, 2 dc) in same st, ★ (ch 1, work Picot Shell in next dc) across to next corner loop, sc in corner loop, work Picot Shell in next dc; repeat from ★ 3 times **more**, ch 1, (work Picot Shell in next dc, ch 1) across; join with slip st to first dc, finish off.

See Washing and Blocking, page 140.

SIMPLE POTPOURRI HOLDERS

Finished Size: Small Holder - approximately
3¹/₂" in diameter x 2" high
Large Holder - approximately
5" in diameter x 2" high

MATERIALS

Bedspread Weight Cotton Thread (size 10), approximately:
Small Holder - 55 yards
Large Holder - 70 yards
Steel crochet hook, size 6 (1.80 mm) **or** size needed for gauge
Starching materials: Commercial fabric stiffener, plastic wrap, resealable plastic bag, terry towel, paper towels, and stainless steel pins

GAUGE: Rnds 1-4 = 2¹/₂"

BOTTOM

Ch 6; join with slip st to form a ring.
Rnd 1 (Right side)**:** Ch 3 **(counts as first dc, now and throughout)**, 23 dc in ring; join with slip st to first dc: 24 dc.
Rnd 2: Ch 4 **(counts as first dc plus ch 1, now and throughout)**, (dc in next dc, ch 1) around; join with slip st to first dc: 24 ch-1 sps.
Rnd 3: Ch 5, (dc in next dc, ch 2) around; join with slip st to third ch of beginning ch-5.
Rnd 4: Ch 4, dc in first ch-2 sp, ch 1, ★ dc in next dc, ch 1, dc in next ch-2 sp, ch 1; repeat from ★ around; join with slip st to first dc: 48 ch-1 sps.
Rnd 5: Ch 4, (dc in next dc, ch 1) around; join with slip st to first dc.

Continued on page 24.

HEIRLOOM ROSE PILLOW

Finished Size: Approximately 13½" square
including Edging

MATERIALS

Crochet Cotton Thread (size 5), approximately:
495 yards
Steel crochet hook, size 3 (2.10 mm) **or** size needed
for gauge
12" Purchased pillow form **or**
½ yard 44/45" wide fabric and polyester stuffing

GAUGE: 28 dc and 12 rows = 4"

BASIC CHART STITCHES

BEGINNING SPACE

Ch 5 (counts as first dc plus ch 2), turn; dc in next dc.

SPACE OVER SPACE

Ch 2, dc in next dc.

SPACE OVER BLOCK

Ch 2, skip next 2 dc, dc in next dc.

BLOCK OVER SPACE

2 Dc in next ch-2 sp, dc in next dc.

BLOCK OVER BLOCK

Dc in next 3 dc.

PLACEMENT DIAGRAM

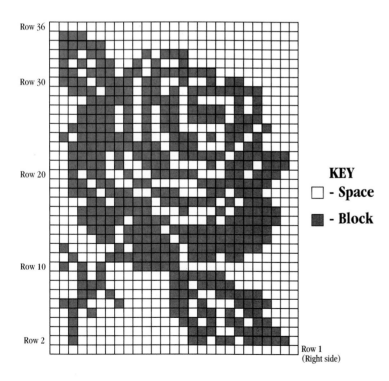

KEY

☐ - Space

■ - Block

Row 36
Row 30
Row 20
Row 10
Row 2
Row 1 (Right side)

**On right side rows, follow Chart from right to left;
on wrong side rows, follow Chart from left to right.**

BACK

Ch 84 **loosely**.

Row 1 (Right side)**:** Dc in fourth ch from hook and in each ch
across: 82 sts.

Note: Loop a short piece of thread around any stitch to mark
last row as **right** side.

Rows 2-36: Ch 3 **(counts as first dc, now and
throughout)**, turn; dc in next dc and in each st across.
Finish off.

FRONT

Ch 86 **loosely**.

Row 1 (Right side)**:** Dc in eighth ch from hook, (ch 2, skip
next 2 chs, dc in next ch) across: 27 sps.

Note: Mark last row as **right** side.

Row 2: Work Beginning Space, work Space over Space, work
Block over Space, continue to follow Chart across.

Rows 3-36: Follow Chart; do **not** finish off.

PATTERN STITCH

SHELL

(2 Dc, ch 3, slip st in third ch from hook, dc) in sc indicated.

FINISHING

Make pillow form, if desired, page 140.

EDGING

Rnd 1 (Joining rnd)**:** Ch 1, turn; holding Front and Back with
wrong sides together, Front facing and working through **both**
pieces, 2 sc in first dc, sc in each ch and in each dc across to
last dc, 3 sc in last dc; work 80 sc evenly spaced across end of
rows; working in free loops and in skipped chs of beginning
ch *(Fig. 21b, page 138)*, 3 sc in first ch, sc in each ch across
to last sp, sc in next 2 chs, 3 sc in next ch; working across
Front **only**, work 80 sc evenly spaced across end of rows, sc in
same st as first sc; join with slip st to first sc: 332 sc.

Rnd 2: Ch 3, dc in same st, ch 3, slip st in third ch from hook,
(dc, ch 1, dc) in same st, ch 3, slip st in third ch from hook,
ch 1, work Shell in same st, skip next 3 sc, work Shell in next
sc, (skip next 2 sc, work Shell in next sc) across to within 3 sc
of next corner sc, skip next 3 sc, ★ work (Shell, ch 1, dc, ch 3,
slip st in third ch from hook, ch 1, Shell) in corner sc, skip
next 3 sc, work Shell in next sc, (skip next 2 sc, work Shell in
next sc) across to within 3 sc of next corner sc, skip next 3 sc;
repeat from ★ 2 times **more**; join with slip st to first dc,
finish off.

Insert Pillow form, then sew remaining seam.

LACY THROW RUG

Finished Size: Approximately 48" in diameter

MATERIALS

Worsted Weight Yarn, approximately:
34 ounces, (970 grams, 2,235 yards)
Crochet hook, size P (10.00 mm) **or** size needed for gauge

Note: Rug is worked holding 3 strands of yarn together.

GAUGE: Rnd 1 = 3½"

PATTERN STITCHES

BEGINNING CLUSTER

Ch 2, ★ YO, insert hook in same sp, YO and pull up a loop, YO and draw through 2 loops on hook; repeat from ★ once **more**, YO and draw through all 3 loops on hook *(Figs. 10a & b, page 134)*.

CLUSTER

★ YO, insert hook in sp indicated, YO and pull up a loop, YO and draw through 2 loops on hook; repeat from ★ 2 times **more**, YO and draw through all 4 loops on hook.

Ch 5; join with slip st to form a ring.

Rnd 1 (Right side)**:** Work beginning Cluster in ring, ch 3, (work Cluster, ch 3) 5 times in ring; join with slip st to top of beginning Cluster: 6 Clusters.

Rnd 2: Ch 1, sc in same st, ch 3, sc in next ch-3 sp, ★ ch 3, sc in next Cluster, ch 3, sc in next ch-3 sp; repeat from ★ around, ch 1, hdc in first sc to form last sp: 12 sps.

Rnd 3: Ch 1, sc in same sp, (ch 3, sc in next ch-3 sp) around, ch 1, hdc in first sc to form last sp.

Rnd 4: Ch 1, sc in same sp, ch 3, (sc, ch 3) twice in next ch-3 sp, ★ sc in next ch-3 sp, ch 3, (sc, ch 3) twice in next ch-3 sp; repeat from ★ around; join with slip st to first sc: 18 ch-3 sps.

Rnd 5: Slip st in first ch-3 sp, work beginning Cluster, ch 2, (work Cluster in next ch-3 sp, ch 2) around; join with slip st to top of beginning Cluster: 18 Clusters.

Rnd 6: Ch 1, sc in same st, 3 sc in next ch-2 sp, (sc in next Cluster, 3 sc in next ch-2 sp) around; join with slip st to first sc: 72 sc.

Rnd 7: Ch 3 **(counts as first dc, now and throughout)**, dc in next sc and in each sc around; join with slip st to first dc: 72 dc.

Rnd 8: Ch 1, sc in same st and in next 10 dc, 2 sc in next dc, (sc in next 11 dc, 2 sc in next dc) around; join with slip st to first sc: 78 sc.

Rnd 9: Ch 1, sc in same st, (ch 3, skip next sc, sc in next sc) around to last sc, ch 1, skip last sc, hdc in first sc to form last sp: 39 sps.

Rnds 10-12: Ch 1, sc in same sp, (ch 3, sc in next ch-3 sp) around, ch 1, hdc in first sc to form last sp.

Rnd 13: Ch 1, sc in same sp, ch 3, sc in next ch-3 sp, (ch 3, sc) twice in next ch-3 sp, ★ (ch 3, sc in next ch-3 sp) twice, (ch 3, sc) twice in next ch-3 sp; repeat from ★ around, ch 1, hdc in first sc to form last sp: 52 sps.

Rnd 14: Ch 1, sc in same sp, (ch 3, sc in next ch-3 sp) around, ch 1, hdc in first sc to form last sp.

Rnd 15: Ch 1, sc in same sp, ch 3, (sc in next ch-3 sp, ch 3) around; join with slip st to first sc.

Rnd 16: Repeat Rnd 5: 52 Clusters.

Rnd 17: Ch 1, sc in same st, 2 sc in next ch-2 sp, (sc in next Cluster, 2 sc in next ch-2 sp) around; join with slip st to first sc: 156 sc.

Rnd 18: Ch 3, dc in next sc and in each sc around; join with slip st to first dc: 156 dc.

Rnd 19: Ch 1, sc in same st and in each dc around; join with slip st to first sc: 156 sc.

Rnd 20: Repeat Rnd 9: 78 sps.

Rnds 21-26: Ch 1, sc in same sp, (ch 3, sc in next ch-3 sp) around, ch 1, hdc in first sc to form last sp.

Rnd 27: Ch 1, sc in same sp, (ch 3, sc in next ch-3 sp) 4 times, (ch 3, sc) twice in next ch-3 sp, ★ (ch 3, sc in next ch-3 sp) 5 times, (ch 3, sc) twice in next ch-3 sp; repeat from ★ around, ch 1, hdc in first sc to form last sp: 91 sps.

Rnds 28-30: Ch 1, sc in same sp, (ch 3, sc in next ch-3 sp) around, ch 1, hdc in first sc to form last sp.

Rnd 31: Work beginning Cluster, ch 2, (work Cluster in next ch-3 sp, ch 2) around; join with slip st to top of beginning Cluster: 91 Clusters.

Rnds 32 and 33: Repeat Rnds 17 and 18: 273 dc.

Rnd 34: Ch 1, sc in same st, skip next 3 dc, dc in next dc, (ch 1, dc) 4 times in same dc, skip next 3 dc, sc in next dc, skip next 3 dc, dc in next dc, (ch 1, dc) 4 times in same dc, skip next 2 dc, ★ sc in next dc, skip next 2 dc, dc in next dc, (ch 1, dc) 4 times in same dc, skip next 2 dc; repeat from ★ around; join with slip st to first sc, finish off: 45 scallops.

FOR THE BATH

*T*he bathroom is a great spot to show off your crochet skills, whether you want to add a country touch or lacy elegance. (Below) Fanciful edgings bring instant beauty to a towel set. A pretty picot edging graces the bath and hand towels, while the washcloth is given a simpler finish. Trimmed with ruffles and ribbons, a tissue box cover crocheted with worsted weight yarn completes the collection. (Opposite) Fashioned in fabrics that coordinate with your bathroom decor, a rag rug is pretty as well as functional! Worked with a jumbo hook, this oval rug and matching wastebasket cover get their soft look from a harmony of pastel fabrics.

17

Quick BERIBBONED TISSUE BOX COVER

MATERIALS

Worsted Weight Yarn, approximately:
  2 ounces, (60 grams, 130 yards)
Crochet hook, size G (4.00 mm) **or** size needed for gauge
Yarn needle
Sewing needle and thread
3/8" Ribbon - 2¼ yards

GAUGE: 12 dc and 6 rows = 3"

SIDES

Ch 72 **loosely**; begin careful not to twist ch, join with slip st to form a ring.

Rnd 1: Ch 1, sc in back ridge of each ch around *(Fig. 2a, page 133)*; join with slip st to first sc: 72 sc.

Rnd 2 (Right side): Ch 3 **(counts as first dc, now and throughout)**, turn; dc in next sc and in each sc around; join with slip st to first dc: 72 dc.

Note: Loop a short piece of yarn around any stitch to mark last round as **right** side.

Rnd 3: Ch 4, turn; skip next dc, (dc in next dc, ch 1, skip next dc) around; join with slip st to third ch of beginning ch-4: 36 ch-1 sps.

Rnd 4: Ch 3, turn; dc in next ch-1 sp, (dc in next dc, dc in next ch-1 sp) around; join with slip st to first dc: 72 dc.

Rnds 5-10: Repeat Rnds 3 and 4, 3 times.

Rnd 11: Ch 1, turn; sc in each dc around; join with slip st to first sc, finish off.

TOP

Ch 20 **loosely**.

Row 1: Dc in fourth ch from hook and in each ch across: 18 dc.

Rows 2-4: Ch 3, turn; dc in next dc and in each dc across.

Row 5 (Right side): Ch 3, turn; dc in next 3 dc, ch 10 **loosely** (opening), skip next 10 dc, dc in last 4 dc.

Note: Mark last row as **right** side.

Row 6: Ch 3, turn; dc in next 3 dc, dc in back ridge of next 10 chs, dc in last 4 dc: 18 dc.

Rows 7-9: Ch 3, turn; dc in next dc and in each dc across. Finish off.

Sew Top to inside loops of Sides.

BOTTOM EDGING

With **right** side facing and working in Back Loops Only of beginning ch *(Fig. 20, page 138)*, join yarn with slip st in first ch; ch 2, 2 dc in same st, skip next 2 chs, ★ (slip st, ch 2, 2 dc) in next ch, skip next 2 chs; repeat from ★ around; join with slip st to first st, finish off.

TOP EDGING

With **right** side facing, bottom edge toward you, and working in free loops on Rnd 11 of Sides *(Fig. 21a, page 138)*, join yarn with slip st in any corner sc; ch 2, dc in same st, skip next 2 sc, ★ (slip st, ch 2, dc) in next sc, skip next 2 sc; repeat from ★ around; join with slip st to first st, finish off.

Weave ribbon through ch-1 sps, alternating sps on each rnd; tack in place.

ELEGANT TOWEL SET

Finished Size: Washcloth Edging - approximately 3/4" wide
Towel Edgings - approximately 1¼" wide

MATERIALS

Bedspread Weight Cotton Thread (size 10), approximately:
  Washcloth - 70 yards (cloth measuring 12¼" wide)
  Hand towel - 35 yards (towel measuring 16" wide)
  Bath towel - 60 yards (towel measuring 27" wide)
Washcloth
Hand towel
Bath towel
Steel crochet hook, size 7 (1.65 mm) **or** size needed for gauge
Straight pins
Sewing needle and thread

GAUGE: 18 sc = 2"

PATTERN STITCHES

PICOT SHELL
(2 Dc, ch 3, slip st in last dc made, 2 dc) in sp indicated.

PUFF STITCH
★ YO, insert hook in sp indicated, YO and pull up a loop even with loop on hook; repeat from ★ 3 times **more** (9 loops on hook) *(Fig. 12, page 134)*, YO and draw through 8 loops on hook, YO and draw through 2 loops on hook.

WASHCLOTH EDGING
BEGINNING CHAIN

Make a chain to fit around the washcloth. The number of chains must be divisible by 4. For example, as in ours, 440 (4 goes into 440, 110 times evenly). Count the chains and adjust as needed. Being careful not to twist ch, join with slip st to form a ring.

Rnd 1 (Right side): Ch 1, sc in same st, ★ ch 5, skip next 3 chs, sc in next ch; repeat from ★ around to last 3 chs, ch 2, skip last 3 chs, dc in first sc to form last loop.

Note: Loop a short piece of thread around any stitch to mark last round as **right** side.

Rnd 2: Ch 1, sc in same loop, ch 3, (sc in next loop, ch 3) around; join with slip st to first sc.

Row 3: Work Picot Shell in next ch-3 sp, (slip st in next sc, work Picot Shell in next ch-3 sp) around; join with slip st to first st; finish off.

TOWEL EDGING
BEGINNING CHAIN

Make a chain to fit across the width of the towel plus 5 chs. The number of chains must be divisible by 3 with 2 left over. For example, as in our hand towel, 149 (3 goes into 149, 49 times with 2 left over). Count the chains and adjust as needed.

Row 1: Dc in eighth ch from hook, (ch 2, skip next 2 chs, dc in next ch) across.

Row 2 (Right side): Ch 3, turn; (work Puff St in next ch-2 sp, ch 2) across to last sp, (work Puff St, dc) in last sp.

Note: Loop a short piece of thread around any stitch to mark last row as **right** side.

Row 3: Ch 1, turn; skip first dc, sc in next Puff St, (ch 3, sc in next Puff St) across to last st, leave remaining st unworked.

Row 4: Turn; slip st in first sc, (work Picot Shell in next ch-3 sp, slip st in next sc) across; finish off.

FINISHING

See Washing and Blocking, page 140.
Using photo as a guide, pin Edging along hem on right side. Hand sew to secure.

SOFT RAG RUG AND WASTEBASKET COVER

Quick

Finished Size: Rug - approximately 25" x 40"
Wastebasket Cover - approximately 8" in diameter x 13" high

MATERIALS

100% Cotton Fabric, 44/45" wide, approximately:
Color A (Pink Floral):
Rug - 7 yards
Cover - 2 yards
Color B (Blue Checked):
Rug - 4 yards
Cover - 3 1/2 yards
Color C (Dark Pink):
Rug - 3 yards
Cover - 2 yards
Color D (Blue Floral):
Rug - 2 yards
Cover - 2 yards
Crochet hook, size Q (15.00 mm)
10 Quart wastebasket - 9" diameter x 11" tall
Bias tape maker (optional)

Prepare fabric and tear into 1 1/2" strips *(see Preparing Fabric Strips and Joining Fabric Strips, page 139)*.

PATTERN STITCH
PICOT
Ch 4, sc in top of last st made.

RUG
GAUGE: Foundation Row through Rnd 2 = 6" x 21"

With Color A, ch 18 **loosely**.
Foundation Row (Right side): Sc in second ch from hook and in each ch across: 17 sc.
Note: Begin working in rounds.
Rnd 1: Ch 3 **(counts as first dc, now and throughout)**, 8 dc in end of row; working in free loops of beginning ch *(Fig. 21b, page 138)*, skip first ch, dc in next 15 chs, skip last ch; working across Foundation Row, 9 dc in first sc, dc in next sc and in each sc across to last sc, skip last sc; join with slip st to first dc: 48 dc.

Continued on page 24.

IN THE KITCHEN

*S*pice up your kitchen with cute crocheted creations! With this trio of vegetables (shown below and opposite), *you can produce a colorful crop of carrots, peas, and radishes to hold messages on the refrigerator, dress up market baskets, or garnish a window wreath. Worked holding two strands of red yarn, a hexagon-shaped pot holder (below) coordinates beautifully with our plaid valance (opposite), which is fashioned from kitchen towels and finished with a lovely picot edging.*

20

21

VERSATILE VEGGIES

MATERIALS

Worsted Weight Yarn, approximately:

Pea Pod

Light Green - 4 yards **each**

Dark Green - 4 yards **each**

Radish

White - 2 yards **each**

Red - 3 yards **each**

Green - 3 yards **each**

Carrot

Orange - 6 yards **each**

Green - 3 yards **each**

Crochet Hook, size E (3.50 mm)

Yarn needle

Radish: Polyester stuffing

Note: Gauge is not important. Pieces can be smaller or larger without changing the overall effect.

PEA POD

PEAS

With Light Green, ch 4 **loosely**; being careful not to twist ch, join with slip st to form a ring.

Rnd 1 (Right side): 2 Sc in each ch around; do **not** join, place marker *(see Markers, page 138)*: 8 sc.

Rnd 2: Sc in each sc around.

Rnd 3: (Skip next sc, sc in next sc) around: 4 sc.

Rnd 4: 2 Sc in each sc around: 8 sc.

Rnds 5-8: Repeat Rnds 2-4 once, then repeat Rnd 2 once **more** changing to Dark Green in last sc on Rnd 8 *(Fig. 22a, page 138)*; do **not** finish off: 8 sc.

POD

Row 1: ★ Slip st in Front Loop Only of next sc *(Fig. 20, page 138)*, ch 11 **loosely**, working in back ridge *(Fig. 2a, page 133)*, slip st in second ch from hook, sc in next ch, hdc in next ch, dc in last 7 chs, slip st in same st at base of ch-11 (half of Pod made); repeat from ★ once **more**, sc in **both** loops of last 6 sc.

Note: Begin working in rounds.

Rnd 1: Sc in next 2 free loops behind Pod *(Fig. 21a, page 138)*, (skip next sc, sc in next sc) 3 times: 5 sc.

Rnd 2: Sc in next sc, (skip next sc, sc in next sc) twice; slip st in next sc, finish off.

RADISH

With White and leaving a 2" end, ch 4 **loosely**; being careful not to twist ch, join with slip st to form a ring.

Rnd 1: 2 Sc in each ch around; do **not** join, place marker *(see Markers, page 138)*: 8 sc.

Note: Loop a short piece of yarn around the **back** of any stitch to mark **right** side *(Figs. 19a & b, page 137)*.

Rnd 2: 2 Sc in each sc around: 16 sc.

Rnd 3: Sc in each sc around changing to Red in last sc *(Fig. 22a, page 138)*.

Rnds 4-6: Sc in each sc around.

Rnd 7: (Skip next sc, sc in next sc) around changing to Green in last sc: 8 sc.

Stuff **lightly**.

Rnd 8: Skip next sc, sc in next sc, (skip next 2 sc, sc in next sc) twice: 3 sc.

Rnd 9: ★ Slip st in next sc, ch 3 **loosely**, (sc, hdc, dc, tr, dc, hdc, sc) in second ch from hook, sc in next ch (Leaf made); repeat from ★ around; join with slip st to first st, finish off: 3 Leaves.

CARROT

With Orange and leaving a 2" end, ch 4 **loosely**; being careful not to twist ch, join with slip st to form a ring.

Rnd 1: 2 Sc in same ch, sc in each ch around; do **not** join, place marker *(see Markers, page 138)*: 5 sc.

Note: Loop a short piece of yarn around the **back** of any stitch to mark **right** side *(Figs. 19a & b, page 137)*.

Rnds 2-8: 2 Sc in next sc, sc in each sc around: 12 sc.

Rnd 9: Sc in each sc around.

Rnd 10: (Skip next sc, sc in next sc) around changing to Green in last sc *(Fig. 22a, page 138)*: 6 sc.

Rnds 11 and 12: Work Loop St in each st around *(Figs. 17a-c, page 136)*.

Rnd 13: (Skip next st, work Loop St in next st) around; join with slip st to first st, finish off.

FINISHING

Pea Pod: Using photo as a guide for placement, sew center edges of Pod together and tack Peas to Pod.

Radish and Carrot: Separate plies of beginning end; tie plies in a knot close to Veggie and trim ends.

Veggies can be added to a wreath or used as magnets.

CHARMING VALANCE EDGING

Finished Size: Approximately 1⅝" wide

MATERIALS

Bedspread Weight Cotton Thread (size 10),
  approximately 160 yards for an Edging 55"
Steel crochet hook, size 7 (1.65 mm) **or** size needed
  for gauge
Cotton dish towels
Straight pins
Sewing needle and thread

GAUGE: 18 dc = 2"

VALANCE

Make Valance desired size. We made ours out of 3 dish towels sewn together to measure 55" wide x 15" high, including casing.

BEGINNING CHAIN

Make a chain the length of the Valance plus 1". The number of chains must be divisible by 8 with 4 left over. For example, as in ours, 492 (8 goes into 492, 61 times with 4 left over). Count the chains and adjust as needed.

PATTERN STITCH
CLUSTER

★ YO, insert hook in dc indicated, YO and pull up a loop, YO and draw through 2 loops on hook; repeat from ★ once **more**, YO and draw through all 3 loops on hook *(Figs. 10a & b, page 134)*.

EDGING

Row 1 (Right side): Dc in back ridge of fourth ch from hook and in each ch across *(Fig. 2a, page 133)*.
Note: Loop a short piece of thread around any stitch to mark last row as **right** side.
Row 2: Ch 3, turn; dc in next dc, (ch 2, skip next 2 sts, dc in next 2 sts) across.
Row 3: Ch 1, turn; sc in first 2 dc, (2 sc in next ch-2 sp, sc in next 2 sts) across.
Row 4: Ch 5, turn; skip first 2 sc, slip st in next sc, hdc in next sc, slip st in next sc, ch 5, ★ skip next sc, slip st in next sc, hdc in next sc, slip st in next sc, ch 5; repeat from ★ across to last sc, slip st in last sc.
Row 5: Turn; slip st in first loop, ch 1, 3 sc in same loop, (5 dc in next loop, 3 sc in next loop) across.
Row 6: Ch 1, turn; sc in first 2 sc, skip next 2 sts, dc in next dc, ch 1, 3 dc in next dc, ch 1, dc in next dc, ★ skip next 2 sts, sc in next sc, skip next 2 sts, dc in next dc, ch 1, 3 dc in next dc, ch 1, dc in next dc; repeat from ★ across to last 4 sts, skip next 2 sts, sc in last 2 sc.

Row 7: Ch 1, turn; sc in first sc, (sc, ch 3, sc) in next sc, ★ sc in next dc and in next ch-1 sp, (slip st, ch 2, dc, work Cluster) in next dc, ch 1, work Cluster in next dc, ch 3, slip st in top of last Cluster made, ch 1, (work Cluster, dc, ch 2, slip st) in next dc, sc in next ch-1 sp and in next dc, (sc, ch 3, sc) in next sc; repeat from ★ across to last sc, sc in last sc; finish off.

FINISHING

See Washing and Blocking, page 140.
Using photo as a guide, pin Edging along hem on right side. Hand sew to secure.

Quick RED-HOT POT HOLDER

Finished Size: Approximately 8" (from side to side)

MATERIALS

Worsted Weight Yarn, approximately:
  1¼ ounces, (35 grams, 70 yards)
Crochet hook, size K (6.50 mm) **or** size needed for gauge

GAUGE: Rnds 1 and 2 = 2½" (from side to side)

Rnd 1 (Right side): Holding 2 strands of yarn together, ch 4, 11 dc in fourth ch from hook; join with slip st to top of beginning ch: 12 sts.
Rnd 2: Ch 1, sc in same st, (sc, tr) in next dc, ★ sc in next dc, (sc, tr) in next dc; repeat from ★ around; join with slip st to first sc: 18 sts.
Rnd 3: Ch 3 **(counts as first dc, now and throughout)**, dc in next sc, 3 dc in next tr, (dc in next 2 sc, 3 dc in next tr) around; join with slip st to first dc: 30 dc.
Rnd 4: Ch 1, sc in same st, 2 sc in next dc, sc in next dc, (sc, tr) in next dc, ★ sc in next 2 dc, 2 sc in next dc, sc in next dc, (sc, tr) in next dc; repeat from ★ around to last dc, sc in last dc; join with slip st to first sc: 42 sts.
Rnd 5: Ch 3, dc in next 4 sc, 3 dc in next tr, (dc in next 6 sc, 3 dc in next tr) around to last sc, dc in last sc; join with slip st to first dc: 54 dc.
Rnd 6: Ch 1, sc in same st and in next 4 dc, 2 sc in next dc, tr in next dc, 2 sc in next dc, ★ sc in next 6 dc, 2 sc in next dc, tr in next dc, 2 sc in next dc; repeat from ★ around to last dc, sc in last dc; join with slip st to first sc: 66 sts.
Rnd 7: Ch 1, sc in same st and in next 6 sc, (3 sc in next tr, sc in next 10 sc) 5 times, 2 sc in next tr, ch 8, sc in same st and in last 3 sc; join with slip st to first sc, finish off.

SIMPLE POTPOURRI HOLDERS

Continued from page 13.

Small Holder Only - Rnd 6: Ch 3, dc in each ch-1 sp and in each dc around; join with slip st to first dc: 96 dc.

Large Holder Only

Rnds 6 and 7: Ch 5, (dc in next dc, ch 2) around; join with slip st to third ch of beginning ch-5.

Rnd 8: Ch 3, 2 dc in first ch-2 sp, (dc in next dc, 2 dc in next ch-2 sp) around; join with slip st to first dc: 144 dc.

SIDES

Rnd 1: Ch 1, sc in Back Loop Only of each dc around *(Fig. 20, page 138)*; join with slip st to both loops of first sc.

Rnd 2: Ch 4, skip next sc, working in both loops, (dc in next sc, ch 1, skip next sc) twice, dc in next 3 sc, ★ ch 1, (skip next sc, dc in next sc, ch 1) 6 times, skip next sc, dc in next 3 sc; repeat from ★ around to last 7 sc, ch 1, skip next sc, (dc in next sc, ch 1, skip next sc) 3 times; join with slip st to first dc.

Rnd 3: Ch 4, dc in next dc, ch 1, dc in next dc, dc in next ch-1 sp and in next dc, ch 3, skip next dc, dc in next dc and in next ch-1 sp, ★ dc in next dc, (ch 1, dc in next dc) 5 times, dc in next ch-1 sp and in next dc, ch 3, skip next dc, dc in next dc and in next ch-1 sp; repeat from ★ around to last 3 dc, (dc in next dc, ch 1) 3 times; join with slip st to first dc.

Rnd 4: Ch 4, dc in next dc, dc in next ch-1 sp and in next dc, ch 3, sc in next ch-3 sp, ch 3, skip next 2 dc, dc in next dc and in next ch-1 sp, ★ dc in next dc, (ch 1, dc in next dc) 3 times, dc in next ch-1 sp and in next dc, ch 3, sc in next ch-3 sp, ch 3, skip next 2 dc, dc in next dc and in next ch-1 sp; repeat from ★ around to last 2 dc, (dc in next dc, ch 1) twice; join with slip st to first dc.

Rnd 5: Ch 3, dc in next ch-1 sp and in next dc, ch 4, sc in next ch-3 sp, sc in next sc and in next ch-3 sp, ch 4, skip next 2 dc, dc in next dc, dc in next ch-1 sp and in next dc, ch 1, ★ dc in next dc, dc in next ch-1 sp and in next dc, ch 4, sc in next ch-3 sp, sc in next sc and in next ch-3 sp, ch 4, skip next 2 dc, dc in next dc, dc in next ch-1 sp and in next dc, ch 1; repeat from ★ around; join with slip st to first dc.

Rnd 6: Ch 4, skip next dc, dc in next dc, 2 dc in next ch-4 sp, ch 3, skip next sc, sc in next sc, ch 3, 2 dc in next ch-4 sp, dc in next dc, ch 1, ★ skip next dc, (dc in next dc, ch 1) twice, skip next dc, dc in next dc, 2 dc in next ch-4 sp, ch 3, skip next sc, sc in next sc, ch 3, 2 dc in next ch-4 sp, dc in next dc, ch 1; repeat from ★ around to last 2 dc, skip next dc, dc in last dc, ch 1; join with slip st to first dc.

Rnd 7: Ch 4, dc in next dc, ch 1, skip next dc, dc in next dc, 2 dc in next ch-3 sp, ch 1, 2 dc in next ch-3 sp, dc in next dc, ch 1, ★ skip next dc, (dc in next dc, ch 1) 4 times, skip next dc, dc in next dc, 2 dc in next ch-3 sp, ch 1, 2 dc in next ch-3 sp, dc in next dc, ch 1; repeat from ★ around to last 3 dc, skip next dc, (dc in next dc, ch 1) twice; join with slip st to first dc.

Rnd 8: Ch 4, (dc in next dc, ch 1) twice, skip next dc, dc in next dc, dc in next ch-1 sp and in next dc, ch 1, ★ skip next dc, (dc in next dc, ch 1) 6 times, skip next dc, dc in next dc, dc in next ch-1 sp and in next dc, ch 1; repeat from ★ around to last 4 dc, skip next dc, (dc in next dc, ch 1) 3 times; join with slip st to first dc.

Rnd 9: Ch 1, sc in same st and in each ch-1 sp and each dc around; join with slip st to first sc.

Rnd 10: Ch 1, work Reverse sc in each sc around *(Figs. 14a-d, page 135)*; join with slip st to first st, finish off.

See Starching and Blocking, page 142.

SOFT RAG RUG AND WASTEBASKET COVER

Continued from page 19.

Rnd 2: Ch 1, 2 sc in same st and in next dc, † work (sc, Picot, sc) in next dc, 2 sc in next dc, work (2 sc, Picot, 2 sc) in next dc, 2 sc in next dc, work (sc, Picot, sc) in next dc, 2 sc in each of next 2 dc, work Picot, (sc in next 5 sc, work Picot) 3 times †, 2 sc in each of next 2 dc, repeat from † to † once; join with slip st to first sc changing to Color B *(Fig. 22b, page 138)*: 14 Picots.

Rnd 3: Ch 3, skip next 3 sc, dc in next sc, † (ch 4, skip next Picot, dc in next sc, skip next 3 sc, dc in next sc) 3 times †, (ch 3, skip next Picot, dc in next sc, skip next 3 sc, dc in next sc) 4 times, repeat from † to † once, ch 3, (skip next Picot, dc in next sc, skip next 3 sc, dc in next sc, ch 3) 3 times; join with slip st to first dc changing to Color C: 14 sps.

Rnd 4: Ch 1, working **around** sts and sps on Rnd 3, ★ sc in center sc on Rnd 2, dc in next Picot on Rnd 2, (ch 1, dc) 3 times in same sp; repeat from ★ around; join with slip st to first sc changing to Color D: 14 4-dc groups.

Rnd 5: Ch 3, 3 dc in same st, † work Picot, skip next dc, sc in next dc, 3 sc in next ch-1 sp, sc in next dc, work Picot, (5 dc in next sc, work Picot, skip next dc, sc in next dc, 3 sc in next ch-1 sp, sc in next dc, work Picot) twice, 4 dc in next sc, skip next ch-1 sp, work (sc, Picot, sc) in next ch-1 sp, [3 dc in next sc, skip next ch-1 sp, work (sc, Picot, sc) in next ch-1 sp] 3 times †, 4 dc in next sc, repeat from † to † once; join with slip st to first dc changing to Color C: 20 Picots.

Rnd 6: Ch 3, skip next 2 dc, dc in next dc, † (ch 4, skip next Picot, dc in next st, skip next 3 sts, dc in next st) 6 times †, (ch 3, skip next Picot, dc in next st, skip next 3 sts, dc in next st) 4 times, repeat from † to † once, (ch 3, skip next Picot, dc in next st, skip next 3 sts, dc in next st) 3 times, ch 3; join with slip st to first dc changing to Color B: 20 sps.

Rnd 7: Ch 1, working **around** sts and sps on Rnd 6, sc in next dc on Rnd 5, dc in next Picot on Rnd 5, (ch 1, dc) 3 times in same sp, ★ sc in center st on Rnd 5, dc in next Picot on Rnd 5, (ch 1, dc) 3 times in same sp; repeat from ★ around; join with slip st to first sc changing to Color A: 20 4-dc groups.

Rnd 8: Ch 3, 2 dc in same st, skip next ch-1 sp, 2 sc in next ch-1 sp, (5 dc in next sc, skip next ch-1 sp, 2 sc in next ch-1 sp) 5 times, (3 dc in next sc, skip next ch-1 sp, 2 sc in next ch-1 sp) 5 times, (5 dc in next sc, skip next ch-1 sp, 2 sc in next sc) 5 times, (3 dc in next sc, skip next ch-1 sp, 2 sc in next ch-1 sp) 4 times; join with slip st to first dc: 80 dc.

Rnd 9: Ch 1, sc in each st around; join with slip st to first sc changing to Color B: 120 sc.

Rnd 10: Ch 1, sc in each sc around; join with slip st to Back Loop Only of first sc changing to Color C *(Fig. 20, page 138)*.

Rnd 11: Ch 1, sc in Back Loop Only of each sc around; join with slip st to first sc changing to Color B.

Rnd 12: Ch 1, sc in Back Loop Only of each sc around; join with slip st to first sc changing to Color A.

Rnd 13: Ch 1, sc in Back Loop Only of each sc around; join with slip st to both loops of first sc.

Rnd 14: Working in both loops, skip next 2 sc, 5 dc in next sc, skip next 2 sc, ★ slip st in next sc, skip next 2 sc, 5 dc in next sc, skip next 2 sc; repeat from ★ around; join with slip st to first st, finish off: 20 5-dc groups.

WASTEBASKET COVER

GAUGE: Rnds 1-3 of Bottom = 8"

BOTTOM

Rnd 1 (Right side): With Color B, ch 2, 8 sc in second ch from hook; join with slip st to first sc.

Rnd 2: Ch 3 **(counts as first dc, now and throughout)**, 2 dc in same st, 3 dc in next sc and in each sc around; join with slip st to first sc: 24 dc.

Rnd 3: Ch 3, 2 dc in next dc, (dc in next dc, 2 dc in next dc) around; join with slip st to Back Loop Only of first dc *(Fig. 20, page 138)*, do **not** finish off: 36 dc.

SIDES

Rnd 1: Ch 1, sc in Back Loop Only of each dc around; join with slip st to both loops of first sc.

Rnd 2: Ch 3, dc in both loops of next sc and in each sc around; join with slip st to first dc.

Rnd 3: Ch 1, sc in each dc around; join with slip st to first sc.

Rnd 4: Ch 3, dc in next sc and in each sc around; join with slip st to first dc.

Rnd 5: Ch 1, pull up a loop in first 2 sts, YO and draw through all 3 loops on hook, sc in next dc and in each dc around; join with slip st to first st: 35 sts.

Rnd 6: Ch 3, dc in next sc and in each sc around; join with slip st to first dc changing to Color D *(Fig. 22b, page 138)*.

Rnd 7: Ch 1, sc in same st and in next 4 dc, work Picot, (sc in next 5 dc, work Picot) around; join with slip st to first sc changing to Color C: 7 Picots.

Rnd 8: Ch 3, skip next 3 sc, dc in next sc, ch 3, skip next Picot, ★ dc in next sc, skip next 3 sc, dc in next sc, ch 3, skip next Picot; repeat from ★ around; join with slip st to first dc changing to Color B: 7 ch-3 sps.

Rnd 9: Ch 1, working **around** sts and sps on Rnd 8, ★ sc in center sc on Rnd 7, dc in next Picot on Rnd 7, (ch 1, dc) 3 times in same sp; repeat from ★ around; join with slip st to first sc changing to Color A: 7 4-dc groups.

Rnd 10: Ch 3, 2 dc in same st, skip next ch-1 sp, 2 sc in next ch-1 sp, ★ 3 dc in next sc, skip next ch-1 sp, 2 sc in next ch-1 sp; repeat from ★ around; join with slip st to first dc changing to Color C: 21 dc.

Rnd 11: Ch 1, sc in each st around; join with slip st to first sc changing to Color B: 35 sc.

Rnd 12: Ch 1, 2 sc in same st, sc in next sc and in each sc around; join with slip st to first sc changing to Color A: 36 sc.

Rnd 13: Skip next 2 sc, 5 dc in next sc, skip next 2 sc, ★ slip st in next sc, skip next 2 sc, 5 dc in next sc, skip next 2 sc; repeat from ★ around; join with slip st to first st, finish off: 6 5-dc groups.

Slide wastebasket into Cover.

wrapped up in afghans

Handmade afghans are labors of love and warm reflections of your personal tastes. This charming collection has something to please everyone — from traditional patterns to new looks that will soon become favorites as well. You'll even find some afghans designed especially for quilt lovers. All the warmth and charm of crochet is yours when you wrap yourself in afghans!

Quick SHADES OF AUTUMN

These afghans make it fast and easy to fill your den with the rich shades of evergreens and falling leaves. Deceptively simple slant stitches create the intricate texture of the solid throw, and long stitches in vivid tones give the striped afghan an autumn air. Worked holding two strands of yarn, the heavy throws are guaranteed to keep you toasty.

SLANT STITCH AFGHAN

Finished Size: Approximately 48" x 62"

MATERIALS
Worsted Weight Yarn, approximately:
   61 ounces, (1,730 grams, 4,185 yards)
Crochet hook, size N (9.00 mm) **or** size needed for gauge

Note: Entire Afghan is worked holding 2 strands of yarn
together.

GAUGE: In pattern, 8 sts = 3" and 4 rows = 3¹/₂"

Note: Afghan is worked from side to side.

BODY
Ch 160 **loosely**.
Row 1: Dc in fourth ch from hook and in next 2 chs, work Slant St *(Fig. 16, page 135)*, ★ skip next ch, dc in next 3 chs, work Slant St; repeat from ★ across to last 2 chs, skip next ch, dc in last ch: 39 Slant Sts.

Row 2: Ch 3 **(counts as first dc, now and throughout)**, turn; dc in next 3 sts, work Slant St, ★ skip next dc, dc in next 3 sts, work Slant St; repeat from ★ across to last 2 sts, skip next dc, dc in last st.
Repeat Row 2 until Afghan measures approximately 46" from beginning ch; do **not** finish off.

EDGING
Rnd 1: Ch 1, 2 sc in end of each row across; working in free loops of beginning ch *(Fig. 21b, page 138)*, sc in each ch across; 2 sc in end of each row across; working across last row, sc in each st across; join with slip st to first sc.
Rnd 2: Ch 1, do **not** turn; working from **left** to **right**, hdc in same st, ch 1, skip next sc, ★ work Reverse hdc in next sc *(Figs. 15a-d, page 135)*, ch 1, skip next sc; repeat from ★ around; join with slip st to first hdc, finish off.

LONG STITCH AFGHAN

Finished Size: Approximately 48" x 62"

MATERIALS

Worsted Weight Yarn, approximately:
Color A (Copper) - 21 ounces, (600 grams, 1,440 yards)
Color B (Green) - 21 ounces, (600 grams, 1,440 yards)
Color C (Burgundy) - 20 ounces, (570 grams, 1,370 yards)
Color D (Gold) - 20 ounces, (570 grams, 1,370 yards)
Crochet hook, size N (9.00 mm) **or** size needed for gauge

Note: Entire Afghan is worked holding 2 strands of yarn together.

GAUGE: In pattern, 9 sc = 4" and 16 rows = 5"

COLOR SEQUENCE

4 Rows each Color A *(Fig. 22a, page 138)*, ★ Color B, Color C, Color D, Color A; repeat from ★ throughout.

BODY

With Color A, ch 108 **loosely**.
Row 1: Sc in second ch from hook and in each ch across: 107 sc.
Rows 2-4: Ch 1, turn; sc in each sc across.
Row 5 (Right side)**:** Ch 1, turn; sc in first 2 sc, ★ work Long sc in sc 1 row **below** next sc *(Figs. 5a & b, page 133)*, work Long sc in sc 2 rows **below** next sc, work Long sc in sc 3 rows **below** next sc, work Long sc in sc 2 rows **below** next sc, work Long sc in sc 1 row **below** next sc, sc in next 2 sc; repeat from ★ across.
Note: Loop a short piece of yarn around any stitch to mark last row as **right** side.
Rows 6-8: Ch 1, turn; sc in each sc across.
Rows 9-196: Repeat Rows 5-8, 47 times.
Finish off.

EDGING

With **right** side facing, join Color B with slip st in any st; ch 1, sc evenly around working 3 sc in each corner; join with slip st to first sc, finish off.

Quick RAINBOW SOFT

Waves of color as pretty as a rainbow make this afghan a sweet addition to your bedroom. Quick to crochet with worsted weight yarn, the ripple pattern gets its fancy look from simple V-stitches.

Finished Size: Approximately 49" x 63"

MATERIALS

Worsted Weight Yarn, approximately:
MC (White) - 9 ounces, (260 grams, 595 yards)
Color A (Pink) - 5 ounces, (140 grams, 330 yards)
Color B (Peach) - 5 ounces, (140 grams, 330 yards)
Color C (Yellow) - 5 ounces, (140 grams, 330 yards)
Color D (Green) - 5 ounces, (140 grams, 330 yards)
Color E (Blue) - 5 ounces, (140 grams, 330 yards)
Color F (Lavender) - 5 ounces, (140 grams, 330 yards)
Crochet hook, size I (5.50 mm) **or** size needed for gauge

GAUGE: In pattern, 14 sts (point to point) = 3$\frac{1}{2}$"
8 rows = 5$\frac{1}{4}$"

PATTERN STITCHES

DECREASE (uses next 3 sts or sps)
★ YO, insert hook in **next** st or sp, YO and pull up a loop, YO and draw through 2 loops on hook; repeat from ★ 2 times **more**, YO and draw through all 4 loops on hook.
V-ST
(Dc, ch 1, dc) in st indicated.

COLOR SEQUENCE

★ † 3 Rows Color A *(Fig. 22a, page 138)*, 1 row MC, 3 rows Color B, 1 row MC, 3 rows Color C, 1 row MC, 3 rows Color D, 1 row MC, 3 rows Color E, 1 row MC, 3 rows Color F †, 1 row MC; repeat from ★ 2 times **more**, then repeat from † to † once.

BODY

With Color A, ch 199 **loosely**.

Row 1 (Right side)**:** 2 Dc in fourth ch from hook, dc in next 3 chs, decrease twice, dc in next 3 chs, ★ work V-St in next 2 chs, dc in next 3 chs, decrease twice, dc in next 3 chs; repeat from ★ across to last ch, 3 dc in last ch: 26 V-Sts.

Note: Loop a short piece of yarn around any stitch to mark last row as **right** side.

Row 2: Ch 3 **(counts as first dc, now and throughout)**, turn; 2 dc in same st, skip next dc, work V-St in next dc, skip next dc, decrease twice, skip next dc, work V-St in next dc, ★ skip next ch, work V-St in next 2 dc, skip next ch, work V-St in next dc, skip next dc, decrease twice, skip next dc, work V-St in next dc; repeat from ★ across to last 2 sts, skip next dc, 3 dc in last st: 54 V-Sts.

Row 3: Ch 3, turn; 2 dc in same st, dc in next 3 dc, decrease twice, ★ dc in next 2 dc and in next ch-1 sp, work V-St in next 2 dc, dc in next ch-1 sp and in next 2 dc, decrease twice; repeat from ★ across to last 4 dc, dc in next 3 dc, 3 dc in last dc.

Rows 4-95: Repeat Rows 2 and 3, 46 times.

Finish off.

DRESDEN PLATE FAVORITE

Quilt enthusiasts will recognize the colorful motif on this pretty throw — it was inspired by a favorite old pattern, the Dresden Plate. Fashioned in soft country colors, the "plates" are centered in lacy blocks that are pieced together to resemble a quilt.

Finished Size: Approximately 50" x 66"

MATERIALS
Worsted Weight Yarn, approximately:
- MC (Off-White) - 37 ounces, (1,050 grams, 2,160 yards)
- Color A (Light Rose) - 5 ounces, (140 grams, 290 yards)
- Color B (Blue) - 5 ounces, (140 grams, 290 yards)
- Color C (Green) - 5 ounces, (140 grams, 290 yards)
- Color D (Dark Rose) - 5 ounces, (140 grams, 290 yards)
- Color E (Light Blue) - 5 ounces, (140 grams, 290 yards)
- Color F (Rose) - 5 ounces, (140 grams, 290 yards)
- Color G (Peach) - 5 ounces, (140 grams, 290 yards)
- Color H (Dark Blue) - 5 ounces, (140 grams, 290 yards)

Crochet hook, size F (3.75 mm) **or** size needed for gauge
Yarn needle

GAUGE: Each Motif = 8"
18 sc and 16 rows = 4"

MOTIF (Make 48)
CENTER
Rnd 1 (Right side): With MC, ch 2, 8 sc in second ch from hook; join with slip st to first sc.

Note: Loop a short piece of yarn around any stitch to mark last round as **right** side.

Rnd 2: Ch 1, 2 sc in each sc around; join with slip st to first sc changing to Color A *(Fig. 22b, page 138)*: 16 sc.

PETALS
Color Sequence: 8 Rows each Color A *(Fig. 22a, page 138)*, Color B, Color C, Color D, Color E, Color F, Color G, Color H.

Ch 11 **loosely**.
Row 1: Hdc in third ch from hook and in next ch, sc in next 4 chs, slip st in last 3 chs and in same sc as joining: 11 sts.
Note: Work in Back Loops Only throughout Petals *(Fig. 20, page 138)*.
Row 2: Turn; skip first slip st, slip st in next 3 slip sts, sc in next 4 sc, hdc in last 3 sts: 10 sts.
Row 3: Ch 2 **(counts as first hdc, now and throughout)**, turn; hdc in next 2 hdc, sc in next 4 sc, slip st in last 3 slip sts and in **same** sc on Rnd 2 of Center: 11 sts.
Row 4: Turn; skip first slip st, slip st in next 3 slip sts, sc in next 4 sc, hdc in last 3 sts: 10 sts.

Row 5: Ch 2, turn; hdc in next 2 hdc, sc in next 4 sc, slip st in last 3 slip sts and in **next** sc on Rnd 2 of Center: 11 sts.
Rows 6-64: Repeat Rows 2-5, 14 times, then repeat Rows 2-4 once **more**; at end of Row 64, do **not** change color and do **not** finish off.
Joining Row: Turn; with **right** side together and working in Back Loop Only of each st on Row 64 **and** in free loops of beginning ch *(Fig. 21b, page 138)*, slip st in each st across; finish off.

BORDER
Rnd 1: With **right** side facing and working in end of rows, join MC with slip st in last row; ch 1, 3 sc in same row, skip next row, (3 sc in next row, skip next row) around; join with slip st to first sc: 96 sc.
Rnd 2: Ch 4 **(counts as first tr)**, (2 tr, ch 2, 3 tr) in same st, ★ † ch 1, skip next 3 sc, 2 dc in next sc, ch 1, skip next 3 sc, 2 hdc in next sc, ch 1, skip next 3 sc, 2 sc in next sc, ch 1, skip next 3 sc, 2 hdc in next sc, ch 1, skip next 3 sc, 2 dc in next sc, ch 1, skip next 3 sc †, (3 tr, ch 2, 3 tr) in next sc; repeat from ★ 2 times **more**, then repeat from † to † once; join with slip st to first tr: 24 tr.
Rnd 3: Ch 1, sc in same st and in next 2 tr, 3 sc in next corner ch-2 sp, sc in each st and in each ch-1 sp around working 3 sc in each corner ch-2 sp; join with slip st to first sc: 100 sc.
Rnd 4: Ch 1, sc in each sc around, working 3 sc in each corner sc; join with slip st to first sc, finish off: 108 sc.

ASSEMBLY
Using MC, whipstitch Motifs together, forming 6 vertical strips of 8 Motifs each *(Fig. 27b, page 140)*; then whipstitch strips together.

EDGING
Rnd 1: With **right** side facing, join MC with slip st in top right corner sc; ch 1, 3 sc in same st, † work 183 sc evenly spaced across to next corner sc, 3 sc in corner sc, work 243 sc evenly spaced across to next corner sc †, 3 sc in corner sc, repeat from † to † once; join with slip st to first sc: 864 sc.
Rnd 2: Ch 2, ★ † sc in next sc, hdc in next sc, dc in next sc, 3 tr in next sc, dc in next sc †, hdc in next sc; repeat from ★ around to last 5 sc, then repeat from † to † once; join with slip st to top of beginning ch-2, finish off: 144 scallops.

CLASSIC DIAMONDS

Popcorn stitches form a rich pattern of diamonds in this classic throw, which features delicate eyelet borders. Trimmed with a lush fringe, the country-blue wrap has the appearance of joined panels, but it works up easily in one piece.

Finished Size: Approximately 46" x 56"

MATERIALS
Worsted Weight Yarn, approximately:
66 ounces, (1,870 grams, 3,850 yards)
Crochet hook, size G (4.00 mm) **or** size needed for gauge

GAUGE: In pattern, 16 dc and 12 rows = 4"

PATTERN STITCH

POPCORN
5 Dc in next sc, drop loop from hook, insert hook in first dc of 5-dc group, hook dropped loop and draw through, ch 1 to close.

BODY

Ch 181 **loosely.**

Row 1 (Right side): Dc in fourth ch from hook and in each ch across: 179 sts.

Row 2 AND ALL WRONG SIDE ROWS: Ch 1, turn; sc in each st or sp across: 179 sc.

Row 3: Ch 3 **(counts as first dc, now and throughout)**, turn; dc in next 11 sc, work Popcorn, (dc in next 21 sc, work Popcorn) across to last 12 sc, dc in last 12 sc: 8 Popcorns.

Row 5: Ch 3, turn; dc in next 9 sc, work Popcorn, dc in next 3 sc, work Popcorn, ★ dc in next 17 sc, work Popcorn, dc in next 3 sc, work Popcorn; repeat from ★ across to last 10 sc, dc in last 10 sc: 16 Popcorns.

Row 7: Ch 3, turn; (dc in next 7 sc, work Popcorn) twice, ★ dc in next 13 sc, work Popcorn, dc in next 7 sc, work Popcorn; repeat from ★ across to last 8 sc, dc in last 8 sc.

Row 9: Ch 3, turn; dc in next 5 sc, work Popcorn, dc in next 5 sc, ch 1, skip next sc, dc in next 5 sc, work Popcorn, ★ dc in next 9 sc, work Popcorn, dc in next 5 sc, ch 1, skip next sc, dc in next 5 sc, work Popcorn; repeat from ★ across to last 6 sc, dc in last 6 sc.

Row 11: Ch 3, turn; dc in next 3 sc, work Popcorn, dc in next 6 sc, ch 1, skip next sc, dc in next sc, ch 1, skip next sc, dc in next 6 sc, work Popcorn, ★ dc in next 5 sc, work Popcorn, dc in next 6 sc, ch 1, skip next sc, dc in next sc, ch 1, skip next sc, dc in next 6 sc, work Popcorn; repeat from ★ across to last 4 sc, dc in last 4 sc.

Row 13: Repeat Row 9.

Row 15: Repeat Row 7.

Row 17: Repeat Row 5.

Row 19: Repeat Row 3.

Row 21: Ch 3, turn; dc in next sc and in each sc across.

Row 23 (Eyelet row): Ch 3, turn; dc in next sc, (ch 1, skip next sc, dc in next sc) across to last 3 sc, ch 1, skip next sc, dc in last 2 sc: 88 ch-1 sps.

Row 25: Ch 3, turn; dc in next sc and in each sc across.
Repeat Rows 2-25 for pattern until Afghan measures approximately 55", ending by working Row 21; do **not** finish off.

EDGING

Rnd 1: Ch 1, work 221 sc evenly spaced across end of rows; working in free loops of beginning ch **(Fig. 21b, page 138)**, 3 sc in first ch, sc in each ch across to last ch, 3 sc in last ch; work 221 sc evenly spaced across end of rows; 3 sc in first dc, sc in each dc across to last dc, 3 sc in last dc; join with slip st to first sc: 808 sc.

Rnd 2 (Eyelet rnd): Slip st in next sc, ch 4, skip next sc, dc in next sc, ★ (ch 1, skip next sc, dc in next sc) across to next corner sc, ch 3, skip corner sc, dc in next sc; repeat from ★ around to last sc, ch 1, skip last sc; join with slip st to third ch of beginning ch-4, finish off: 404 sps.

Add fringe **(Figs. 28a & b, page 141)**.

GRANNY'S DOGWOOD

Stitched in spring colors, this Granny Square afghan brings to mind the beauty of a dogwood tree in full bloom. The "blossoms" are worked in squares with clusters and double crochet stitches and then whipstitched together.

Finished Size: Approximately 48" x 66"

MATERIALS
Worsted Weight Yarn, approximately:
Color A (Rose) - 18 ounces, (510 grams, 1,235 yards)
Color B (Off-White) - 14 ounces, (400 grams, 960 yards)
Color C (Green) - 11 ounces, (310 grams, 755 yards)
Crochet hook, size J (6.00 mm) **or** size needed for gauge
Yarn needle

GAUGE: One Square = 9"

PATTERN STITCHES

TR CLUSTER
★ YO twice, insert hook in ring, YO and pull up a loop, (YO and draw through 2 loops on hook) twice; repeat from ★ 2 times **more**, YO and draw through all 4 loops on hook *(Figs. 10a & b, page 134)*.

BEGINNING DC CLUSTER
Ch 2, ★ YO, insert hook in same sp, YO and pull up a loop, YO and draw through 2 loops on hook; repeat from ★ once **more**, YO and draw through all 3 loops on hook.

DC CLUSTER
★ YO, insert hook in sp indicated, YO and pull up a loop, YO and draw through 2 loops on hook; repeat from ★ 2 times **more**, YO and draw through all 4 loops on hook.

SQUARE (Make 35)
With Color A, ch 6; join with slip st to form a ring.
Rnd 1 (Right side): Ch 3, ★ YO twice, insert hook in ring, YO and pull up a loop, (YO and draw through 2 loops on hook) twice; repeat from ★ once **more**, YO and draw through all 3 loops on hook, ch 3, (work tr Cluster, ch 3) 7 times; join with slip st to top of beginning tr Cluster, finish off: 8 Clusters.
Note: Loop a short piece of yarn around any stitch to mark last round as **right** side.
Rnd 2: With **right** side facing, join Color B with slip st in any ch-3 sp; work (beginning dc Cluster, ch 3, dc Cluster) in same sp (corner), ch 3, hdc in next ch-3 sp, ch 3, ★ work (dc Cluster, ch 3, dc Cluster) in next ch-3 sp, ch 3, hdc in next ch-3 sp, ch 3; repeat from ★ around; join with slip st to top of beginning dc Cluster, finish off: 8 Clusters.

Rnd 3: With **right** side facing, join Color C with slip st in any corner ch-3 sp; work (beginning dc Cluster, ch 3, dc Cluster) in same sp, ch 3, (work dc Cluster in next ch-3 sp, ch 3) twice, ★ work (dc Cluster, ch 3, dc Cluster) in next corner ch-3 sp, ch 3, (work dc Cluster in next ch-3 sp, ch 3) twice; repeat from ★ around; join with slip st to top of beginning dc Cluster, finish off: 16 Clusters.

Rnd 4: With **right** side facing, join Color A with slip st in any corner ch-3 sp; ch 1, 7 sc in same sp, 4 sc in each of next 3 ch-3 sps, ★ 7 sc in next corner ch-3 sp, 4 sc in each of next 3 ch-3 sps; repeat from ★ around; join with slip st to first sc, finish off: 76 sc.

Rnd 5: With **right** side facing, join Color B with slip st in center sc of any corner 7-sc group; ch 1, sc in same st, ch 3, (skip next 2 sc, sc in next 2 sc, ch 3) 4 times, skip next 2 sc, ★ sc in next sc, ch 3, (skip next 2 sc, sc in next 2 sc, ch 3) 4 times, skip next 2 sc; repeat from ★ around; join with slip st to first sc: 36 sc.

Rnd 6: Slip st in first ch-3 sp, ch 1, (sc, 3 hdc, sc) in same sp and in next 4 ch-3 sps, ch 1, ★ (sc, 3 hdc, sc) in next 5 ch-3 sps, ch 1; repeat from ★ around; join with slip st to first sc, finish off: 60 hdc.

Rnd 7: With **right** side facing, join Color C with slip st in any corner ch-1 sp; ch 3, 4 dc in same sp, ★ † skip next 2 sts, (hdc, sc, hdc) in next hdc, [skip next 4 sts, (hdc, sc, hdc) in next hdc] 4 times, skip next 2 sts †, 5 dc in next corner ch-1 sp; repeat from ★ 2 times **more**, then repeat from † to † once; join with slip st to top of beginning ch-3, finish off: 80 sts.

Rnd 8: With **right** side facing, skip first 2 sts and join Color A with slip st in next dc; ch 2 **(counts as first hdc, now and throughout)**, 2 hdc in same st, ★ sc in next st and in each st across to center dc of next corner 5-dc group, 3 hdc in next dc; repeat from ★ 2 times **more**, sc in next st and in each st across; join with slip st to first hdc: 88 sts.

Rnd 9: Ch 2, 3 hdc in next hdc, ★ hdc in next st and in each st across to center hdc of next corner 3-hdc group, 3 hdc in next hdc; repeat from ★ 2 times **more**, hdc in next st and in each st across; join with slip st to first hdc, finish off: 96 hdc.

ASSEMBLY
Using Color A, whipstitch Squares together, forming 5 vertical strips of 7 Squares each *(Fig. 27a, page 140)*; then whipstitch strips together.

EDGING

Rnd 1: With **right** side facing, join Color C with slip st in center hdc of any corner 3-hdc group; ch 2, 4 hdc in same st, ★ † hdc in next 24 hdc, 2 hdc in joining, (hdc in next 25 hdc, 2 hdc in joining) across to last Square, hdc in next 24 hdc †, 5 hdc in next hdc; repeat from ★ 2 times **more**, then repeat from † to † once; join with slip st to first hdc, finish off: 652 hdc.

Rnd 2: With **right** side facing, join Color B with slip st in center hdc of any corner 5-hdc group; ch 1, 3 sc in same st, sc in next hdc and in each hdc across to center hdc of next corner 5-hdc group, ★ 3 sc in next hdc, sc in next hdc and in each hdc across to center hdc of next corner 5-hdc group; repeat from ★ around; join with slip st to first sc: 660 sc.

Rnd 3: Slip st in next sc, ch 1, sc in same st, ch 3, skip next 2 sc, ★ sc in next sc, ch 3, skip next 2 sc; repeat from ★ around; join with slip st to first sc: 220 ch-3 sps.

Rnd 4: Slip st in next ch-3 sp, ch 1, 4 sc in same sp, ★ 4 sc in each ch-3 sp across to next corner, ch 1; repeat from ★ around; join with slip st to first sc, finish off.

COZY MILE-A-MINUTE

Because this peachy mile-a-minute throw works up so easily, you'll be enjoying its warm comfort long before winter's chill arrives. Simple chain spaces and double crochet stitches create the openwork centers of the strips.

Finished Size: Approximately 49½" x 68"

MATERIALS

Worsted Weight Yarn, approximately:
MC (Cream) - 28 ounces, (800 grams, 1,840 yards)
Color A (Peach) - 9 ounces, (260 grams, 595 yards)
Color B (Dark Peach) - 7 ounces, (200 grams, 460 yards)
Crochet hook, size I (5.50 mm) **or** size needed for gauge
Yarn needle

GAUGE: In pattern, 6 Center rows = 4"
One Strip = 4½" wide

STRIP (Make 11)
CENTER
With Color A, ch 7 **loosely**.

Row 1 (Right side): Dc in fourth ch from hook, ch 1, skip next ch, dc in last 2 chs: 5 sts.

Note: Loop a short piece of yarn around any stitch to mark last row as **right** side and bottom edge.

Row 2: Ch 3 **(counts as first dc, now and throughout)**, turn; dc in next dc, ch 1, dc in last 2 dc: 4 dc.

Rows 3-97: Repeat Row 2.
Finish off.

EDGING
Rnd 1: With **right** side facing and working in end of rows, join MC with slip st in Row 97; ch 3, 4 dc in same sp, † (skip next row, 5 dc in next row) across to last 2 rows, skip next row, 3 dc in next row, place marker around last dc made, 2 dc in same row; 5 dc in ch-1 sp at end †; working in end of rows, 5 dc in first row, repeat from † to † once; join with slip st to first dc, finish off: 100 5-dc groups.

Rnd 2: With **right** side facing, join Color B with sc in first marked dc **(see Joining With Sc, page 138)**; remove marker and place around last sc made; sc in each dc and in each sp **before** 5-dc groups across to marked dc, sc in next dc, remove marker and place around last sc made, sc in each dc and in each sp **before** 5-dc groups around; join with slip st to first sc, finish off.

Rnd 3: With **right** side facing and working in Back Loops Only **(Fig. 20, page 138)**, join MC with slip st in marked sc; ch 2 **(counts as first hdc, now and throughout)**, remove marker and place around last hdc made, hdc in next sc and in each sc across to next marked sc, hdc in marked sc, remove marker and place around last hdc made, hdc in each sc around; join with slip st to first hdc.

Rnd 4: Ch 2, hdc in same st, (hdc in next hdc, 2 hdc in next hdc) 7 times, hdc in each hdc across to marked hdc, 2 hdc in marked hdc, (hdc in next hdc, 2 hdc in next hdc) 7 times, hdc in each hdc across; join with slip st to first hdc, finish off.

ASSEMBLY
Using MC, whipstitch Strips together, placing bottom edges at the same end, matching sts, and always working from the same direction between markers **(Fig. 27b, page 140)**.

VICTORIAN ELEGANCE

This elegant afghan is reminiscent of the fanciful throws found in Victorian homes. Simple crown stitches — formed with a series of chains and single crochet stitches — create the royal texture. Clusters make up the intricate scalloped edging, which is trimmed with satin ribbon.

Finished Size: Approximately 46" x 58"

MATERIALS

Worsted Weight Yarn, approximately:
 37 ounces, (1,050 grams, 2,160 yards)
Crochet hook, size G (4.00 mm) **or** size needed for gauge
3/8" Ribbon - 10 yards
Yarn needle

GAUGE: In pattern, 3 Crown Sts = 6½"
 12 rows = 5¼"

PATTERN STITCHES

CROWN ST
Sc in st indicated, (ch 7, sc) 3 times in same st.

CLUSTER
★ YO, insert hook in sp indicated, YO and pull up a loop, YO and draw through 2 loops on hook; repeat from ★ 2 times **more**, YO and draw through all 4 loops on hook *(Figs. 10a & b, page 134)*.

DECREASE (uses next 2 dc)
★ YO, insert hook in **next** dc, YO and pull up a loop, YO and draw through 2 loops on hook; repeat from ★ once **more**, YO and draw through all 3 loops on hook.

BODY

Ch 157 **loosely**.

Row 1: Work Crown St in twelfth ch from hook, ch 4, skip next 4 chs, dc in next ch, ★ ch 4, skip next 4 chs, work Crown St in next ch, ch 4, skip next 4 chs, dc in next ch; repeat from ★ across: 15 Crown Sts.

Row 2 (Right side): Ch 1, turn; sc in first dc, ch 1, skip next ch-4 sp, sc in next loop, (ch 3, sc in next loop) twice, ch 1, ★ skip next ch-4 sp, sc in next dc, ch 1, skip next ch-4 sp, sc in next loop, (ch 3, sc in next loop) twice, ch 1; repeat from ★ across to last loop, skip next 4 chs, sc in next ch: 61 sc.

Note: Loop a short piece of yarn around any stitch to mark last row as **right** side.

Row 3: Ch 8, turn; (sc, ch 7, sc) in first sc, ch 4, skip next ch-3 sp, dc in next sc, ch 4, ★ skip next sc, work Crown St in next sc, ch 4, skip next ch-3 sp, dc in next sc, ch 4; repeat from ★ across to last 2 sc, skip next sc, (sc, ch 7, sc, ch 3, tr) in last sc: 14 Crown Sts.

Row 4: Ch 1, turn; sc in first tr, ch 3, sc in next loop, ch 1, skip next ch-4 sp, sc in next dc, ch 1, ★ skip next ch-4 sp, sc in next loop, (ch 3, sc in next loop) twice, ch 1, skip next ch-4 sp, sc in next dc, ch 1; repeat from ★ across to last ch-4 sp, skip next ch-4 sp, sc in next loop, ch 3, sc in last loop: 61 sc.

Row 5: Ch 7, turn; skip next sc, work Crown St in next sc, ch 4, skip next ch-3 sp, dc in next sc, ★ ch 4, skip next sc, work Crown St in next sc, ch 4, skip next ch-3 sp, dc in next sc; repeat from ★ across: 15 Crown Sts.

Repeat Rows 2-5 until Afghan measures approximately 46" from beginning ch, ending by working Row 4; do **not** finish off.

EDGING

Rnd 1: Ch 1, work 205 sc evenly spaced across end of rows to next corner loop, work 6 sc in corner loop; working in free loops of beginning ch *(Fig. 21b, page 138)* and in ch-4 sps, work 148 sc evenly spaced across to next corner loop, work 6 sc in corner loop; work 205 sc evenly spaced across end of rows to next corner; working across last row, work 156 sc evenly spaced across; join with slip st to first sc: 726 sc.

Rnd 2 (Eyelet rnd): Turn; slip st in Front Loop Only of next 2 sc *(Fig. 20, page 138)*, ch 5, **turn;** skip next 2 sc, (dc in Back Loop Only of next sc, ch 2, skip next 2 sc) around; join with slip st to third ch of beginning ch-5: 242 ch-2 sps.

Rnd 3: Ch 1, sc in Back Loop Only of each ch and in each dc around; join with slip st to first sc: 726 sc.

Rnd 4: Working in both loops, slip st in next sc, ch 3 **(counts as first dc, now and throughout)**, dc in next sc, ch 5, skip next 3 sc, sc in next sc, (ch 3, skip next 2 sc, sc in next sc) 5 times, ch 5, ★ skip next 4 sc, dc in next 2 sc, ch 5, skip next 4 sc, sc in next sc, (ch 3, skip next 2 sc, sc in next sc) 5 times, ch 5; repeat from ★ around to last 3 sc, skip last 3 sc; join with slip st to first dc: 196 sps.

Rnd 5: Slip st in next dc, ch 3, dc in same st, ch 7, skip next loop, sc in next ch-3 sp, (ch 3, sc in next ch-3 sp) 4 times, ch 7, 2 dc in next dc, ch 1, ★ 2 dc in next dc, ch 7, skip next loop, sc in next ch-3 sp, (ch 3, sc in next ch-3 sp) 4 times, ch 7, 2 dc in next dc, ch 1; repeat from ★ around; join with slip st to first dc.

Rnd 6: Ch 3, dc in next dc, ch 7, sc in next ch-3 sp, (ch 3, sc in next ch-3 sp) 3 times, ch 7, dc in next 2 dc, ch 2, ★ dc in next 2 dc, ch 7, sc in next ch-3 sp, (ch 3, sc in next ch-3 sp) 3 times, ch 7, dc in next 2 dc, ch 2; repeat from ★ around; join with slip st to first dc.

Rnd 7: Ch 3, dc in next dc, ch 7, sc in next ch-3 sp, (ch 3, sc in next ch-3 sp) twice, ch 7, dc in next 2 dc, † ch 2, work Cluster in next ch-2 sp, ch 2, dc in next 2 dc, ch 7, sc in next ch-3 sp, (ch 3, sc in next ch-3 sp) twice, ch 7, dc in next 2 dc †, repeat from † to † across to next corner ch-2 sp, ch 5, work Cluster in corner ch-2 sp, ch 5, ★ dc in next 2 dc, ch 7, sc in next ch-3 sp, (ch 3, sc in next ch-3 sp) twice, ch 7, dc in next 2 dc, repeat from † to † across to next corner ch-2 sp, ch 5,

work Cluster in corner ch-2 sp, ch 5; repeat from ★ around; join with slip st to first dc.

Rnd 8: Ch 3, dc in next dc, ch 7, sc in next ch-3 sp, ch 3, sc in next ch-3 sp, ch 7, dc in next 2 dc, † ch 3, (work Cluster in next ch-2 sp, ch 3) twice, dc in next 2 dc, ch 7, sc in next ch-3 sp, ch 3, sc in next ch-3 sp, ch 7, dc in next 2 dc †, repeat from † to † across to next corner loop, ch 7, (work Cluster in next loop, ch 7) twice, ★ dc in next 2 dc, ch 7, sc in next ch-3 sp, ch 3, sc in next ch-3 sp, ch 7, dc in next 2 dc, repeat from † to † across to next corner loop, ch 7, (work Cluster in next loop, ch 7) twice; repeat from ★ around; join with slip st to first dc.

Rnd 9: Ch 3, dc in next dc, ch 7, sc in next ch-3 sp, ch 7, dc in next 2 dc, † ch 3, (work Cluster in next ch-3 sp, ch 3) 3 times, dc in next 2 dc, ch 7, sc in next ch-3 sp, ch 7, dc in next 2 dc †, repeat from † to † across to next corner loop, ch 5, (work Cluster, ch 5) twice in each of next 3 loops, ★ dc in next 2 dc, ch 7, sc in next ch-3 sp, ch 7, dc in next 2 dc, repeat from † to † across to next corner loop, ch 5, (work Cluster, ch 5) twice in each of next 3 loops; repeat from ★ around; join with slip st to first dc.

Rnd 10: Ch 3, dc in next dc, ch 1, dtr in next sc, ch 1, dc in next 2 dc, † ch 5, (work Cluster in next ch-3 sp, ch 5) 4 times, dc in next 2 dc, ch 1, dtr in next sc, ch 1, dc in next 2 dc †, repeat from † to † across to next corner loop, ch 5, (work Cluster in next loop, ch 5) 7 times, ★ dc in next 2 dc, ch 1, dtr in next sc, ch 1, dc in next 2 dc, repeat from † to † across to next corner loop, ch 5, (work Cluster in next loop, ch 5) 7 times; repeat from ★ around; join with slip st to first dc.

Rnd 11: Ch 2, dc in next dc, dc in next dtr, decrease, † (4 dc, hdc) in next loop, sc in next Cluster, [(hdc, 4 dc, hdc) in next loop, sc in next Cluster] 3 times, (hdc, 4 dc) in next loop, decrease, dc in next dtr, decrease †, repeat from † to † across to next corner loop, (4 dc, hdc) in next loop, sc in next Cluster, [(hdc, 4 dc, hdc) in next loop, sc in next Cluster] 6 times, (hdc, 4 dc) in next loop, ★ decrease, dc in next dtr, decrease, repeat from † to † across to next corner loop, (4 dc, hdc) in next loop, sc in next Cluster, [(hdc, 4 dc, hdc) in next loop, sc in next Cluster] 6 times, (hdc, 4 dc) in next loop; repeat from ★ around; skip beginning ch-2 and join with slip st to first dc, finish off.

FINISHING

Weave ribbon through Eyelet rnd along one side of Afghan, leaving 25" at each end. Repeat for remaining three sides. Tie ends in a bow at each corner.

LOG CABIN COMFORT

This old-fashioned set was adapted from the long-popular Log Cabin quilt pattern. To give the throw an authentic quilt look, we fashioned the afghan in blocks of varying sizes and color combinations and then pieced them together with narrow strips. The pillow is simply two blocks slip stitched together.

Finished Size: Afghan - approximately 45" x 56"
Pillow - approximately 10" square

MATERIALS
Worsted Weight Yarn, approximately:
    MC (Granite) - 22 ounces, (620 grams, 1,385 yards)
    Color A (Gold) - 11 ounces, (310 grams, 690 yards)
    Color B (Blue) - 11 ounces, (310 grams, 690 yards)
    Color C (Red) - 3 ounces, (90 grams, 190 yards)
    Crochet hook, size H (5.00 mm) **or** size needed for gauge
    10" Purchased pillow form
    or ½ yard 44/45" wide fabric and polyester stuffing
    Yarn needle

GAUGE: 8 sc = 2"
        Block A = 10" x 10"
        Block B = 10" x 11"
        Block C = 10" x 12"

AFGHAN
BLOCK A (Make 10)
CENTER
Color Sequence: 3 Rows MC *(Fig. 22a, page 138)*, 3 rows Color A, 7 rows Color C, 3 rows Color A, 3 rows MC.

With MC, ch 12 **loosely**.
Row 1 (Right side): Sc in back ridge of second ch from hook and in each ch across *(Fig. 2a, page 133)*: 11 sc.
Note: Loop a short piece of yarn around any stitch to mark last row as **right** side.
Row 2: Ch 2 **(counts as turning ch, now and throughout)**, turn; hdc in next sc, hdc around post of last hdc made *(Fig. 1)*, (skip next sc, hdc in next sc, hdc around post of last hdc made) across to last sc, hdc in last sc: 11 hdc.

Fig. 1

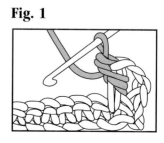

Row 3: Ch 1, turn; sc in each hdc across, leave turning ch unworked: 11 sc.

Row 4: Ch 1, turn; sc in each sc across.

Rows 5-7: Repeat Rows 2-4.

Rows 8-11: Repeat Rows 2 and 3 twice.

Rows 12-19: Repeat Rows 2-4 twice, then repeat Rows 2 and 3 once **more**.

Finish off.

FIRST SIDE

Row 1: With **right** side facing and working in end of rows, join Color B with slip st in first row; ch 1, sc in same row, work 2 sc in each hdc row and 1 sc in each sc row across: 26 sc.

Row 2: Ch 2, turn; hdc in next sc, hdc around last hdc made, (skip next sc, hdc in next sc, hdc around last hdc made) across to last 2 sc, skip next sc, hdc in last sc: 25 hdc.

Row 3: Ch 1, turn; sc in each hdc across, changing to MC in last sc, leave turning ch unworked: 25 sc.

Row 4: Ch 1, turn; sc in each sc across.
Row 5: Ch 2, turn; hdc in next sc, hdc around last hdc made, (skip next sc, hdc in next sc, hdc around last hdc made) across to last sc, hdc in last sc: 25 hdc.
Row 6: Ch 1, turn; sc in each hdc across, leave turning ch unworked; finish off.

SECOND SIDE
Work same as First Side.

TOP
Row 1: With **right** side facing and working in end of rows on Sides and across Center, join Color A with slip st in first row; ch 1, sc in same row, 2 sc in next row, sc in next 2 rows, 2 sc in next row, sc in next row, sc in next 11 sts, sc in next row, 2 sc in next row, sc in next 2 rows, 2 sc in next row, sc in last row: 27 sc.
Row 2: Ch 2, turn; hdc in next sc, hdc around last hdc made, (skip next sc, hdc in next sc, hdc around last hdc made) across to last sc, hdc in last sc: 27 hdc.
Row 3: Ch 1, turn; sc in each hdc across, changing to MC in last sc, leave turning ch unworked: 27 sc.
Row 4: Ch 1, turn; sc in each sc across.
Row 5: Repeat Row 2.
Row 6: Ch 1, turn; sc in each hdc across, leave turning ch unworked, finish off.

BOTTOM
Work same as Top.

FIRST EDGE
Row 1: With **right** side facing and working in end of rows on Top and Bottom, and across Row 6 on Side, join Color B with slip st in first row; ch 1, sc in same row, 2 sc in next row, sc in next 2 rows, 2 sc in next row, sc in next row, sc in next 25 sc, sc in next row, 2 sc in next row, sc in next 2 rows, 2 sc in next row, sc in last row: 41 sc.
Row 2: Ch 2, turn; hdc in next sc, hdc around last hdc made, (skip next sc, hdc in next sc, hdc around last hdc made) across to last sc, hdc in last sc: 41 hdc.
Row 3: Ch 1, turn; sc in each hdc across, changing to MC in last sc, leave turning ch unworked: 41 hdc.
Row 4: Ch 1, turn; sc in each sc across.

Row 5: Ch 2, turn; hdc in next sc, hdc around last hdc made, (skip next sc, hdc in next sc, hdc around last hdc made) across to last sc, hdc in last sc: 41 hdc.
Row 6: Ch 1, turn; sc in each hdc across, leave turning ch unworked; finish off.

SECOND EDGE
Work same as First Edge.

BLOCK B (Make 4)
CENTER
Color Sequence: 3 Rows MC, 3 rows Color B, 7 rows Color C, 3 rows Color B, 3 rows MC.

FIRST SIDE
Beginning with Color A, work same as Block A.

SECOND SIDE
Work same as First Side.

TOP
Beginning with Color B, work same as Block A.

BOTTOM
Work same as Top.

FIRST EDGE
Beginning with Color A, work same as Block A.

SECOND EDGE
Work same as First Edge, changing to Color A in last sc on Row 6; do **not** finish off.
Rows 7-9: Repeat Rows 4-6.

BLOCK C (Make 6)
Work same as Block B, working First Edge same as Second Edge.

FINISHING
ASSEMBLY
Following Placement Diagram, page 43, whipstitch 5 Blocks into 4 vertical strips *(Fig. 27a, page 140)*.

PLACEMENT DIAGRAM

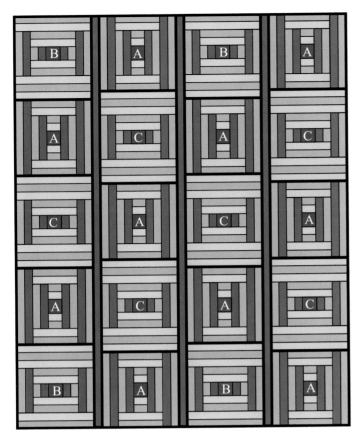

VERTICAL STRIP (Make 3)

Note: Work along left edge of 3 strips, leaving outside edge unworked.

Row 1: With **right** side of strip facing, working in end of rows and in sc across Blocks, join Color B with slip st in corner of strip; ch 1, sc in each sc across working 2 sc in each hdc row and 1 sc in each sc row.

Row 2: Ch 2, turn; hdc in next sc, hdc around last hdc made, (skip next sc, hdc in next sc, hdc around last hdc made) across to last sc, hdc in last sc.

Row 3: Ch 1, turn; sc in each hdc across; finish off.

With **wrong** sides together, whipstitch strips together.

BORDER

Rnd 1: With **right** side facing and working in end of rows and in sc across Blocks, join MC with slip st in first row on top right corner; ch 1, ★ 3 sc in corner, sc in each sc across working 2 sc in each hdc row and 1 sc in each sc row; repeat from ★ around; join with slip st to first sc.

Rnd 2: Ch 2, hdc in each sc around working 3 hdc in each corner sc; join with slip st to top of beginning ch-2.

Rnd 3: Ch 1, working in Back Loops Only *(Fig. 20, page 138)*, sc in same st and in each hdc around working 3 sc in each corner hdc; join with slip st to first sc, finish off.

PILLOW

BLOCK A
Work same as Afghan Block A.

BLOCK B
Work same as Afghan Block B through First Edge.

SECOND EDGE
Work same as First Edge.

BORDER

Rnd 1: With **right** side of Block facing and working in end of rows and in sc across Block, join MC with slip st in any corner; ch 1, ★ 3 sc in corner, sc in each sc across working 2 sc in each hdc row and 1 sc in each sc row; repeat from ★ around; join with slip st to first sc.

Rnd 2: Ch 2, hdc in each sc around working 3 hdc in each corner sc; join with slip st to top of beginning ch-2.

Rnd 3: Ch 1, working in Back Loops Only *(Fig. 20, page 138)*, sc in same st and in each hdc around working 3 sc in each corner hdc; join with slip st to first sc, finish off.

FINISHING

Make pillow form, if desired, page 140.

Holding **wrong** sides of Blocks together, matching sts and working through **both** loops of **both** pieces, join MC with slip st in sc at top right corner; slip st in each sc around inserting pillow form before closing; join with slip st to first slip st, finish off.

gifts for all

Finding just the right present for someone special is what makes gift-giving such an art. The ideas in this collection offer some exciting options — from dainty crocheted coasters for a dear friend to novelty button covers for a little girl. You'll enjoy making these presents as much as your friends and family will love receiving them!

Quick APPLE PILLOW

This luscious pillow makes an "a-peel-ing" gift for a favorite teacher or a friend who loves country things. Crocheted using fabric strips and a large hook, the pillow takes shape fast. And you don't have to worry about gauge — in any size, this gift earns an A⁺! A leafy stem provides a realistic finish.

Finished Size: Approximately 14½" wide x 15½" tall

MATERIALS

100% Cotton Fabric, 44/45" wide, approximately:
Apple (Red) - 7 yards
Leaf (Green) - ½ yard
Stem (Brown) - ¼ yard
Crochet hook, size N (9.00 mm)
Polyester stuffing
Yarn needle
Bias tape maker (optional)

Prepare fabric and tear all fabric except ½ yard of Red for pillow form, into 1½" strips *(see Preparing Fabric Strips and Joining Fabric Strips, page 139)*.

Note: Gauge is not important. Pillow can be smaller or larger without changing the overall effect.

APPLE
BODY
With Red, ch 22 **loosely**.

Row 1: 2 Sc in second ch from hook, (skip next ch, pull up a loop in next ch) 3 times, YO and draw through all 4 loops on hook, skip next ch, sc in next 5 chs, (skip next ch, pull up a loop in next ch) 3 times, YO and draw through all 4 loops on hook, skip next ch, 2 sc in last ch: 11 sts.

Row 2 (Right side)**:** Ch 1, turn; 2 sc in first sc, sc in each st across to last sc, 2 sc in last sc: 13 sc.

Note: Loop a short piece of fabric around any stitch to mark last row as **right** side and **bottom** edge.

Row 3: Ch 1, turn; sc in each sc across.

Rows 4 and 5: Ch 1, turn; 2 sc in first sc, sc in each sc across to last sc, 2 sc in last sc: 17 sc.

Rows 6-15: Ch 1, turn; sc in each sc across.

Row 16: Ch 1, turn; skip first sc, sc in each sc across to last sc, slip st in last sc, do **not** finish off: 15 sc.

LEFT TOP
Row 1: Ch 1, turn; skip first sc, sc in next 4 sc, slip st in next sc, leave remaining sts unworked: 4 sc.

Row 2: Ch 1, turn; skip first slip st, sc in next 3 sc, (sc, slip st) in last sc; finish off.

RIGHT TOP
Row 1: With **wrong** side facing, skip 3 sc from Left Top and join Red with slip st in next sc; ch 1, sc in next 4 sc, slip st in last sc: 4 sc.

Row 2: Ch 1, turn; skip first slip st, sc in first 3 sc, (sc, slip st) in last sc; do **not** finish off.

EDGING

Ch 1, sc in end of next row, skip next slip st, sc in next sc, (sc, ch 1, sc) in next sc, sc in next sc and in end of next row, sc in next 4 sc across Left Top; skip first row, sc in end of next 17 rows; working in free loops of beginning ch *(Fig. 21b, page 138)*, sc in next 7 chs, skip next ch, sc in next 5 chs, skip next ch, sc in last 7 chs; sc in end of next 17 rows; sc in next 4 sc across Right Top; join with slip st to first sc, finish off: 67 sc.

Repeat for second side; do **not** finish off.

FINISHING

Make pillow form, page 140.

JOINING

Holding **wrong** sides of Apple together, bottom edges at same end, and working through **both** loops of **both** pieces, slip st in each sc around, matching sts and inserting pillow form before closing; join with slip st to first slip st, finish off.

LEAF

With Green, ch 12 **loosely**.

Row 1: 2 Dc in fourth ch from hook, dc in next 3 chs, hdc in next 3 chs, sc in next ch, 3 slip sts in last ch; working in free loops of beginning ch, sc in next ch, hdc in next 3 chs, dc in next 3 chs, 2 sc in next ch; join with slip st to top of beginning ch, finish off leaving a long end for sewing.

STEM

With Brown, ch 9 **loosely**.

Row 1: Slip st in fourth ch from hook, hdc in each ch across, finish off leaving a long end for sewing.

Sew Leaf and Stem to Apple.

Quick BATH BASKET

*D*eliver this pretty bath basket to a friend who would enjoy some pampering, and you'll be greeted with delight. After the scented accessories are gone, she'll find lots of uses for the handy-sized basket, which works up quickly using strips of rose-patterned chintz fabric.

Finished Size: Approximately 10" in diameter x 10" high

MATERIALS

100% Cotton Fabric, 44/45" wide, approximately: 3 yards
Crochet hook, size N (9.00 mm)
1¼" Ribbon - 1½ yards
Wire - 1½ yards
Bias tape maker (optional)
Sewing needle and thread
Silk rose

Prepare fabric and tear into 1½" strips *(see Preparing Fabric Strips and Joining Fabric Strips, page 139)*.

GAUGE: Rnds 1-4 of Bottom = 5"

BOTTOM

Rnd 1 (Right side): Ch 2, 8 sc in second ch from hook; do **not** join, place fabric marker *(see Markers, page 138)*.

Rnd 2: 2 Sc in each sc around: 16 sc.

Rnd 3: (Sc in next sc, 2 sc in next sc) around: 24 sc.

Rnd 4: (Sc in next 3 sc, 2 sc in next sc) around; remove marker, slip st in next sc: 30 sc.

Rnd 5 (Ruffle): Turn; working in Back Loops Only *(Fig. 20, page 138)*, ★ (slip st, ch 3, dc) in next sc, skip next 2 sc; repeat from ★ around; join with slip st to first slip st, do **not** finish off: 10 scallops.

SIDES

Rnd 1: Ch 1, **turn;** working in free loops on Rnd 4 *(Fig. 21a, page 138)*, sc in each sc around; join with slip st to first sc: 30 sc.

Rnds 2-4: Ch 1, do **not** turn; sc in each sc around; join with slip st to first sc.

Rnd 5 (Eyelet rnd): Ch 5, skip next 2 sc, ★ dc in next sc, ch 2, skip next 2 sc; repeat from ★ around; join with slip st to third ch of beginning ch-5: 10 ch-2 sps.

Rnd 6: Ch 1, sc in each dc and in each ch around; join with slip st to first sc: 30 sc.

Rnd 7: Ch 1, **turn**; sc in first 3 sc, † hdc in next sc, dc in next sc, 2 dc in each of next 6 sc, dc in next sc, hdc in next sc †, sc in next 5 sc, repeat from † to † once, sc in last 2 sc; join with slip st to first sc: 42 sts.

Prepare wire as follows: Cut a length of wire equal to Rnd 7 plus approximately 3". Fold 1¹/₂" at each end and form loop; hook loops together and twist ends to secure. Place wire along top of Rnd 7, shaping wire to fit.

Rnd 8 (Ruffle)**:** Ch 3, do **not** turn; working over wire *(Fig. 23, page 138)*, dc in same st, skip next 2 sts, (slip st, ch 3, dc) in next st, [skip next st, (slip st, ch 3, dc) in next st] 6 times, [skip next 2 sts, (slip st, ch 3, dc) in next st] 3 times, [skip next st, (slip st, ch 3, dc) in next st] 6 times, skip next 2 sts, (slip st, ch 3, dc) in next st, skip last 2 sts; join with slip st to same st as joining, finish off: 18 scallops.

HANDLE

Row 1: With **wrong** side facing, join fabric strip with slip st around post of first dc on Eyelet rnd *(Fig. 13, page 135)*; ch 36 **loosely**, skip next 4 dc on Eyelet rnd, being careful not to twist ch, slip st around post of next dc.

Prepare wire as follows: Cut a length of wire equal to length of Handle plus approximately 5". Fold 2¹/₂" at each end and form loop; wrap loop around same dc as Handle and twist ends to secure. Shape wire to fit Handle.

Row 2: Ch 1, turn; working over wire, slip st around same dc; sc in back ridge of each ch across *(Fig. 2a, page 133)*, slip st around same dc as joining; finish off.

Using photo as a guide for placement, weave ribbon through Eyelet rnd and tie in a bow. Tack rose to center of bow.

RING BEARER'S PILLOW

To make a couple's wedding day even more memorable, present them with this lacy ring bearer's pillow for the ceremony. Featuring ribbon trim and a satin lining in the bride's chosen colors, the delicate pillow is a gift that will always be treasured. Miniature wedding bells set a joyful tone.

Finished Size: Approximately 11" square including Edging

MATERIALS

Bedspread Weight Cotton Thread (size 10), approximately 730 yards

Steel crochet hook, size 7 (1.65 mm) **or** size needed for gauge

Satin fabric - 2 pieces 9" x 9" **each**

Polyester stuffing

Tapestry needle

Sewing needle and thread

Finishing materials: Ribbon, glue gun, pearls

Starching materials: Commercial fabric stiffener, blocking board, transparent tape, plastic wrap, resealable plastic bag, terry towel, paper towels, and stainless steel pins

GAUGE: In pattern, 3 Fans and 12 rows = $3^{1}/_{2}$"

PATTERN STITCH

FAN

Tr in st or sp indicated, (ch 2, tr) 4 times in same st or sp.

BACK

Ch 67 **loosely**.

Row 1 (Right side): Sc in second ch from hook, ch 1, ★ skip next 4 chs, work Fan in next ch, ch 1, skip next 4 chs, sc in next ch, ch 1; repeat from ★ across to last 5 chs, skip next 4 chs, tr in last ch, (ch 2, tr) twice in same ch: 6 Fans.

Note: Loop a short piece of thread around any stitch to mark last row as **right** side.

Row 2: Ch 1, turn; sc in first tr, ch 3, skip next ch-2 sp, dc in next ch-2 sp, ★ ch 2, skip next 2 ch-1 sps, dc in next ch-2 sp, ch 3, skip next tr, sc in next tr, ch 3, skip next ch-2 sp, dc in next ch-2 sp; repeat from ★ across to last ch-1 sp, ch 1, skip last ch-1 sp, tr in last sc: 20 ch-sps.

Row 3: Ch 6 **(counts as first tr plus ch 2, now and throughout)**, turn; (tr, ch 2, tr) in next ch-1 sp, ch 1, sc in next sc, ★ ch 1, skip next ch-3 sp, work Fan in next ch-2 sp, ch 1, sc in next sc; repeat from ★ across: 6 Fans.

Row 4: Ch 5 **(counts as first tr plus ch 1, now and throughout)**, turn; dc in next ch-2 sp, ch 3, skip next tr, sc in next tr, ★ ch 3, skip next ch-2 sp, dc in next ch-2 sp, ch 2, skip next 2 ch-1 sps, dc in next ch-2 sp, ch 3, skip next tr, sc in next tr; repeat from ★ across: 20 ch-sps.

Row 5: Ch 1, turn; sc in first sc, ch 1, ★ skip next ch-3 sp, work Fan in next ch-2 sp, ch 1, sc in next sc, ch 1; repeat from ★ across to last 2 sps, skip next dc, tr in last tr, (ch 2, tr) twice in same st: 6 Fans.

Rows 6-26: Repeat Rows 2-5, 5 times, then repeat Row 2 once **more**.

Finish off.

FRONT

Work same as Back; do **not** finish off.

Make pillow form, page 140.

EDGING

Rnd 1 (Joining rnd): Ch 1, turn; holding Front and Back with **wrong** sides together, Front facing, and working through **both** pieces, 2 sc in first tr; work 71 sc evenly spaced across to last sc, 3 sc in last sc; work 71 sc evenly spaced across end of rows; working in free loops and in ch-sps of beginning ch *(Fig. 21b, page 138)*, 3 sc in first ch, work 71 sc evenly spaced across to last ch, 3 sc in last ch; working in Front **only**, work 71 sc evenly spaced across end of rows, sc in same st as first sc; join with slip st to first sc: 296 sc.

Rnd 2: Ch 3 **(counts as first dc, now and throughout)**, dc in same st, ★ dc in next sc and in each sc across to next corner sc, 3 dc in corner sc; repeat from ★ 2 times **more**, dc in each sc across, dc in same st as first dc; join with slip st to first dc: 304 dc.

Rnd 3: Ch 3, dc in same st, ch 3, ★ skip next 3 dc, (dc in next 3 dc, ch 3, skip next 3 dc) across to next corner dc, 3 dc in corner dc, ch 3; repeat from ★ 2 times **more**, (skip next 3 dc, dc in next 3 dc, ch 3) across to last 3 dc, skip last 3 dc, dc in same st as first dc; join with slip st to first dc: 52 ch-3 sps.

Rnd 4: Ch 3, dc in same st, ★ dc in next dc and in each dc and each ch across to next corner dc, 3 dc in corner dc; repeat from ★ 2 times **more**, dc in next dc and in each dc and each ch across, dc in same st as first dc; join with slip st to first dc: 320 dc.

Rnd 5: Ch 6, (tr, ch 2, tr) in same st, ch 1, skip next 4 dc, sc in next dc, ch 1, ★ skip next 4 dc, work Fan in next dc, ch 1, skip next 4 dc, sc in next dc, ch 1; repeat from ★ around to last 4 dc, skip last 4 dc, (tr, ch 2) twice in same st as first tr; join with slip st to first tr: 32 Fans.

Rnd 6: Ch 1, sc in same st, ch 3, skip next ch-2 sp, dc in next ch-2 sp, ch 2, skip next 2 ch-1 sps, dc in next ch-2 sp, ch 3, ★ skip next tr, sc in next tr, ch 3, skip next ch-2 sp, dc in next ch-2 sp, ch 2, skip next 2 ch-1 sps, dc in next ch-2 sp, ch 3; repeat from ★ around; join with slip st to first sc: 96 ch-sps.

Rnd 7: Ch 1, sc in same st, ch 1, skip next ch-3 sp, work Fan in next ch-2 sp, ch 1, ★ sc in next sc, ch 1, skip next ch-3 sp, work Fan in next ch-2 sp, ch 1; repeat from ★ around; join with slip st to first sc, finish off.

49

BELL (Make 2)

Rnd 1 (Right side): Ch 2, 10 sc in second ch from hook; do **not** join, place marker *(see Markers, page 138)*.
Note: Loop a short piece of thread around any stitch to mark last round as **right** side.
Rnd 2: 2 Sc in each sc around: 20 sc.
Rnds 3-9: Sc in each sc around.
Rnd 10: (Sc in next 4 sc, 2 sc in next sc) around: 24 sc.
Rnd 11: (Sc in next 3 sc, 2 sc in next sc) around: 30 sc.
Rnd 12: (Sc in next 2 sc, 2 sc in next sc) around; slip st in next sc, finish off: 40 sc.

FINISHING

Insert pillow form, then sew remaining seam.
Starch Bells, see Starching and Blocking, page 142.
Weave ribbon through ch-3 sps on Rnd 3 of Edging; tack ends together.
Tie a knot at the end of an 16" piece of ribbon. Thread pearl onto ribbon, then insert ribbon through top of Bell from the inside leaving ribbon long enough for pearl to hang freely inside Bell; lightly glue at top to secure.
Thread opposite end of ribbon through top of second Bell from outside. Thread pearl onto ribbon, then tie a knot at the end of ribbon. Leave ribbon long enough for pearl to hang freely inside Bell; lightly glue at top to secure.
Using photo as guide, attach Bells and decorate as desired.

HANDSOME MUFFLER

Surprise the man in your life with this handsome houndstooth muffler. It makes a great birthday or Christmas gift, and it's a present he's sure to wear close to his heart! The classic pattern is created using sport weight yarn and single crochet stitches.

Finished Size: Approximately 12" x 54"

MATERIALS
Sport Weight Yarn, approximately:
MC (Black) - 6 ounces, (170 grams, 600 yards)
CC (Brown) - 4 ounces, (110 grams, 400 yards)
Crochet hook, size F (3.75 mm) **or** size needed for gauge

GAUGE: 20 sc and 20 rows = 4"

With MC, ch 59 **loosely**.

Row 1 (Right side): Sc in second ch from hook and in each ch across: 58 sc.
Note #1: Loop a short piece of yarn around any stitch to mark last row as **right** side.
Note #2: When changing colors *(Fig. 22a, page 138)*, do **not** cut yarn unless specified, work over unused color carrying yarn along **wrong** side.
Row 2: Ch 1, turn; sc in first 3 sc, with CC sc in next 2 sc, ★ with MC sc in next 5 sc, with CC sc in next 2 sc; repeat from ★ across to last 4 sc, with MC sc in last 4 sc.

Row 3: Ch 1, turn; with MC sc in first 4 sc, with CC sc in next 2 sc, ★ with MC sc in next 5 sc, with CC sc in next 2 sc; repeat from ★ across to last 3 sc, with MC sc in last 3 sc.
Row 4: Ch 1, turn; with MC sc in first 3 sc, with CC sc in next 5 sc, ★ with MC sc in next 2 sc, with CC sc in next 5 sc; repeat from ★ across to last sc, with MC sc in last sc.
Rows 5 and 6: Ch 1, turn; with MC sc in first sc, with CC sc in next 5 sc, ★ with MC sc in next 2 sc, with CC sc in next 5 sc; repeat from ★ across to last 3 sc, with MC sc in last 3 sc.
Row 7: Ch 1, turn; with MC sc in first 3 sc, with CC sc in next 5 sc, ★ with MC sc in next 2 sc, with CC sc in next 5 sc; repeat from ★ across to last sc, with MC sc in last sc.
Row 8: Ch 1, turn; with MC sc in first 4 sc, with CC sc in next 2 sc, ★ with MC sc in next 5 sc, with CC sc in next 2 sc; repeat from ★ across to last 3 sc, with MC sc in last 3 sc.
Row 9: Ch 1, turn; with MC sc in first 3 sc, with CC sc in next 2 sc, ★ with MC sc in next 5 sc, with CC sc in next 2 sc; repeat from ★ across to last 4 sc, with MC sc in last 4 sc.
Rows 10-265: Repeat Rows 2-9, 32 times.
Cut CC.
Row 266: Ch 1, turn; sc in each sc across; do **not** finish off.

EDGING

Rnd 1: Ch 1, turn; 3 sc in first sc, sc in each sc across to last sc, 3 sc in last sc; sc in end of each row across; working in free loops of beginning ch *(Fig. 21b, page 138)*, 3 sc in first ch, sc in each ch across to last ch, 3 sc in last ch; sc in end of each row across; join with slip st to first sc: 656 sc.

Rnd 2: Ch 1, sc in first 62 sc, ch 3, (skip next 2 sc, sc in next sc, ch 3) across to within 3 sc of next corner sc, skip next 2 sc; sc in next 62 sc; ch 3, skip next 2 sc, (sc in next sc, ch 3, skip next 2 sc) across; join with slip st to first sc, finish off.

SIDE EDGING TRIM

With **right** side facing and working across long edge, join CC with slip st in first ch-3 sp; ch 3, ★ drop loop from hook, insert hook in next ch-3 sp, hook dropped loop and draw through to right side, ch 4; repeat from ★ across to last ch-3 sp, slip st in last ch-3 sp, finish off.

Repeat on second long edge.

With MC add fringe *(Figs. 28a & b, page 141)*.

51

FLORAL SACHETS

Scented sachets make nice little gifts, and they work up quickly, too! Made with bedspread weight cotton thread, this pretty set features flowers that signify love, youth, and good thoughts. For a delicate fragrance, sprinkle scented oil or your favorite cologne on the filling before you finish.

Finished Size: Approximately 4" square

MATERIALS
Bedspread Weight Cotton Thread (size 10), approximately:
All
    MC (White) - 55 yards **each**
    Color A (Green) - 6 yards **each**
Primrose
    Color B (Yellow) - 2 yards
    Color C (Pink) - 10 yards
Pansy
    Color B (Yellow) - 2 yards
    Color C (Lavender) - 10 yards
    Color D (Black) - 2 yards
Rose
    Color B (Rose) - 11 yards
Steel crochet hook, size 5 (1.90 mm) **or** size needed
    for gauge
Cotton balls or polyester stuffing
Tapestry needle
Scented oil

GAUGE: Rnds 1-4 = 1¾"

PATTERN STITCHES
BEGINNING CLUSTER
Ch 2, ★ YO, insert hook in same st or sp, YO and pull up a loop, YO and draw through 2 loops on hook; repeat from ★ once **more**, YO and draw through all 3 loops on hook **(Figs. 10a & b, page 134)**.
CLUSTER
★ YO, insert hook in st or sp indicated, YO and pull up a loop, YO and draw through 2 loops on hook; repeat from ★ 2 times **more**, YO and draw through all 4 loops on hook.
DECREASE (uses next 3 dc)
★ YO, insert hook in **next** dc, YO and pull up a loop, YO and draw through 2 loops on hook; repeat from ★ 2 times **more**, YO and draw through all 4 loops on hook.

BACK
With MC, ch 3; join with slip st to form a ring.
Rnd 1 (Right side): Ch 1, 8 sc in ring; join with slip st to first sc.

Note: Loop a short piece of thread around any stitch to mark last round as **right** side.
Rnd 2: Ch 1, 2 sc in Back Loop Only of each sc around **(Fig. 20, page 138)**; join with slip st to first sc: 16 sc.
Rnd 3: Ch 5, working in Back Loops Only, dc in same st, (dc, ch 2, dc) in each sc around; join with slip st to third ch of beginning ch-5: 16 ch-2 sps.
Rnd 4: Slip st in first ch-2 sp, work beginning Cluster, ch 2, (work Cluster in next ch-2 sp, ch 2) around; join with slip st to top of beginning Cluster: 16 Clusters.
Rnd 5: Ch 4, working in both loops, (tr, ch 4, 2 tr) in same st, ch 1, dc in next ch-2 sp, ch 2, (work Cluster in next Cluster, ch 2) 3 times, dc in next ch-2 sp, ch 1, ★ (2 tr, ch 4, 2 tr) in next Cluster, ch 1, dc in next ch-2 sp, ch 2, (work Cluster in next Cluster, ch 2) 3 times, dc in next ch-2 sp, ch 1; repeat from ★ around; join with slip st to top of beginning ch-4.
Rnd 6: Slip st in next tr and in first ch-4 sp, work (beginning Cluster, ch 4, Cluster) in same sp, ch 2, 3 dc in next dc, ch 2, (work Cluster in next Cluster, ch 2) 3 times, 3 dc in next dc, ch 2, ★ work (Cluster, ch 4, Cluster) in next ch-4 sp, ch 2, 3 dc in next dc, ch 2, (work Cluster in next Cluster, ch 2) 3 times, 3 dc in next dc, ch 2; repeat from ★ around; join with slip st to top of beginning Cluster.
Rnd 7: Work beginning Cluster, ch 2, work (Cluster, ch 4, Cluster) in next ch-4 sp, ch 2, work Cluster in next Cluster, ch 2, decrease, ch 2, (work Cluster in next Cluster, ch 2) 3 times, decrease, ch 2, ★ work Cluster in next Cluster, ch 2, work (Cluster, ch 4, Cluster) in next ch-4 sp, ch 2, work Cluster in next Cluster, ch 2, decrease, ch 2, (work Cluster in next Cluster, ch 2) 3 times, decrease, ch 2; repeat from ★ around; join with slip st to top of beginning Cluster.
Rnd 8: Ch 1, sc in each st and 2 sc in each ch-2 sp around working 5 sc in each corner ch-4 sp; join with slip st to first sc, finish off leaving a long end for sewing: 120 sc.

FRONT
With Color B, ch 3; join with slip st to form a ring.
Rnds 1 and 2: Work same as Back: 16 sc.
Finish off.
Rnd 3: With **right** side facing and working in Back Loops Only, join Color A with slip st in any sc; ch 5, dc in same st, (dc, ch 2, dc) in each sc around; join with slip st to third ch of beginning ch-5: 16 ch-2 sps.

Rnd 4: Work same as Back; finish off.

Rnd 5: With **right** side facing, join MC with slip st in any Cluster; ch 4, working in both loops, (tr, ch 4, 2 tr) in same st, ch 1, dc in next ch-2 sp, ch 2, (work Cluster in next Cluster, ch 2) 3 times, dc in next ch-2 sp, ch 1, ★ (2 tr, ch 4, 2 tr) in next Cluster, ch 1, dc in next ch-2 sp, ch 2, (work Cluster in next Cluster, ch 2) 3 times, dc in next ch-2 sp, ch 1; repeat from ★ around; join with slip st to top of beginning ch-4.

Rnds 6 and 7: Work same as Back.
Finish off.

Note: Work Rnd 8 with Color C for Primrose and Pansy and with Color B for Rose.

Rnd 8: With **right** side facing, join thread with slip st in same st as joining; ch 1, sc in each st and 2 sc in each ch-2 sp around working 5 sc in each corner ch-4 sp; join with slip st to first sc, finish off: 120 sc.

RUFFLE

Rnd 1: With **right** side facing and working in Front Loops Only on Rnd 8, join MC with slip st in same st as joining; ch 1, sc in same st, ch 3, skip next sc, (sc in next sc, ch 3, skip next sc) around; join with slip st to first sc: 60 ch-3 sps.

Rnd 2: Slip st in first ch-3 sp, work (beginning Cluster, ch 3, Cluster) in same sp, ch 2, sc in next ch-3 sp, ch 2, ★ work (Cluster, ch 3, Cluster) in next ch-3 sp, ch 2, sc in next ch-3 sp, ch 2; repeat from ★ around; join with slip st to top of beginning Cluster, finish off.

PRIMROSE

With **right** side facing and working in free loops on Rnd 2 of Front *(Fig. 21a, page 138)*, join Color C with slip st in any sc; ch 3, 2 dc in same st, (2 tr, dtr) in next sc, (dtr, 2 tr) in next sc, ★ (2 dc, ch 3, slip st, ch 3, 2 dc) in next sc, (2 tr, dtr) in next sc, (dtr, 2 tr) in next sc; repeat from ★ around to last sc, (2 dc, ch 3, slip st) in last sc; join with slip st to first slip st, finish off: 5 petals.

PANSY

Rnd 1: With **right** side facing and working in free loops on Rnd 1 of Front *(Fig. 21a, page 138)*, join Color D with slip st in any sc; ch 1, (sc, hdc, sc) in same st and in next sc, (sc, ch 1, dc) in next sc, (dc, ch 1, sc) in next sc, (sc, ch 1, tr) in next sc, (tr, ch 1, sc) in next sc, (sc, ch 1, dc) in next sc, (dc, ch 1, sc) in last sc; join with slip st to first sc; finish off.

Rnd 2: With **right** side facing, join Color C with slip st in first sc; ch 4, tr in same st, 2 tr in next hdc, (2 dc, ch 3, slip st) in next sc, (slip st, ch 3, 2 dc) in next sc, 2 tr in next hdc, (tr, ch 4, slip st) in next sc, slip st in next sc, ch 4, 2 tr in next ch-1 sp, 2 tr in each of next 2 dc and in next ch-1 sp, ch 4, slip st in next 2 sc, ch 4, 2 tr in next ch-1 sp, 4 tr in each of next 2 tr, 2 tr in next ch-1 sp, ch 4, slip st in next 2 sc, ch 4, 2 tr in next ch-1 sp, 2 tr in each of next 2 dc and in next ch-1 sp, ch 4, slip st in last sc; join with slip st to first slip st, finish off: 5 petals.

ROSE

Rnd 1: With **right** side facing and working in free loops of Rnd 1 on Front *(Fig. 21a, page 138)*, join Color B with slip st in any sc; ch 2, (2 dc, hdc) in same st, (hdc, 2 dc, hdc) in next sc and in each sc around to last sc, (hdc, 2 dc, ch 2, slip st) in last sc.

Rnd 2: Working in free loops on Rnd 2, slip st in first sc, ch 2, (dc, 3 tr, dc, hdc) in same st, (hdc, dc, 3 tr, dc, hdc) in next sc and in each sc around; join with slip st to top of beginning ch-2, finish off.

Sprinkle scented oil on the stuffing.
Thread needle with long end and whipstitch Front to Back, stuffing before closing *(Fig. 27b, page 140)*.

~~Quick~~ ICE CREAM BUTTON COVERS

These delectable button covers let you indulge a special little girl with two favorite treats — ice cream and pretty clothes! Fashioned from bedspread weight cotton thread in pastel shades, the quick-to-make covers offer a whimsical way to dress up a plain blouse.

Finished Size: Approximately 1½" tall

MATERIALS

Bedspread Weight Cotton Thread (size 10), approximately:
    MC (Brown) - 3 yards **each**
    CC (Various) - 6 yards **each**
Steel crochet hook, size 8 (1.50 mm)

Polyester stuffing
Tapestry needle
Glue gun
Button cover(s)

Note: Gauge is not important. Cover can be smaller or larger without changing the overall effect.

PATTERN STITCH
DECREASE
Pull up a loop in next 2 sts, YO and draw through all 3 loops on hook (counts as one sc).

CONE
Rnd 1: With MC, ch 2; 6 sc in second ch from hook; do **not** join, place marker *(see Markers, page 138)*.
Rnd 2: (2 Sc in next sc, sc in next 2 sc) twice: 8 sc.
Rnd 3: (2 Sc in next sc, sc in next 3 sc) twice: 10 sc.
Rnd 4: (2 Sc in next sc, sc in next 4 sc) twice: 12 sc.
Rnd 5: (2 Sc in next sc, sc in next 5 sc) twice: 14 sc.
Rnd 6: (2 Sc in next sc, sc in next 6 sc) twice: 16 sc.
Rnd 7: (2 Sc in next sc, sc in next 7 sc) twice: 18 sc.
Rnd 8: (2 Sc in next sc, sc in next 8 sc) twice: 20 sc.
Rnd 9: Sc in each sc around.
Rnd 10: Sc in each sc around; join with slip st in next sc changing to CC *(Fig. 22b, page 138)*.

ICE CREAM
Rnd 1: Ch 1, 2 sc in same st, sc in next sc, (2 sc in next sc, sc in next sc) around: 30 sc.
Rnd 2: Working in Front Loops Only *(Fig. 20, page 138)*, (slip st in next sc, ch 2) around: 30 ch-2 sps.
Rnd 3: Working in free loops of Rnd 1 *(Fig. 21a, page 138)*, slip st in first sc, ch 1, sc in each sc around: 30 sc.
Rnd 4: Decrease, (sc in next 2 sc, decrease) around: 22 sc.
Rnd 5: Sc in each sc around.
Rnd 6: Sc in next 2 sc, (decrease, sc in next 3 sc) around: 18 sc.
Rnd 7: Sc in each sc around.
Rnds 8 and 9: (Sc in next sc, decrease) around: 8 sc.
Stuff lightly.
Rnd 10: Decrease around; slip st in next sc, finish off leaving a long end for sewing: 4 sc.

FINISHING
Thread needle with end and weave through remaining sts; gather tightly and secure.
Glue Ice Cream Cone to button cover.

Quick HOUSEWARMING SET

Celebrate a friend's move into a new home with this gift basket filled with kitchen essentials. A dishcloth, crocheted in colors matching her kitchen decor, makes a thoughtful gift, along with a pot scrubber that features a color-coordinated crocheted backing. A purchased kitchen towel and stylish cutlery set round out your gift.

Finished Size: Dishcloth - approximately 8½" square
Pot Scrubber - approximately 5" x 5¾"

MATERIALS
100% Cotton Worsted Weight Yarn, approximately:
Dishcloth
MC (Black) - 1 ounce, (30 grams, 50 yards)
CC (White) - 1 ounce, (30 grams, 50 yards)
Pot Scrubber
¾ ounce, (20 grams, 40 yards)
Crochet hook, size G (4.00 mm) **or** size needed for gauge
3" x 4" Scrubber
Sharp pointed tool

DISHCLOTH
GAUGE: 4 Blocks = 3"
Rows 1-5 = 3¾" x 3¾" x 5" (triangle)

PATTERN STITCHES
BEGINNING BLOCK
Ch 5, turn; 3 dc in fourth ch from hook.
BLOCK
Slip st in ch-3 sp on next Block, ch 3, 3 dc in same sp.

Note #1: See Symbol Crochet Chart, page 136, for illustration of Rows 1-5.
Note #2: When changing colors *(Fig. 22a, page 138)*, cut old yarn and weave in later.

Row 1 (Right side): With MC, ch 5, 3 dc in fifth ch from hook, changing to CC in last dc.
Note: Loop a short piece of yarn around any stitch to mark last row as **right** side.
Row 2: Work Beginning Block, slip st around beginning ch of previous Block *(Fig. 18a, page 136)*, ch 3, 3 dc in same sp *(Fig. 18b, page 136)* changing to MC in last dc: 2 Blocks.
Row 3: Work Beginning Block, slip st in ch-3 sp on first Block, ch 3, 3 dc in same sp, work Block changing to CC in last dc: 3 Blocks.
Row 4: Work Beginning Block, slip st in ch-3 sp on first Block, ch 3, 3 dc in same sp, work Blocks across changing to MC in last dc: 4 Blocks.

Row 5: Work Beginning Block, slip st in ch-3 sp on first Block, ch 3, 3 dc in same sp, work Blocks across changing to CC in last dc: 5 Blocks.
Rows 6-11: Repeat Rows 4 and 5, 3 times; at end of Row 11, do **not** change colors: 11 Blocks.
Row 12: Turn; slip st in first 3 dc, cut MC; with CC, slip st in first ch-3 sp, ch 3, 3 dc in same sp, work Blocks across to last Block, slip st in ch-3 sp on last Block: 10 Blocks.
Row 13: Turn; slip st in first 3 dc, cut CC; with MC, slip st in first ch-3 sp, ch 3, 3 dc in same sp, work Blocks across to last Block, slip st in ch-3 sp on last Block: 9 Blocks.
Rows 14-20: Repeat Rows 12 and 13, 3 times, then repeat Row 12 once **more**: 2 Blocks.
Row 21: Turn; slip st in first 3 dc, cut CC; with MC, slip st in first ch-3 sp, ch 3, 3 dc in same sp, slip st in ch-3 sp on last Block: 1 Block.
Edging: Ch 1, sc evenly around, working 3 sc in each corner; join with slip st to first sc, finish off.

POT SCRUBBER
GAUGE: In pattern, 5 sts = 3" and 6 rows = 2½"

TOP
Ch 16 **loosely**.
Row 1: Sc in second ch from hook, (ch 1, skip next ch, sc in next ch) across: 7 ch-1 sps.
Row 2 (Right side): Ch 4 **(counts as first dc plus ch 1)**, turn; (YO, insert hook in **next** ch-1 sp, YO and pull up a loop, YO and draw through 2 loops on hook) twice, YO and draw through all 3 loops on hook, ch 1, ★ YO, insert hook in **same** ch-1 sp, YO and pull up a loop, YO and draw through 2 loops on hook, YO, insert hook in **next** ch-1 sp, YO and pull up a loop, YO and draw through 2 loops on hook, YO and draw through all 3 loops on hook, ch 1; repeat from ★ across, dc in last sc: 7 sps.
Note: Mark last row as **right** side.
Row 3: Ch 1, turn; sc in first dc, (ch 1, skip next ch, sc in next st) across: 8 sc.
Rows 4-12: Repeat Rows 2 and 3, 4 times, then repeat Row 2 once **more**; at end of Row 12, finish off.

SCRUBBER PREPARATION

With sharp, pointed tool, make a hole in each corner of scrubber, then make 3 holes evenly spaced across each short side and 6 holes evenly spaced across each long side.

BOTTOM

Rnd 1 (Right side)**:** Join yarn with slip st in any corner hole on scrubber; ch 1, 2 sc in same hole, ch 1, (sc in next hole, ch 1) across to next corner, ★ 3 sc in corner hole, ch 1, (sc in next hole, ch 1) across to next corner; repeat from ★ around, sc in same hole as first sc; join with slip st to first sc: 30 sc.

Note: Loop a short piece of yarn around any stitch to mark last round as **right** side.

Rnd 2: Ch 3 **(counts as first dc)**, 2 dc in same st, dc in next sc and in each sc and each ch-1 sp across to next corner sc, ★ 3 dc in corner sc, dc in next sc and in each sc and each ch-1 sp across to next corner sc; repeat from ★ around; join with slip st to first dc, do **not** finish off: 60 dc.

JOINING

Ch 1, holding Top and Bottom with **wrong** sides together, Top facing, and working through **both** loops of **both** pieces, sc evenly across to next corner, ★ 3 sc in corner, sc evenly across to next corner; repeat from ★ once **more**, leave remaining sts unworked; finish off.

PRETTY COASTERS

Just to let her know she's special, present a dear friend with our pretty coasters. The dainty set, crocheted with bedspread weight cotton thread, will bring old-fashioned elegance to her table. Pastel accents add sweetness to the pattern of petite pineapples.

Finished Size: Approximately 5½" in diameter

MATERIALS

Bedspread Weight Cotton Thread (size 10), approximately:
  MC (Ecru) - 55 yards **each**
  CC (Various) - 6 yards **each**
Steel crochet hook, size 9 (1.40 mm) **or** size needed for gauge

GAUGE: Rnds 1-5 = 2¼"

PATTERN STITCHES

BEGINNING SHELL

Ch 3, (dc, ch 2, 2 dc) in sp indicated.

SHELL

(2 Dc, ch 2, 2 dc) in sp indicated.

DECREASE

Pull up a loop in next 2 dc, YO and draw through all 3 loops on hook.

With CC, ch 10; join with slip st to form a ring.

Rnd 1 (Right side): Ch 3 **(counts as first dc, now and throughout)**, 19 dc in ring; join with slip st to first dc, finish off: 20 dc.

Note: Loop a short piece of thread around any stitch to mark last round as **right** side.

Rnd 2: With **right** side facing, join MC with slip st in any dc; ch 4, (dc in next dc, ch 1) around; join with slip st to third ch of beginning ch-4: 20 ch-1 sps.

Rnd 3: Ch 5, (dc in next dc, ch 2) around; join with slip st to third ch of beginning ch-5.

Rnd 4: Slip st in first ch-2 sp, ch 1, sc in same sp, ch 5, (sc in next ch-2 sp, ch 5) around; join with slip st to first sc, finish off.

Rnd 5: With **right** side facing, join CC with slip st in any loop; work beginning Shell in same loop, work Shell in next loop and in each loop around; join with slip st to first dc, finish off: 20 Shells.

Rnd 6: With **right** side facing, join MC with slip st in any Shell (ch-2 sp); work beginning Shell in same sp, ch 1, work (2 dc, ch 5, 2 dc) in next Shell, ch 1, work Shell in next Shell, ch 3, sc in next Shell, ch 3, ★ work Shell in next Shell, ch 1, work (2 dc, ch 5, 2 dc) in next Shell, ch 1, work Shell in next Shell, ch 3, sc in next Shell, ch 3; repeat from ★ around; join with slip st to first dc: 5 sc.

Rnd 7: Slip st in next dc and in first ch-2 sp, work beginning Shell in same sp, 7 dc in next loop, work Shell in next Shell, ch 3, (sc in next ch-3 sp, ch 3) twice, ★ work Shell in next Shell, 7 dc in next loop, work Shell in next Shell, ch 3, (sc in next ch-3 sp, ch 3) twice; repeat from ★ around; join with slip st to first dc.

Rnd 8: Slip st in next dc and in first ch-2 sp, work beginning Shell in same sp, dc in next dc, (ch 1, dc in next dc) 6 times, work Shell in next Shell, ch 3, (sc in next ch-3 sp, ch 3) 3 times, ★ work Shell in next Shell, dc in next dc, (ch 1, dc in next dc) 6 times, work Shell in next Shell, ch 3, (sc in next ch-3 sp, ch 3) 3 times; repeat from ★ around; join with slip st to first dc.

Rnd 9: Slip st in next dc and in first ch-2 sp, work beginning Shell in same sp, ch 1, sc in next ch-1 sp, (ch 3, sc in next ch-1 sp) 5 times, ch 1, work Shell in next Shell, ch 1, sc in next ch-3 sp, (ch 3, sc in next ch-3 sp) 3 times, ch 1, ★ work Shell in next Shell, ch 1, sc in next ch-1 sp, (ch 3, sc in next ch-1 sp) 5 times, ch 1, work Shell in next Shell, ch 1, sc in next ch-3 sp, (ch 3, sc in next ch-3 sp) 3 times, ch 1; repeat from ★ around; join with slip st to first dc.

Rnd 10: Slip st in next dc and in first ch-2 sp, work beginning Shell in same sp, ch 3, (sc in next ch-3 sp, ch 3) 5 times, work Shell in next Shell, ch 1, sc in next ch-3 sp, (ch 3, sc in next ch-3 sp) twice, ch 1, ★ work Shell in next Shell, ch 3, (sc in next ch-3 sp, ch 3) 5 times, work Shell in next Shell, ch 1, sc in next ch-3 sp, (ch 3, sc in next ch-3 sp) twice, ch 1; repeat from ★ around; join with slip st to first dc.

Rnd 11: Slip st in next dc and in first ch-2 sp, work beginning Shell in same sp, ch 5, skip next ch-3 sp, sc in next ch-3 sp, (ch 3, sc in next ch-3 sp) 3 times, ch 5, work Shell in next Shell, ch 1, sc in next ch-3 sp, ch 3, sc in next ch-3 sp, ch 1, ★ work Shell in next Shell, ch 5, skip next ch-3 sp, sc in next ch-3 sp, (ch 3, sc in next ch-3 sp) 3 times, ch 5, work Shell in next Shell, ch 1, sc in next ch-3 sp, ch 3, sc in next ch-3 sp, ch 1; repeat from ★ around; join with slip st to first dc.

Rnd 12: Slip st in next dc, ch 3, dc in same st, work Shell in next ch-2 sp, 2 dc in next dc, ch 5, sc in next ch-3 sp, (ch 3, sc in next ch-3 sp) twice, ch 5, skip next dc, 2 dc in next dc, work Shell in next ch-2 sp, 2 dc in next dc, ch 1, sc in next ch-3 sp, ch 1, skip next dc, ★ 2 dc in next dc, work Shell in next ch-2 sp, 2 dc in next dc, ch 5, sc in next ch-3 sp, (ch 3, sc in next ch-3 sp) twice, ch 5, skip next dc, 2 dc in next dc, work Shell in next ch-2 sp, 2 dc in next dc, ch 1, sc in next ch-3 sp, ch 1, skip next dc; repeat from ★ around; join with slip st to first dc.

Rnd 13: Slip st in next dc, ch 3, dc in same st and in next 2 dc, 4 dc in next ch-2 sp, dc in next 2 dc, 2 dc in next dc, ch 5, sc in next ch-3 sp, ch 3, sc in next ch-3 sp, ch 5, ★ † skip next dc, 2 dc in next dc, dc in next 2 dc, 4 dc in next ch-2 sp, dc in next 2 dc, 2 dc in next dc †, skip next 2 ch-1 sps, repeat from † to † once, ch 5, sc in next ch-3 sp, ch 3, sc in next ch-3 sp, ch 5; repeat from ★ 3 times **more**, then repeat from † to † once, skip next 2 ch-1 sps; join with slip st to first dc.

Rnd 14: Slip st in next dc, ch 1, 2 sc in same st, (sc in next dc, 2 sc in next dc) 5 times, sc in next ch-5 sp, ch 7, sc in next ch-3 sp, ch 7, sc in next ch-5 sp, ★ † 2 sc in next dc, (sc in next dc, 2 sc in next dc) 5 times †, decrease, repeat from † to † once, sc in next ch-5 sp, ch 7, sc in next ch-3 sp, ch 7, sc in next ch-5 sp; repeat from ★ 3 times **more**, then repeat from † to † once, decrease; join with slip st to first sc, finish off.

See Washing and Blocking, page 140.

just for fun

When you want to crochet something just for fun, turn to this playful collection. It includes projects to tickle everyone's fancy — from sophisticated sweaters for your dog to dandy dinosaurs that will add an adventurous touch to any child's room. Filled with bright colors and whimsical ideas, these accents are delightfully different!

TV PILLOWS

Fashioned with colorful Granny Square motifs, these jumbo pillows are perfect for lounging in front of the television. Coordinating stripes border both of the pillows, which work up quickly holding double strands of yarn.

Finished Size: Approximately 24" square

MATERIALS
Worsted Weight Yarn, approximately:
  Pillow #1
    MC (Black) - 18 ounces, (510 grams, 1,020 yards)
    Color A (Green) - ¹/₂ ounce, (20 grams, 30 yards)
    Color B (Red) - 1 ounce, (30 grams, 60 yards)
    Color C (Blue) - 1¹/₂ ounces, (40 grams, 85 yards)
    Color D (Yellow) - 1 ounce, (30 grams, 60 yards)
    Color E (Purple) - 6 yards
    Color F (Orange) - 1 ounce, (30 grams, 60 yards)
  Pillow #2
    MC (Black) - 16 ounces, (450 grams, 905 yards)
    Color A (Green) - 1 ounce, (30 grams, 60 yards)
    Color B (Red) - 1¹/₂ ounces, (40 grams, 85 yards)
    Color C (Blue) - 1¹/₂ ounces, (40 grams, 85 yards)
    Color D (Yellow) - 1¹/₂ ounces, (40 grams, 85 yards)
Crochet hook, size N (9.00 mm) **or** size needed for gauge
Yarn needle
24" Purchased pillow form **or**
  1¹/₂ yards 44/45" wide fabric and polyester stuffing

Note: Entire Pillow is worked holding two strands of yarn together.

BACK
GAUGE: Rnds 1 and 2 = 4¹/₂"

With MC, ch 5; join with slip st to form a ring.
Rnd 1: Ch 3 **(counts as first dc, now and throughout)**, 2 dc in ring, ch 1, (3 dc in ring, ch 1) 3 times; join with slip st to first dc: 12 dc.
Rnd 2 (Right side): Turn; slip st in first ch-1 sp, ch 3, 2 dc in same sp, (3 dc, ch 1, 3 dc) in next 3 ch-1 sps, 3 dc in same sp as first dc, ch 1; join with slip st to first dc: 24 dc.
Note: Loop a short piece of yarn around any stitch to mark last round as **right** side.
Rnd 3: Turn; slip st in first ch-1 sp, ch 3, 2 dc in same sp, 3 dc in sp **between** 3-dc groups, ★ (3 dc, ch 1, 3 dc) in next corner ch-1 sp, 3 dc in sp **between** 3-dc groups; repeat from ★ around, 3 dc in same sp as first dc, ch 1; join with slip st to first dc: 36 dc.
Rnds 4-16: Turn; slip st in first ch-1 sp, ch 3, 2 dc in same sp, 3 dc in each sp **between** 3-dc groups across to next corner ch-1 sp, ★ (3 dc, ch 1, 3 dc) in corner ch-1 sp, 3 dc in each sp **between** 3-dc groups across to next corner ch-1 sp; repeat from ★ 2 times **more**, 3 dc in same sp as first dc, ch 1; join with slip st to first dc: 192 dc.
Finish off.

61

PATTERN STITCHES

2-DC CLUSTER

★ YO, insert hook in sp indicated, YO and pull up a loop, YO and draw through 2 loops on hook; repeat from ★ once **more**, YO and draw through all 3 loops on hook *(Figs. 10a & b, page 134)*.

3-DC CLUSTER

★ YO, insert hook in sp indicated, YO and pull up a loop, YO and draw through 2 loops on hook; repeat from ★ 2 times **more**, YO and draw through all 4 loops on hook *(Figs. 10a & b, page 134)*.

2-TR CLUSTER

★ YO twice, insert hook in st indicated, YO and pull up a loop, (YO and draw through 2 loops on hook) twice; repeat from ★ once **more**, YO and draw through all 3 loops on hook.

FRONT - PILLOW #1

GAUGE: Each Square = 9½"

SQUARE A

Make 2 Squares, working one Square in each of the following Color Sequences:

Color Sequence #1: 1 Rnd Color A *(Fig. 22b, page 138)*, 2 rnds Color B, 2 rnds MC.

Color Sequence #2: 1 Rnd Color F, 2 rnds Color C, 2 rnds MC.

With first color, ch 4; join with slip st to form a ring.

Rnd 1 (Right side)**:** Ch 4, (dc in ring, ch 1) 11 times; join with slip st to third ch of beginning ch-4 changing to new color: 12 ch-1 sps.

Note: Mark last round as **right** side.

Rnd 2: Ch 6 **(counts as first tr plus ch 2, now and throughout)**, (work 3-dc Cluster in next ch-1 sp, ch 2) 3 times, ★ tr in next dc, ch 2, (work 3-dc Cluster in next ch-1 sp, ch 2) 3 times; repeat from ★ around; join with slip st to first tr: 12 3-dc Clusters.

Rnd 3: Ch 6, 5 dc in next ch-2 sp, ch 2, skip next Cluster, sc in next Cluster, ch 2, skip next Cluster, 5 dc in next ch-2 sp, ch 2, ★ tr in next tr, ch 2, 5 dc in next ch-2 sp, ch 2, skip next Cluster, sc in next Cluster, ch 2, skip next Cluster, 5 dc in next ch-2 sp, ch 2; repeat from ★ around; join with slip st to first tr changing to MC: 40 dc.

Rnd 4: Slip st in first ch-2 sp, ch 3 **(counts as first dc, now and throughout)**, dc in same sp, ★ † skip next dc, dc in next 4 dc and in next ch-2 sp, work 2-tr Cluster in next sc, dc in next ch-2 sp and in next 4 dc, skip next dc, 2 dc in next ch-2 sp, ch 2 †, 2 dc in next ch-2 sp; repeat from ★ 2 times **more**, then repeat from † to † once; join with slip st to first dc: 56 dc.

Rnd 5: Ch 3, ★ dc in next dc and in each dc and each Cluster across to next corner ch-2 sp, (2 dc, ch 2, 2 dc) in corner ch-2 sp; repeat from ★ around; join with slip st to first dc, finish off: 76 dc.

SQUARE B

Make 2 Squares, working one Square in each of the following Color Sequences:

Color Sequence #1: 1 Rnd each Color D, Color E, Color F, 2 rnds MC.

Color Sequence #2: 1 Rnd each Color B, Color C, Color D, 2 rnds MC.

With first color, ch 4; join with slip st to form a ring.

Rnd 1 (Right side)**:** Ch 1, ★ sc in ring, ch 5, work 2-dc Cluster in ring, ch 5; repeat from ★ 3 times **more**; join with slip st to first sc, finish off: 8 loops.

Note: Mark last round as **right** side.

Rnd 2: With **right** side facing, join new color with slip st in loop to left of any 2-dc Cluster; ch 3 **(counts as first dc, now and throughout)**, 2 dc in same loop, ch 2, (3 dc in next loop, ch 2) around; join with slip st to first dc, finish off: 24 dc.

Rnd 3: With **right** side facing, join new color with slip st in same st as joining; ch 1, sc in same st, ★ † ch 1, skip next dc, sc in next dc, work 3-dc Cluster in next ch-2 sp, sc in next dc, ch 1, skip next dc, sc in next dc, work 2-dc Cluster in next corner ch-2 sp, (ch 1, work 2-dc Cluster) twice in same sp †, sc in next dc; repeat from ★ 2 times **more**, then repeat from † to † once; join with slip st to first sc, finish off.

Rnd 4: With **right** side facing, join MC with slip st in any corner 2-dc Cluster; ch 3, (dc, ch 2, 2 dc) in same st, ★ † dc in next ch-1 sp and in next 2 sts, working **around** next ch, dc in skipped dc on Rnd 2, dc in next 3 sts, working **around** next ch, dc in skipped dc on Rnd 2, dc in next 2 sts and in next ch-1 sp †, (2 dc, ch 2, 2 dc) in next Cluster; repeat from ★ 2 times **more**, then repeat from † to † once; join with slip st to first dc: 60 dc.

Rnd 5: Ch 3, dc in next dc, (2 dc, ch 2, 2 dc) in next corner ch-2 sp, ★ dc in each dc across to next corner ch-2 sp, (2 dc, ch 2, 2 dc) in corner ch-2 sp; repeat from ★ 2 times **more**, dc in each dc across; join with slip st to first dc, finish off: 76 dc.

ASSEMBLY

With MC, whipstitch each Square A to a Square B *(Fig. 27a, page 140)*.

Whipstitch strips together, placing Square A and B together.

Continued on page 72.

DOLLY DRAFT DODGER

*Hanging around doorknobs is what this darling miss does best —
when she's not keeping drafts from creeping in under the door! Designed
to resemble an old-fashioned rag doll, she makes a fun country accent.*

Finished Size: Approximately 35" tall

MATERIALS
Worsted Weight Yarn, approximately:
    Color A (White) - 4 ounces, (110 grams, 250 yards)
    Color B (Blue) - 3½ ounces, (100 grams, 220 yards)
    Color C (Beige) - 8 ounces, (230 grams, 505 yards)
    Color D (Red) - 2½ ounces, (70 grams, 160 yards)
    Color E (Black) - ¾ ounce, (20 grams, 50 yards)
Crochet hook, size G (4.00 mm) **or** size needed for gauge
Yarn needle
Sewing needle and thread
Polyester stuffing
Red and White felt
Fusible interfacing
¾" Shank buttons - 2
Fabric (for bow and cheeks)
Glue gun

GAUGE: 16 dc and 8 rows = 4"
              12 Clusters and 8 rows = 4"

PATTERN STITCH
CLUSTER
YO, insert hook in **same** st, YO and pull up a loop, YO and draw through 2 loops on hook, YO, insert hook in **next** st, YO and pull up a loop, YO and draw through 2 loops on hook, YO and draw through all 3 loops on hook.

HEAD
FRONT
Rnd 1 (Right side)**:** With Color A, ch 2, 8 sc in second ch from hook; do **not** join, place marker *(see Markers, page 138)*.
Note: Loop a short piece of yarn around any stitch to mark last round as **right** side.
Rnd 2: 2 Sc in each sc around: 16 sc.

Rnd 3: (Sc in next sc, 2 sc in next sc) around: 24 sc.
Rnd 4: (Sc in next 2 sc, 2 sc in next sc) around: 32 sc.
Rnd 5: Sc in next sc, 2 sc in next sc, (sc in next 3 sc, 2 sc in next sc) 7 times, sc in next 2 sc: 40 sc.
Rnd 6: Sc in each sc around.
Rnd 7: (Sc in next 4 sc, 2 sc in next sc) around: 48 sc.
Rnd 8: Sc in next 2 sc, 2 sc in next sc, (sc in next 5 sc, 2 sc in next sc) 7 times, sc in next 3 sc: 56 sc.
Rnd 9: (Sc in next 6 sc, 2 sc in next sc) around: 64 sc.
Rnd 10: Sc in next 4 sc, 2 sc in next sc, (sc in next 7 sc, 2 sc in next sc) 7 times, sc in next 3 sc: 72 sc.
Rnd 11: (Sc in next 8 sc, 2 sc in next sc) around: 80 sc.
Rnd 12: Sc in next 4 sc, 2 sc in next sc, (sc in next 9 sc, 2 sc in next sc) 7 times, sc in next 5 sc: 88 sc.
Neck: Slip st in next sc, sc in next sc, hdc in next sc, 2 dc in each of next 6 sc, hdc in next sc, sc in next sc, slip st in next sc, leave remaining sts unworked; finish off.

BACK

Rnds 1-12: With Color D, work same as Front; at end of Rnd 12, slip st in next sc, finish off.
Neck: With **right** side facing and working in Back Loops Only *(Fig. 20, page 138)*, join Color A with slip st in first sc; sc in next sc, hdc in next sc, 2 dc in each of next 6 sc, hdc in next sc, sc in next sc, slip st in next sc; finish off.

TOE (Make 2)

Rnd 1 (Right side): With Color E, ch 2, 6 sc in second ch from hook; do **not** join, place marker.
Note: Mark last round as **right** side.
Rnd 2: 2 Sc in each sc around: 12 sc.
Rnd 3: (Sc in next 3 sc, 2 sc in next sc) around: 15 sc.
Rnd 4: (Sc in next 4 sc, 2 sc in next sc) around: 18 sc.
Rnds 5-9: Sc in each sc around.
Rnd 10: (Sc in next sc, 2 sc in next sc) around: 27 sc.
Rnd 11: Sc in each sc around; slip st in next sc, finish off leaving a long end for sewing.
Stuff **and** set aside.

LEG (Make 2)

HEEL

Rnd 1 (Right side): With Color E, ch 2, 6 sc in second ch from hook; do **not** join, place marker.
Rnd 2: 2 Sc in each sc around: 12 sc.
Rnd 3: (Sc in next 2 sc, 2 sc in next sc) around: 16 sc.
Rnd 4: (Sc in next 3 sc, 2 sc in next sc) around: 20 sc.
Rnds 5-13: Sc in each sc around; at end of Rnd 13, slip st in next sc, finish off.
Stuff **firmly.**

STOCKING

Rnd 1: With **right** side of Heel facing, join Color D with slip st in first sc; ch 3 **(counts as first dc, now and throughout)**, dc in next sc and in each sc around, drop Color D; join with slip st to first dc changing to Color A *(Fig. 22b, page 138)*: 20 dc.
Note: Carry unused yarn **loosely** along joining on **wrong** side.
Rnd 2: Ch 3, dc in next dc and in each dc around, drop Color A; join with slip st to first dc changing to Color D.
Rnd 3: Ch 3, dc in next dc and in each dc around, drop Color D; join with slip st to first dc changing to Color A.
Note: Stuff lightly as needed while working entire Leg.
Rnds 4-17: Repeat Rnds 2 and 3, 7 times; at end of Rnd 17 change to Color C.

PANTALOONS

Rnd 1: Ch 1, sc in each dc around; join with slip st to Back Loop Only of first sc.
Rnd 2: Ch 1, working in Back Loops Only, sc in same st, dc in next sc, (sc in next sc, dc in next sc) around; join with slip st to first sc.
Rnd 3: Ch 3, **turn;** working in **both** loops, sc in next dc, (dc in next sc, sc in next dc) around; join with slip st to first dc.
Rnd 4: Ch 1, turn; sc in same st, dc in next sc, (sc in next dc, dc in next sc) around; join with slip st to first sc.
Repeat Rnds 3 and 4 until piece measures approximately 18" from bottom of Heel, ending by working a **right** side rnd; finish off.

RUFFLE

With **right** side facing, top towards you and working in free loops on Rnd 1 *(Fig. 21a, page 138)*, join Color C with slip st in first st; ch 1, (sc, ch 1, dc, ch 1) in same st and in each st around; join with slip st to first sc, finish off.

BODY

Rnd 1: Holding previous rnd of left Leg together with joining at center back, and working through **both** loops of front dc and in Front Loops Only of back dc, join Color C with slip st in first sc; ch 3, sc in next dc, (dc in next sc, sc in next dc) across; holding right Leg in same manner, dc in first sc, sc in next dc, (dc in next sc, sc in next dc) across, **turn;** working in **free** loops, (dc in next sc, sc in next dc) across **both** Legs; join with slip st to first dc: 40 sts.
Rnd 2 (Increase rnd): Ch 3, turn; sc in same st, (dc in next sc, sc in next dc) 4 times, ★ (dc, sc) in each of next 2 sts, (dc in next sc, sc in next dc) 4 times; repeat from ★ 2 times **more**, (dc, sc) in last sc; join with slip st to first dc: 48 sts.
Rnd 3: Ch 1, turn; sc in same st, dc in next sc, (sc in next dc, dc in next sc) around; join with slip st to first sc.

Rnd 4: Ch 3, turn; sc in next dc, (dc in next sc, sc in next dc) around; join with slip st to first dc.
Repeat Rnds 3 and 4 until Body measures approximately 5", ending by working a **right** side rnd.
Edging: Slip st in Front Loop Only of each st around; finish off.

BODICE

Rnd 1: With **right** side facing and working in free loops of Body, join Color B with slip st in st at side; ch 3, dc in next st and in each st around; join with slip st to first dc.
Rnd 2: Ch 3, dc in next dc and in each dc around; join with slip st to first dc.
Repeat Rnd 2 until Bodice measures approximately 4¹/₂"; finish off leaving a long end for sewing.
Stuff **lightly**.

Sew top seam.

ARM (Make 2)

Rnd 1 (Right side): With Color A, ch 4, 6 dc in fourth ch from hook; join with slip st to top of beginning ch: 7 sts.
Rnd 2: Ch 3, dc in same st, 2 dc in each dc around; join with slip st to first dc: 14 dc.
Rnd 3: Ch 2, dc in next st, work Clusters around working last Cluster in same st as beginning ch-2; skip beginning ch-2 and join with slip st to first dc: 14 sts.
Rnd 4: Ch 2, dc in next st, work 5 Clusters, 4 dc in same st (thumb), work Clusters around; skip beginning ch-2 and join with slip st to first dc: 18 sts.
Rnd 5: Ch 2, dc in next st, work 4 Clusters, ★ YO, insert hook in **next** dc, YO and pull up a loop, YO and draw through 2 loops on hook; repeat from ★ 4 times **more**, YO and draw through all 6 loops on hook, work Clusters around; skip beginning ch-2 and join with slip st to first dc: 14 sts.
Note: Stuff **lightly** as needed while working Rnds 6-28.
Rnds 6-28: Repeat Rnd 3, 23 times.
Finish off leaving a long end for sewing.

Sew Arms to Bodice.
Flatten each Arm across top of Rnd 14 and sew across forming elbow.

APRON

With Color C, ch 48 **loosely**; being careful not to twist ch, join with slip st to form a ring.
Rnd 1 (Right side): Ch 1, sc in each ch around; join with slip st to first sc: 48 sc.
Note: Mark last round as **right** side.
Rnd 2 (Increase rnd): Ch 1, (sc, dc) in each sc around; join with slip st to first sc: 96 sts.
Rnd 3: Ch 3, turn; sc in next dc, (dc in next sc, sc in next dc) around; join with slip st to first dc.

Rnd 4: Ch 1, turn; sc in same st, dc in next sc, (sc in next dc, dc in next sc) around; join with slip st to first sc.
Repeat Rnds 3 and 4 until Apron measures approximately 9", ending by working a **right** side rnd, do **not** finish off.

BOTTOM APRON RUFFLE

Ch 1, do **not** turn; working in Front Loops Only, (sc, ch 1, dc, ch 1) in each st around; join with slip st to first sc, finish off.

DRESS RUFFLE

Rnd 1: With **right** side facing and working in free loops **behind** Apron Ruffle, join Color B with slip st in first st; ch 3, dc in same st, 2 dc in next st and in each st around; join with slip st to first dc: 192 dc.
Rnds 2 and 3: Ch 3, dc in next dc and in each dc around; join with slip st to first dc.
Finish off.

TOP APRON RUFFLE

Rnd 1: With **right** side facing and working in free loops of beginning ch *(Fig. 21b, page 138)*, join Color C with slip st in first ch; ch 1, sc in each ch around; join with slip st to first sc: 48 sc.
Rnd 2: Ch 3, dc in same st, 2 dc in next sc and in each sc around; join with slip st to first dc, finish off: 96 dc.

TIES (Make 2)
With Color C, ch 38 **loosely**.
Row 1: Dc in fourth ch from hook and in each ch across: 36 sts.
Edging: Slip st twice in end of row, slip st in free loop of each ch across, slip st twice in end of row; join with slip st to first dc, finish off.

Sew Ties to Apron, crossing them in back.

SLEEVE (Make 2)

With Color B and leaving a long end for sewing, ch 20 **loosely**; being careful not to twist ch, join with slip st to form a ring.
Rnd 1: Ch 1, sc in each ch around; join with slip st to first sc: 20 sc.
Rnd 2 (Increase rnd): Ch 3, 2 dc in next sc, (dc in next sc, 2 dc in next sc) around; join with slip st to first dc: 30 dc.
Rnds 3-11: Ch 3, dc in next dc and in each dc around; join with slip st to first dc.
Rnd 12: Ch 2, dc in next dc, ★ (YO, insert hook in **next** dc, YO and pull up a loop, YO and draw through 2 loops on hook) twice, YO and draw through all 3 loops on hook; repeat from ★ around; skip beginning ch-2 and join with slip st to first dc: 15 sts.
Rnd 13: Ch 1, sc in each st around; join with slip st to first sc.

Rnd 14 (Ruffle): Ch 4, dc in same st, ch 1, (dc, ch 1) twice in each sc around; join with slip st to third ch of beginning ch-4, finish off.

FINISHING

Sew Toes to front of Heels.
Slip Arms into Sleeves and sew Sleeves to Bodice.
Sew Front and Back of Head together, working in **both** loops of Front and in inside loop only of Back and leaving 16 Neck sts free.

NECK RUFFLE

Rnd 1: With **right** side facing, join Color C with slip st in first sc at seam; ch 1, sc in each st around; join with slip st to first sc: 32 sc.
Rnd 2: Ch 1, turn; (sc, ch 1, dc, ch 1) in Back Loop Only of same st and in each sc around; join with slip st to first sc, finish off leaving a long end for sewing.
Stuff Head.

Sew Neck Ruffle to Body, working along Rnd 1.
Cut nose from red felt and eyes from white felt using diagrams.
Glue in place.
Cut shank off buttons. Glue button tops to felt eyes.
Iron a 1¹/₂" x 3" piece of fusible interfacing to wrong side of fabric. Cut 2 circles from fabric using diagram.
Glue in place for cheeks.
With Color E, add mouth.
Slip Apron on doll.
Sew hands together firmly.

HAIR

With Color D, add fringe to free loops of Back of Head **(Figs. 28a & b, page 141)**, placing 12 groups of three, 7" strands along nape of Neck and three, 5" strands to remaining loops.
Cut a 1" x 14" piece of fabric. Tie in a bow and sew to Head at hairline.

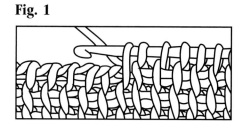

Cheeks

Nose

Eyes

DANDY DINOSAURS

*D*elight a youngster with our dandy dinosaur afghan! The colorful brontosaurus, triceratops, and stegosaurus are easy to cross stitch on blocks of afghan stitches. Textured squares and a simple striped border offer added interest to this playful throw.

Finished Size: Approximately 45" x 60"

MATERIALS

Worsted Weight Yarn, approximately:
    MC (Blue) - 45 ounces, (1,280 grams, 2,545 yards)
    Color A (Red) - 5 ounces, (140 grams, 285 yards)
    Color B (Orange) - ¹/₂ ounce, (15 grams, 30 yards)
    Color C (Yellow) - 2 ounces, (60 grams, 115 yards)
    Color D (Fuchsia) - ³/₄ ounce, (20 grams, 45 yards)
    Color E (Green) - 1¹/₂ ounces, (40 grams, 85 yards)
    Color F (White) - 3 yards
    Color G (Black) - 2 yards
Afghan hook, size J (6.00 mm) **or** size needed for gauge
Crochet hook, size H (5.00 mm) **or** size needed for gauge
Yarn needle

GAUGE: In Afghan Stitch, 16 sts and 14 rows = 4"
        Block before Edging = 13" x 13"
        Edging, 16 sc = 4"

PATTERN STITCHES

AFGHAN STITCH

With yarn in **back**, insert hook from **right** to **left** under next vertical strand **(Fig. 1)**, YO and pull up a loop.

Fig. 1

PUFF STITCH

★ YO, insert hook from right to left under **both** vertical strands of next st, YO and pull up a loop **(Fig. 2)**; repeat from ★ 2 times **more**, YO and draw through 6 loops on hook, ch 1 to close.

Fig. 2

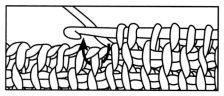

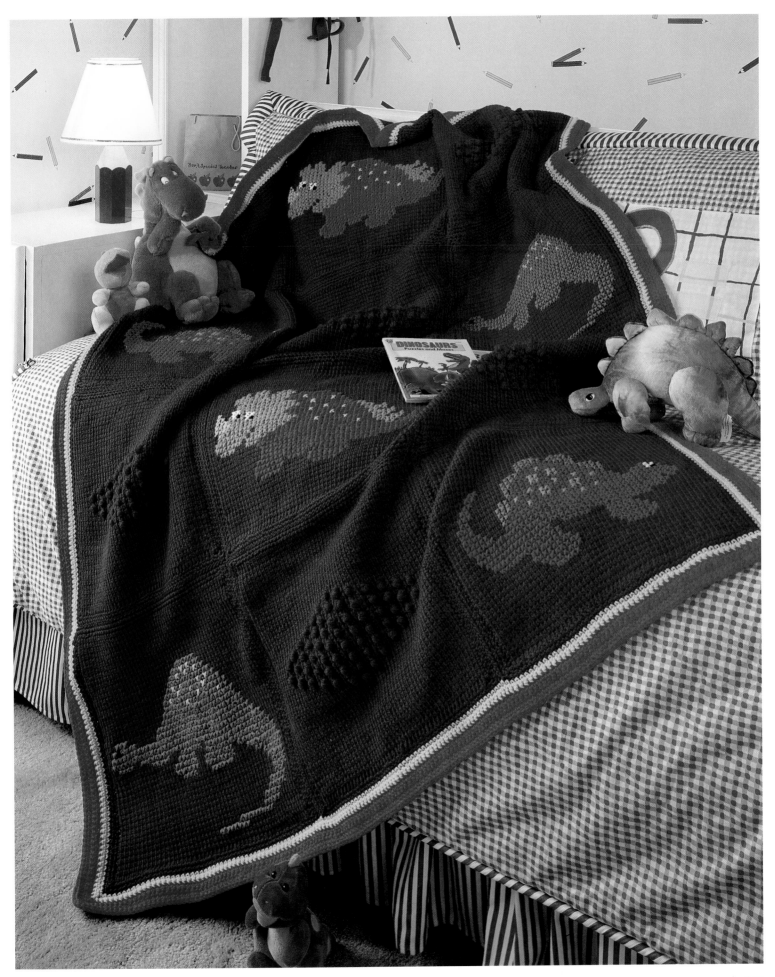

BASIC BLOCK (Make 6)

With afghan hook and MC, ch 52 **loosely**.

Note: Each row is worked in 2 steps, working to the **left** picking up loops and then working to the **right** completing each stitch.

Row 1: Working from right to left and in Top Loops Only, insert hook in second ch from hook, YO and pull up a loop (2 loops on hook), pull up a loop in each ch across *(Fig. 3a)* (52 loops on hook); working from left to right, YO and draw through first loop on hook, ★ YO and draw through 2 loops on hook *(Fig. 3b)*; repeat from ★ across until one loop remains on hook. This is the first stitch of the next row.

Fig. 3a   **Fig. 3b**

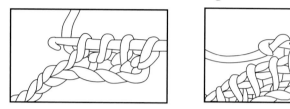

Row 2: Working from right to left, skip first vertical strand, work Afghan St across *(Fig. 1, page 66)* (52 loops on hook); working from left to right, YO and draw through first loop on hook, (YO and draw through 2 loops on hook) across.

Rows 3-46: Repeat Row 2, 44 times.

Note: Loop a short piece of yarn around any stitch on Row 46 to mark **right** side and top.

Last Row: Working from right to left, skip first vertical strand, ★ insert hook under next vertical strand, YO and draw loosely through strand **and** loop on hook *(Fig. 4)*; repeat from ★ across; do **not** finish off.

Fig. 4

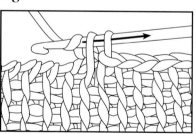

EDGING

Rnd 1: Using a crochet hook, ch 1, sc in end of each row across; working in free loops of beginning ch *(Fig. 21b, page 138)*, 3 sc in first ch, work 46 sc evenly spaced across to last ch, 3 sc in last ch; sc in end of each row across; working across last row, 3 sc in first st, work 46 sc evenly spaced across to last st, 3 sc in last st; join with slip st to first sc: 196 sc.

Rnd 2: Ch 1, sc in each sc around working 3 sc in each corner sc; join with slip st to first sc, finish off: 204 sc.

TEXTURED BLOCK (Make 6)

With afghan hook and MC, ch 52 **loosely**.

Rows 1-16: Work same as Basic Block.

Row 17: Working from right to left, skip first vertical strand, work 25 Afghan Sts, work Puff St *(Fig. 2, page 66)*, work Afghan St across; working from left to right, YO and draw through first loop on hook, (YO and draw through 2 loops on hook) across.

Row 18: Working from right to left, skip first vertical strand, work 22 Afghan Sts, work Puff St, work 5 Afghan Sts, work Puff St, work Afghan St across; working from left to right, YO and draw through first loop on hook, (YO and draw through 2 loops on hook) across.

Row 19: Working from right to left, skip first vertical strand, work 19 Afghan Sts, work Puff St, (work 5 Afghan Sts, work Puff St) twice, work Afghan St across; working from left to right, YO and draw through first loop on hook, (YO and draw through 2 loops on hook) across.

Row 20: Working from right to left, skip first vertical strand, work 16 Afghan Sts, work Puff St, (work 5 Afghan Sts, work Puff St) 3 times, work Afghan St across; working from left to right, YO and draw through first loop on hook, (YO and draw through 2 loops on hook) across.

Row 21: Working from right to left, skip first vertical strand, work 13 Afghan Sts, work Puff St, (work 5 Afghan Sts, work Puff St) 4 times, work Afghan St across; working from left to right, YO and draw through first loop on hook, (YO and draw through 2 loops on hook) across.

Row 22: Working from right to left, skip first vertical strand, work 10 Afghan Sts, work Puff St, (work 5 Afghan Sts, work Puff St) 5 times, work Afghan St across; working from left to right, YO and draw through first loop on hook, (YO and draw through 2 loops on hook) across.

Row 23: Working from right to left, skip first vertical strand, work 7 Afghan Sts, work Puff St, (work 5 Afghan Sts, work Puff St) 6 times, work Afghan St across; working from left to right, YO and draw through first loop on hook, (YO and draw through 2 loops on hook) across.

Rows 24-26: Repeat Rows 22 and 23 once, then repeat Row 22 once **more**.

Row 27: Repeat Row 21.

Row 28: Repeat Row 20.

Row 29: Repeat Row 19.

Row 30: Repeat Row 18.

Row 31: Repeat Row 17.

Rows 32-46: Repeat Row 2, 15 times.

Note: Mark last row as **right** side and top.

Last Row: Working from right to left, skip first vertical strand, ★ insert hook under next vertical strand, YO and draw loosely through strand **and** loop on hook; repeat from ★ across; do **not** finish off.

EDGING
Work same as Basic Block.

FINISHING
CROSS STITCH
Following charts, cross stitch each dinosaur in center of 2 Blocks *(Fig. 29, page 141)*.

TRICERATOPS

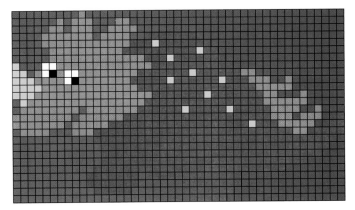

BRONTOSAURUS

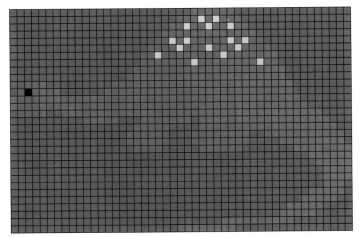

STEGOSAURUS

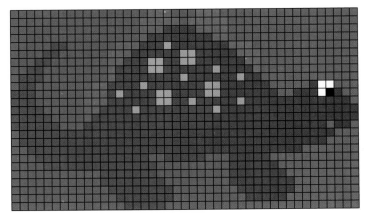

ASSEMBLY
Following Placement Diagram and using MC, whipstitch 4 Blocks into 3 vertical strips *(Fig. 27a, page 140)*; then whipstitch strips together.

PLACEMENT DIAGRAM

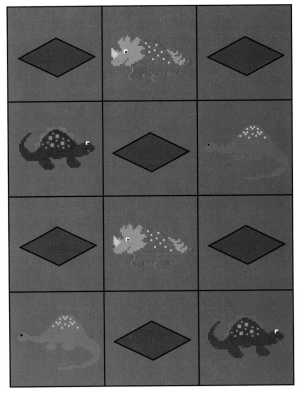

BORDER
Rnd 1: With **right** side facing, join Color C with slip st in any corner sc; ch 1, sc evenly around working 3 sc in each corner sc; join with slip st to first sc.

Rnd 2: Ch 1, turn; sc in each sc around working 3 sc in each corner sc; join with slip st to first sc changing to Color A *(Fig. 22b, page 138)*.

Rnds 3-6: Ch 1, turn; sc in each sc around working 3 sc in each corner sc; join with slip st to first sc.

Rnd 7: Turn; slip st in each sc around; join with slip st to first slip st, finish off.

Quick DOGGIE WEAR

When the weather turns cold, dress your dogs in these sporty sweaters for their nightly walk. Both are extra-easy to make because there aren't any leg holes — the sweaters are secured with a simple strap around your pooch's tummy.

Finished Size: Approximately 12{14-16-18}" from neck to base of tail

Size Note: Instructions are written for size Small with sizes Medium, Large and Extra-Large in braces. Instructions will be easier to read if you circle all the numbers pertaining to your dog's size.

MATERIALS

Worsted Weight Yarn, approximately:

Solid

2$\frac{1}{2}${3-4-5} ounces, [70{90-110-140} grams, 165{200-265-330} yards]

Striped

MC (Blue) - 1$\frac{1}{2}${2-2$\frac{1}{2}$-3} ounces, [40{60-70-90} grams, 100{135-165-200} yards]

Color A (White) - $\frac{3}{4}${1-1$\frac{1}{4}$-1$\frac{1}{2}$} ounces, [20{30-35-40} grams, 50{65-85-100} yards]

Color B (Red) - $\frac{1}{2}${$\frac{1}{2}$-$\frac{3}{4}$-$\frac{3}{4}$} ounce, [15{15-20-20} grams, 35{35-50-50} yards]

Crochet hook, size K (6.50 mm) **or** size needed for gauge

$\frac{3}{4}$" Buttons - 2

Yarn needle

GAUGE: In pattern, 12 sts and 8 rows = 4"

PATTERN STITCH

DECREASE (uses next 2 sts)

★ YO, insert hook in **next** st, YO and pull up a loop, YO and draw through 2 loops on hook; repeat from ★ once **more**, YO and draw through all 3 loops on hook **(counts as one dc)**.

FRONT POST DOUBLE CROCHET *(abbreviated FPdc)*

YO, insert hook from **front** to **back** around post of st indicated *(Fig. 13, page 135)*, YO and pull up a loop even with loop on hook, (YO and draw through 2 loops on hook) twice. Skip st behind FPdc.

BACK POST DOUBLE CROCHET *(abbreviated BPdc)*

YO, insert hook from **back** to **front** around post of st indicated, YO and pull up a loop even with loop on hook, (YO and draw through 2 loops on hook) twice. Skip st in front of BPdc.

SOLID SWEATER

BODY

Ch 28{31-34-37} **loosely.**

Row 1: Dc in fourth ch from hook and in each ch across: 26{29-32-35} sts.

Row 2 (Right side): Ch 3 **(counts as first dc, now and throughout)**, turn; dc in next dc, (work FPdc around next dc, dc in next 2 dc) across: 8{9-10-11} FPdc.

Row 3 (Increase row): Ch 3, turn; dc in same st and in next dc, work BPdc around next st, (dc in next 2 dc, work BPdc around next st) across to last 2 dc, dc in next dc, 2 dc in last dc: 28{31-34-37} sts.

Row 4: Ch 3, turn; (dc in next 2 dc, work FPdc around next st) across to last 3 dc, dc in last 3 dc.

Row 5 (Increase row): Ch 3, turn; dc in same st and in next 2 dc, (work BPdc around next st, dc in next 2 dc) across to last dc, 2 dc in last dc: 30{33-36-39} sts.

Row 6: Ch 3, turn; work FPdc around next st, (dc in next 2 dc, work FPdc around next st) across to last dc, dc in last dc.

Row 7 (Increase row): Ch 3, turn; dc in same st, work BPdc around next st, (dc in next 2 dc, work BPdc around next st) across to last dc, 2 dc in last dc: 32{35-38-41} sts.

Row 8: Ch 3, turn; dc in next dc, (work FPdc around next st, dc in next 2 dc) across.

Rows 9-11: Repeat Rows 3-5: 36{39-42-45} sts.

Repeat Row 6 for a total of 21{25-29-33} rows.

RIGHT NECK SHAPING

Note: Maintain established pattern throughout.

Row 1: Ch 3, turn; work across next 13{14-15-16} sts, leave remaining sts unworked: 14{15-16-17} sts.

Row 2 (Decrease row): Ch 3, turn; decrease, work across: 13{14-15-16} sts.

Row 3 (Decrease row): Ch 3, turn; work across to last 3 sts, decrease, dc in last dc: 12{13-14-15} sts.

Rows 4-7: Repeat Rows 2 and 3 twice: 8{9-10-11} sts.

Row 8: Work across; finish off.

LEFT NECK SHAPING

Row 1: With **right** side facing, skip 8{9-10-11} sts from Right Neck and join yarn with slip st in next st; ch 3, work across: 14{15-16-17} sts.

Row 2 (Decrease row): Ch 3, turn; work across to last 3 sts, decrease, dc in last dc: 13{14-15-16} sts.

Row 3 (Decrease row): Ch 3, turn; decrease, work across: 12{13-14-15} sts.

Rows 4-7: Repeat Rows 2 and 3 twice: 8{9-10-11} sts.
Row 8: Work across; finish off.

STRIPED SWEATER

Work same as Solid Sweater in the following Color Sequence:
★ 3 Rows MC *(Fig. 22a, page 138)*, 1 row each Color A, Color B, Color A; repeat from ★ 3{4-5-5} times **more**, then work 3{3-1-3} rows MC.
For sizes Small & Extra-Large Only: work 1 Row each Color A, Color B.

FINISHING

With **right** sides together and corresponding color, whipstitch end of Right Neck to end of Left Neck *(Fig. 27a, page 140)*.

NECKBAND

Rnd 1: With **right** side facing and MC, join yarn with slip st at seam; ch 1, sc evenly around; join with slip st to first sc.

Rnds 2 and 3: Ch 1, sc in each sc around; join with slip st to first sc.
Finish off.

BAND

Row 1: With **right** side facing, working in end of rows and using MC, join yarn with slip st on left edge of Sweater, 5{6-7-8}" down from seam; ch 3, dc in same st, 2 dc in each of next 5 rows, dc in next row: 13 dc.
Row 2: Ch 3, turn; dc in next dc and in each dc across.
Repeat Row 2 until Band fits snugly around dog's chest.

BUTTONHOLES

Row 1: Ch 1, turn; sc in each dc across.
Row 2: Ch 1, turn; sc in first 3 sc, (ch 2, skip next 2 sc, sc in next 3 sc) twice.
Row 3: Ch 1, turn; sc in each sc and in each ch across: 13 sc.
Row 4: Ch 1, turn; sc in each sc across; finish off.

Add buttons.

GRANNY SQUARE TV PILLOWS

Continued from page 62.

BORDER

Rnd 1: With **right** side facing, join Color B with slip st in any corner ch-2 sp; ch 3, dc in same sp, ★ † dc in each dc across to next joining, dc in next 2 ch-sps, dc in each dc across to next corner ch-2 sp †, (2 dc, ch 1, 2 dc) in corner ch-2 sp; repeat from ★ 2 times **more**, then repeat from † to † once, 2 dc in same sp as first dc, sc in first dc to form last sp changing to Color F *(Fig. 22a, page 138)*: 176 dc.

Rnd 2: Ch 1, 2 sc in same sp, sc in each st across to next corner ch-1 sp, ★ (2 sc, ch 1, 2 sc) in corner ch-1 sp, sc in each st across to next corner ch-1 sp; repeat from ★ around, 2 sc in same sp as first sc, sc in first sc to form last sp changing to Color D: 192 sc.

Rnd 3: Repeat Rnd 2, changing to Color A: 208 sc.

Rnd 4: Repeat Rnd 2, changing to Color C: 224 sc.

Rnd 5: Ch 3, (dc, ch 2, 2 dc) in same sp, dc in each sc across to next corner ch-1 sp, ★ (2 dc, ch 2, 2 dc) in corner ch-1 sp, dc in each sc across to next corner ch-1 sp; repeat from ★ around; join with slip st to first dc, finish off: 240 dc.

FRONT - PILLOW #2

Work 4 Squares same as Square A of Pillow #1, page 62, working in the following Color Sequence:

Color Sequence: 1 Rnd each Color A, Color B, Color C, Color D, MC *(Fig. 22b, page 138)*.

ASSEMBLY

With MC, whipstitch Squares into 2 vertical strips of 2 Squares each *(Fig. 27a, page 140)*; then whipstitch strips together.

BORDER

Rnd 1: With **right** side facing, join Color A with slip st in any corner ch-2 sp; ch 1, 2 sc in same sp, ★ † sc in each dc across to next joining, sc in next 2 ch-sps, sc in each dc across to next corner ch-2 sp †, (2 sc, ch 1, 2 sc) in corner ch-2 sp; repeat from ★ 2 times **more**, then repeat from † to † once, 2 sc in same sp as first sc, sc in first sc to form last sp changing to Color B *(Fig. 22a, page 138)*: 176 sc.

Rnd 2: Ch 3, dc in same sp, dc in each st across to next corner ch-1 sp, ★ (2 dc, ch 1, 2 dc) in corner ch-1 sp, dc in each st across to next corner ch-1 sp; repeat from ★ around, 2 dc in same sp as first dc, sc in first dc to form last sp changing to Color C: 192 dc.

Rnd 3: Repeat Rnd 2, changing to Color D: 208 dc.

Rnd 4: Ch 1, ★ (2 sc, ch 1, 2 sc) in corner sp, sc in each dc across to next corner ch-1 sp; repeat from ★ around; join with slip st to first sc, finish off: 224 sc.

FINISHING

Make pillow form, if desired, page 140.
Whipstitch Front and Back together, inserting pillow form before closing.

Quick CHEERY PLANT POKES

Quick and easy to make, this cheery pair is a fun way to brighten a potted plant. The pokes are crocheted using embroidery floss and a steel hook and are lightly stuffed before finishing.

MATERIALS

Embroidery floss, approximately 1 skein **each**:
    Sun: Yellow, Orange, and Red
    Rainbow: Red, Orange, Yellow, Green, Blue,
        Blue Violet, and Purple
Steel crochet hook, size 6 (1.80 mm)
Polyester stuffing
Glue gun
Wooden stick
Embroidery needle
4 mm Wiggle Eyes - 2

Note #1: Gauge is not important. Pieces can be smaller or larger without changing the overall effect.
Note #2: **Both** projects use 6 strands of floss throughout.

SUN

PATTERN STITCH

CLUSTER (uses 4 sts)
YO, insert hook in same st, YO and pull up a loop, YO and draw through 2 loops on hook, ★ YO, insert hook in **next** sc, YO and pull up a loop, YO and draw through 2 loops on hook; repeat from ★ 2 times **more**, YO and draw through all 5 loops on hook.

Joining Rnd: With **wrong** sides of both pieces together, Front facing, and working through **both** thicknesses, sc in each sc around stuffing **lightly** before closing; slip st in next sc.

Edging: ★ Ch 3, work Cluster, ch 3, slip st in same sc as last st worked and in next sc; repeat from ★ around ending last slip st in same st as beginning ch-3; finish off.

With 6 strands of Red, add Backstitch smile *(Figs. 30a & b, page 142)*.

Glue eyes to Front and stick to Back.

RAINBOW

With Red, ch 16 **loosely**; being careful not to twist ch, join with slip st to form a ring.

Rnd 1 (Right side)**:** Ch 1, sc in same ch, 2 sc in next ch, (sc in next ch, 2 sc in next ch) around, cut Red; join with slip st to first sc changing to Orange *(Fig. 22b, page 138)*: 24 sc.

Rnd 2: Ch 1, sc in first 2 sc, 2 sc in next sc, (sc in next 2 sc, 2 sc in next sc) around, cut Orange; join with slip st to first sc changing to Yellow: 32 sc.

Rnd 3: Ch 1, sc in first 3 sc, 2 sc in next sc, (sc in next 3 sc, 2 sc in next sc) around, cut Yellow; join with slip st to first sc changing to Green: 40 sc.

Rnd 4: Ch 1, sc in first 4 sc, 2 sc in next sc, (sc in next 4 sc, 2 sc in next sc) around, cut Green; join with slip st to first sc changing to Blue: 48 sc.

Rnd 5: Ch 1, sc in first 5 sc, 2 sc in next sc, (sc in next 5 sc, 2 sc in next sc) around, cut Blue; join with slip st to first sc changing to Blue Violet: 56 sc.

Rnd 6: Ch 1, sc in first 6 sc, 2 sc in next sc, (sc in next 6 sc, 2 sc in next sc) around, cut Blue Violet; join with slip st to first sc changing to Purple: 64 sc.

Outside Joining Rnd: Ch 1, fold piece in half with wrong side together and ch-1 at fold, working through **both** thicknesses, sc in each sc across; finish off.

Stuff **lightly**.

Inside Joining Rnd: Matching sts and working through **both** thicknesses of beginning ch, join Red with slip st in first ch; ch 1, sc in each ch across; finish off.

Glue stick to Rainbow.

BACK

Rnd 1 (Right side)**:** With Yellow, ch 2, 8 sc in second ch from hook; do **not** join, place marker *(see Markers, page 138)*. *Note:* Loop a short piece of thread around any stitch to mark last round as **right** side.

Rnd 2: 2 Sc in each sc around: 16 sc.

Rnd 3: (2 Sc in next sc, sc in next sc) around: 24 sc.

Rnd 4: (2 Sc in next sc, sc in next 2 sc) around: 32 sc.

Rnd 5: Sc in each sc around; slip st in next sc, finish off.

FRONT

Rnds 1-4: Work same as Back.

Rnd 5: Sc in each sc around, cut Yellow; slip st in next sc changing to Orange *(Fig. 22b, page 138)*.

BLOOMING TEA SET

This summer serving set will make your refreshment table look as fresh as a flower. Featuring lacy petals in full bloom, the doily is fashioned in layers using bedspread weight cotton thread. The matching coasters start with the same pattern as the center of the doily.

Finished Size: Doily - approximately 11" in diameter
Coaster - approximately 4" in diameter

MATERIALS

Bedspread Weight Cotton Thread (size 10), approximately:
Color A (Yellow) - 100 yards
Color B (Green) - 93 yards
Color C (White) - 50 yards
Steel crochet hook, size 9 (1.40 mm) **or** size needed for gauge

GAUGE: Rnds 1-4 = 3"

PATTERN STITCHES
BEGINNING CLUSTER

Ch 3, ★ YO, insert hook in same sp, YO and pull up a loop, YO and draw through 2 loops on hook; repeat from ★ once **more**, YO and draw through all 3 loops on hook *(Figs. 10a & b, page 134)*.

CLUSTER

★ YO, insert hook in sp indicated, YO and pull up a loop, YO and draw through 2 loops on hook; repeat from ★ 2 times **more**, YO and draw through all 4 loops on hook.

DECREASE (uses next 2 dtr)

★ YO 3 times, insert hook in **next** dtr, YO and pull up a loop, (YO and draw through 2 loops on hook) 3 times; repeat from ★ once **more**, YO and draw through all 3 loops on hook **(counts as one dtr)**.

DOILY
CENTER

Rnd 1 (Right side): With Color A, ch 2, (sc, ch 3) 8 times in second ch from hook; join with slip st to first sc.
Note: Loop a short piece of thread around any stitch to mark last round as **right** side.
Rnd 2: Slip st in first ch-3 sp, work beginning Cluster, ch 3, (work Cluster in next ch-3 sp, ch 3) around; join with slip st to top of beginning Cluster: 8 Clusters.
Rnd 3: Slip st in first ch-3 sp, work (beginning Cluster, ch 3, Cluster) in same sp, ch 3, work Cluster in next ch-3 sp, ch 3, ★ (work Cluster, ch 3) twice in next ch-3 sp, work Cluster in next ch-3 sp, ch 3; repeat from ★ around; join with slip st to top of beginning Cluster: 12 Clusters.

Rnd 4: Slip st in first ch-3 sp, work beginning Cluster, (ch 3, work Cluster) twice in each of next 2 ch-3 sps, ★ ch 3, work Cluster in next ch-3 sp, (ch 3, work Cluster) twice in each of next 2 ch-3 sps; repeat from ★ around, ch 1, hdc in top of beginning Cluster to form last sp: 20 Clusters.
Rnd 5: Work (beginning Cluster, ch 3, Cluster) in same sp, [ch 3, (work Cluster, ch 3) twice in next ch-3 sp, work Cluster in next ch-3 sp] twice, ★ ch 3, (work Cluster, ch 3) twice in each of next 2 ch-3 sps, work Cluster in next ch-3 sp, ch 3, (work Cluster, ch 3) twice in next ch-3 sp, work Cluster in next ch-3 sp; repeat from ★ around, ch 1, hdc in top of beginning Cluster to form last sp: 32 Clusters.
Rnd 6: Work beginning Cluster in same sp, (ch 3, work Cluster in next ch-3 sp) around, ch 1, hdc in top of beginning Cluster to form last sp.
Rnd 7: Ch 1, sc in same sp, ch 8, (sc in next ch-3 sp, ch 8) around; join with slip st to first sc: 32 loops.
Rnd 8: Slip st in first loop, ch 1, (4 sc, ch 3, 4 sc) in same loop, keeping skipped loops to **back** of work, skip next loop, ★ (4 sc, ch 3, 4 sc) in next loop, skip next loop; repeat from ★ around; join with slip st to first sc, finish off: 128 sc.
Rnd 9: With **right** side facing, join Color B with slip st in any ch-3 sp on Rnd 8; ch 1, (sc, ch 3, sc) in same sp, sc in next 3 sc, pull up a loop in next 2 sc, YO and draw through all 3 loops on hook, sc in next 3 sc, ★ (sc, ch 3, sc) in next ch-3 sp, sc in next 3 sc, pull up a loop in next 2 sc, YO and draw through all 3 loops on hook, sc in next 3 sc; repeat from ★ around; join with slip st to first sc, finish off: 16 ch-3 sps.

PETALS

Rnd 1: With **right** side facing, join Color C with slip st in any ch-3 sp on Rnd 9; ch 3 **(counts as first dc, now and throughout)**, [dc, ch 3, dc, (ch 1, dc) 4 times, ch 3, 2 dc] in same sp, [2 dc, ch 3, dc, (ch 1, dc) 4 times, ch 3, 2 dc] in each ch-3 sp around; join with slip st to first dc: 144 dc.
Rnd 2: Ch 3, dc in next dc, ch 3, skip next ch-3 sp, (sc in next ch-1 sp, ch 3) 4 times, skip next ch-3 sp, dc in next 2 dc, ch 1, ★ dc in next 2 dc, ch 3, skip next ch-3 sp, (sc in next ch-1 sp, ch 3) 4 times, skip next ch-3 sp, dc in next 2 dc, ch 1; repeat from ★ around; join with slip st to first dc: 96 ch-sps.

Rnd 3: Ch 3, dc in next dc, ch 3, skip next ch-3 sp, (sc in next ch-3 sp, ch 3) 3 times, dc in next 2 dc, ch 2, ★ dc in next 2 dc, ch 3, skip next ch-3 sp, (sc in next ch-3 sp, ch 3) 3 times, dc in next 2 dc, ch 2; repeat from ★ around; join with slip st to first dc: 80 ch-sps.

Rnd 4: ★ Ch 3, dc in next dc, ch 3, skip next ch-3 sp, (sc in next ch-3 sp, ch 3) twice, dc in next dc, ch 6, **turn**; skip next ch-3 sp, sc in next ch-3 sp, ch 3, dc in last 2 dc, ch 3, **turn**; YO, insert hook in next dc, YO and pull up a loop, YO and draw through 2 loops on hook, YO, skip next sc and next 3 chs, insert hook in next ch, YO and pull up a loop, YO and draw through 2 loops on hook, YO and draw through all 3 loops on hook, ch 3, slip st in last ch worked into, ch 3, slip st in top of next row, ch 3, slip st in next dc on Rnd 3, slip st in next 2 chs and in next dc; repeat from ★ around; finish off.

LEAVES

Rnd 1: With **right** side facing and working behind Petals and in skipped loops on Rnd 7 of Center, join Color B with slip st in any loop; ch 5 **(counts as first dtr, now and throughout)**, (3 dtr, ch 2, 4 dtr) in same loop, ch 2, (4 dtr, ch 2) twice in each loop around; join with slip st to first dtr: 128 dtr.

Rnd 2: Ch 5, dtr in next 3 dtr, ch 2, (dtr in next 4 dtr, ch 2) around; join with slip st to first dtr.

Rnd 3: ★ Ch 5, dtr in next 3 dtr, ch 2, dtr in next 3 dtr, ch 4, **turn**; decrease 3 times, ch 4, **turn**; decrease, ch 4, slip st in top of beginning ch, ch 4, slip st in top of next row, ch 5, slip st in next dtr on Rnd 2, slip st in next 2 chs and in next dtr; repeat from ★ around; finish off.

COASTER (Make 4)

Rnds 1-4: Work same as Doily Center.

Rnd 5: Ch 1, sc in same sp, ch 5, (sc in next ch-3 sp, ch 5) around; join with slip st to first sc: 20 loops.

Rnd 6: Slip st in first loop, ch 1, (2 sc, ch 2, 2 sc) in same loop and in each loop around; join with slip st to first sc, finish off: 20 ch-2 sps.

Rnd 7: With **right** side facing, join Color B with slip st in any ch-2 sp; ch 1, (sc, ch 2, sc) in same sp, sc in next sc, pull up a loop in next 2 sc, YO and draw through all 3 loops on hook, sc in next sc, ★ (sc, ch 2, sc) in next ch-2 sp, sc in next sc, pull up a loop in next 2 sc, YO and draw through all 3 loops on hook, sc in next sc; repeat from ★ around; join with slip st to first sc, finish off.

Wash and Block all pieces, page 140.

rock-a-bye collection

Babies are precious gifts from above, and this heavenly collection will help you celebrate a long-awaited arrival. From afghans to photo frames, these projects all make sweet accessories for the nursery or thoughtful gifts for a new mom. There's even a little guardian angel to keep watch while baby sleeps. You'll find lots of ways to shower baby with love!

HEARTWARMING WRAP

Rows of tiny hearts, fashioned with a unique cluster stitch, perfectly reflect a parent's love on this darling throw. It's sure to make baby's trip home from the hospital a memorable one. Finished with a lacy ruffle and satin ribbon, the afghan looks pretty in pink — or any color!

Finished Size: Approximately 33" x 43"

MATERIALS

Baby Sport Weight Yarn, approximately:
   17 ounces, (480 grams, 1,715 yards)
Crochet hook, size F (3.75 mm) **or** size needed for gauge
1/2" Ribbon - 6 yards

GAUGE: In pattern, 16 dc = 4" and 10 rows = 4¹/₄"

PATTERN STITCHES

DOUBLE CLUSTER

YO, insert hook from **front** to **back** around post of dc **below** last dc worked *(Fig. 13, page 135)*, † YO and pull up a loop, YO and draw through 2 loops on hook, YO, insert hook from **front** to **back** around same dc, YO and pull up a loop, YO and draw through 2 loops on hook †, skip next dc, YO, insert hook from **front** to **back** around post of next dc, repeat from † to † once, YO and draw through all 5 loops on hook.

PUFF ST

★ YO, insert hook in sp indicated, YO and pull up a loop even with loop on hook; repeat from ★ 3 times **more** *(Fig. 12, page 134)*, YO and draw through all 9 loops on hook.

BODY

Ch 107 **loosely**.

Row 1 (Eyelet row): Dc in eighth ch from hook, (ch 2, skip next 2 chs, dc in next ch) across: 34 sps.

Row 2: Ch 5 **(counts as first dc plus ch 2, now and throughout)**, turn; dc in next dc, (2 dc in next ch-2 sp, dc in next dc) across to beginning ch, ch 2, skip next 2 chs, dc in next ch: 99 dc.

Row 3 (Right side): Ch 5, turn; dc in next 2 dc, work double Cluster, ★ dc in same dc and in next 2 dc, work double Cluster; repeat from ★ across to last 2 dc, dc in same dc and in next dc, ch 2, dc in last dc: 24 double Clusters.

Row 4: Ch 5, turn; dc in next 2 dc, dc in each double Cluster and in each dc across to last dc, ch 2, dc in last dc: 99 dc.

Rows 5-83: Repeat Rows 3 and 4, 39 times, then repeat Row 3 once **more**.

Row 84 (Eyelet row): Ch 5, turn; dc in next dc, ch 2, (skip next 2 sts, dc in next st, ch 2) across to last dc, dc in last dc; do **not** finish off: 34 sps.

EDGING

Rnd 1: Ch 1, turn; (sc, ch 5) 3 times in first corner sp, † (sc, ch 5) twice in each sp across to next corner sp, (sc, ch 5) 6 times in next corner sp, (sc, ch 5) twice in next sp, (sc in next sp, ch 5) across to next corner sp †, (sc, ch 5) 6 times in corner sp, repeat from † to † once, sc in first corner sp, (ch 5, sc) twice in same sp, ch 2, dc in first sc to form last loop: 318 loops.

Rnd 2: Ch 1, sc in same loop, (ch 5, sc in next loop) around, ch 2, dc in first sc to form last loop.

Rnd 3: Ch 1, sc in same loop, ch 5, sc in next loop, ch 5, work Puff St in next loop, ★ (ch 5, sc in next loop) twice, ch 5, work Puff St in next loop; repeat from ★ around, ch 2, dc in first sc to form last loop: 106 Puff Sts.

Rnd 4: Ch 1, sc in same loop, ch 5, work Puff St in next loop, ch 5, ★ (sc in next loop, ch 5) twice, work Puff St in next loop, ch 5; repeat from ★ around to last loop, sc in last loop, ch 2, dc in first sc to form last loop.

Rnd 5: Ch 1, work Puff St in same loop, (ch 5, sc in next loop) twice, ★ ch 5, work Puff St in next loop, (ch 5, sc in next loop) twice; repeat from ★ around, ch 2, dc in top of first Puff St to form last loop.

Rnds 6 and 7: Repeat Rnds 3 and 4.

Rnd 8: Ch 1, sc in same loop, ch 5, sc in third ch from hook, ch 2, ★ sc in next loop, ch 5, sc in third ch from hook, ch 2; repeat from ★ around; join with slip st to first sc, finish off.

FINISHING

Weave ribbon through each Eyelet row, leaving 10" at each end. Weave ribbon through ch-2 sps on remaining two sides, leaving 10" at each end. Tie ends into a bow at each corner.

THIRSTY BABY BIBS

Bibs are always nice shower gifts, and when they're handmade, they're extra special. Fashioned from thirsty terry washcloths, this pretty pair gets a lacy look from dainty edgings worked in bedspread weight cotton thread. The bibs look sweet, and they're durable, too!

MATERIALS

Bedspread Weight Cotton Thread (size 10), approximately:
    Edging #1 - 45 yards
    Edging #2 - 65 yards
Steel crochet hook, size 6 (1.80 mm) **or** size needed
    for gauge
Typing paper
Liquid fray preventative
Washcloth - 11" square **each**
⅛" Ribbon - two 11" lengths **each**
Straight pins
Sewing needle and thread

GAUGE: 16 sc = 2"

WASHCLOTH PREPARATION

Fold washcloth in half and pin together at outer corners. Trace pattern onto typing paper; cut out traced pattern. Pin pattern to washcloth with solid line on fold. Before cutting, apply liquid fray preventative to washcloth along edge of pattern (dotted line); allow to dry.
Following dotted line, cut out bib.

EDGING #1

Rnd 1: With **right** side of prepared washcloth facing, join thread with slip st in top right corner of outside edge (left hand side); ch 1, 3 sc in corner, sc evenly around working 3 sc in each corner; join with slip st to first sc.

Note: When working Rnd 2, the total number of stitches worked from center sc on top right corner of outside edge to center sc on top left corner of outside edge must be divisible by 3 with 1 left over. For example, 280 (3 goes into 280, 93 times with 1 left over).

Rnd 2: Slip st in next sc, ch 1, 3 sc in same st, sc in each sc around to center sc on top left corner of outside edge, increasing as necessary to keep piece lying flat, 3 sc in next corner sc, ch 1, (slip st in next sc, ch 1) around; join with slip st to first sc.

Rnd 3: ★ (Slip st, ch 2, 2 dc) in next sc, skip next 2 sc; repeat from ★ around to center sc on top left corner of outside edge, slip st in next sc; finish off.

Sew ribbon ties to bib.

EDGING #2
PATTERN STITCH
CLUSTER

★ YO, insert hook in sp indicated, YO and pull up a loop, YO and draw through 2 loops on hook; repeat from ★ 2 times **more**, YO and draw through all 4 loops on hook.

Rnd 1: With **right** side of prepared washcloth facing, join thread with slip st in top right corner of outside edge (left hand side); ch 1, 3 sc in corner, sc evenly around working 3 sc in each corner; join with slip st to first sc.
Note: When working Rnd 2, the total number of stitches worked from center sc on top right corner of outside edge to center sc on top left corner of outside edge must be divisible by 6 with 4 left over. For example, 280 (6 goes into 280, 46 times with 4 left over).

Rnd 2: Slip st in next sc, ch 1, 3 sc in same st, sc in each sc around, working 3 sc in each corner **and** increasing or decreasing as necessary to keep piece lying flat; join with slip st to first sc.

Rnd 3: Slip st in next sc, ch 1, sc in same st, (ch 3, skip next 2 sc, sc in next sc) around to center sc on top left corner of outside edge, ch 2, skip next sc, (slip st in next sc, ch 2, skip next sc) around; join with slip st to first sc.

Rnd 4: Slip st in first ch-3 sp, ch 1, sc in same sp, ★ ch 1, work Cluster in next ch-3 sp, (ch 3, work Cluster) twice in same sp, ch 1, sc in next ch-3 sp; repeat from ★ around to top left corner of outside edge; finish off.

Sew ribbon ties to bib.

GUARDIAN ANGEL

Ever watchful, guardian angels are believed to keep us from harm's way. Designed to hang in the nursery, this heavenly protector is crocheted in bedspread weight cotton thread.

Finished Size: Approximately 4¹/₂" tall x 8" wide

MATERIALS

Bedspread Weight Cotton Thread (size 10), approximately 160 yards

Steel crochet hook, size 6 (1.80 mm) **or** size needed for gauge

Tapestry needle

1¹/₂" Ring

Polyester stuffing

Starching materials: Commercial fabric stiffener, blocking board, plastic wrap, resealable plastic bag, terry towel, paper towels, and stainless steel pins

¹/₈" Ribbon - 24"

Note: Gauge is not important. Angel can be smaller or larger without changing the overall effect.

PATTERN STITCHES

SC DECREASE

Pull up a loop in next 2 sc, YO and draw through all 3 loops on hook **(counts as one sc)**.

PUFF ST

★ YO, insert hook in st or sp indicated, YO and pull up a loop even with loop on hook; repeat from ★ 3 times **more** *(Fig. 12, page 134)*, YO and draw through all 9 loops on hook.

PICOT

Ch 4, slip st in side of hdc just made.

DC DECREASE (uses next 2 dc)

★ YO, insert hook in **next** dc, YO and pull up a loop, YO and draw through 2 loops on hook; repeat from ★ once **more**, YO and draw through all 3 loops on hook **(counts as one dc)**.

HEAD

Rnd 1(Right side): Ch 2, 3 sc in second ch from hook, place marker around last sc made for Hair placement, 5 sc in same ch; join with slip st to BLO of first sc *(Fig. 20, page 138)*: 8 sc.

Rnd 2: Ch 1, working in BLO, 2 sc in each sc around; join with slip st to **both** loops of first sc: 16 sc.

Rnd 3: Ch 1, working in **both** loops, sc in same st, 2 sc in next sc, (sc in next sc, 2 sc in next sc) around; join with slip st to BLO of first sc: 24 sc.

Rnd 4: Ch 1, working in BLO, sc in same st and in next sc, 2 sc in next sc, (sc in next 2 sc, 2 sc in next sc) around; join with slip st to **both** loops of first sc: 32 sc.

Rnd 5: Ch 1, working in **both** loops, sc in same st and in next 2 sc, 2 sc in next sc, (sc in next 3 sc, 2 sc in next sc) around; join with slip st to BLO of first sc: 40 sc.

Rnd 6: Ch 1, working in BLO, sc in same st and in next 3 sc, 2 sc in next sc, (sc in next 4 sc, 2 sc in next sc) around; join with slip st to **both** loops of first sc: 48 sc.

Rnd 7: Ch 1, sc in **both** loops of each sc around; join with slip st to BLO of first sc.

Rnd 8: Ch 1, sc in BLO of same st and in next 15 sc; sc in **both** loops of next 16 sc; sc in BLO of last 16 sc; join with slip st to **both** loops of first sc.

Rnd 9: Ch 1, sc in **both** loops of each sc around; join with slip st to BLO of first sc.

Rnds 10-16: Repeat Rnds 8 and 9, 3 times; then repeat Rnd 8 once **more**.

Rnd 17: Ch 1, working in **both** loops, sc in same st and in next 3 sc, sc decrease, (sc in next 4 sc, sc decrease) around; join with slip st to first sc: 40 sc.

Rnd 18: Ch 1, sc in same st and in next 2 sc, sc decrease, (sc in next 3 sc, sc decrease) around; join with slip st to first sc: 32 sc.

Rnd 19: Ch 1, sc in same st and in next sc, sc decrease, (sc in next 2 sc, sc decrease) around; join with slip st to first sc: 24 sc.

Rnd 20: Ch 1, sc in each sc around; join with slip st to first sc.

Rnd 21: Ch 1, sc in same st, sc decrease, (sc in next sc, sc decrease) around; join with slip st to first sc; do **not** finish off: 16 sc.

Stuff **firmly**.

BODICE

Rnd 1: Ch 3 **(counts as first dc, now and throughout)**, dc in same st, 2 dc in next sc and in each sc around; join with slip st to first dc: 32 dc.

Rnd 2: Ch 3; working in BLO, dc in next 5 dc, (dc, ch 1, dc) in next dc, dc in next dc, (2 dc in next dc, dc in next dc) 3 times, (dc, ch 1, dc) in next dc, dc in next 7 dc, (dc, ch 1, dc) in next dc, dc in next dc, (2 dc in next dc, dc in next dc) 3 times, (dc, ch 1, dc) in next dc, dc in last dc; join with slip st to first dc: 42 dc.

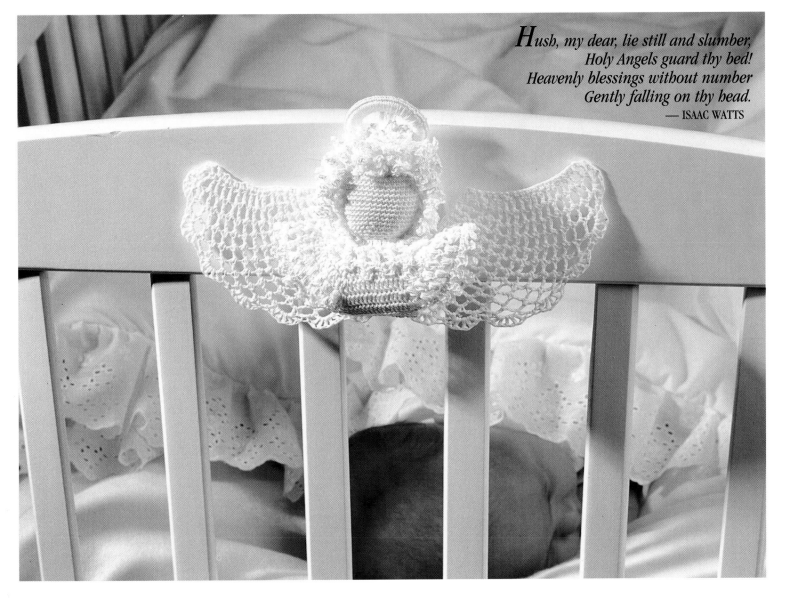

Rnd 3: Ch 3, working in both loops, dc in next 6 dc, (dc, ch 1, dc) in next ch-1 sp, (dc in next dc, 2 dc in next dc) 6 times, (dc, ch 1, dc) in next ch-1 sp, dc in next 9 dc, (dc, ch 1, dc) in next ch-1 sp, (dc in next dc, 2 dc in next dc) 6 times, (dc, ch 1, dc) in next ch-1 sp, dc in last 2 dc; join with slip st to first dc: 62 dc.

Rnd 4: Ch 3, dc in next 7 dc, (dc, ch 1, dc) in next ch-1 sp, dc in next 2 dc, (2 dc in next dc, dc in next dc) 9 times, (dc, ch 1, dc) in next ch-1 sp, dc in next 11 dc, (dc, ch 1, dc) in next ch-1 sp, dc in next 2 dc, (2 dc in next dc, dc in next dc) 9 times, (dc, ch 1, dc) in next ch-1 sp, dc in last 3 dc; join with slip st to first dc: 88 dc.

Rnd 5: Ch 3, dc in next 8 dc, ✝ (dc, ch 1, dc) in next ch-1 sp, work Puff St in next dc, (ch 3, skip next dc, work Puff St in next dc) 15 times, (dc, ch 1, dc) in next ch-1 sp ✝, dc in next 13 dc, repeat from ✝ to ✝ once, dc in last 4 dc; join with slip st to first dc: 32 Puff Sts.

Rnd 6: Ch 3, dc in next 9 dc, ✝ (dc, ch 1, dc) in next ch-1 sp, dc in next dc, ch 1, work Puff St in next ch-3 sp, (ch 2, work Puff St in next ch-3 sp) 14 times, ch 1, dc in next dc, (dc, ch 1, dc) in next ch-1 sp ✝, dc in next 15 dc, repeat from ✝ to ✝ once, dc in last 5 dc; join with slip st to first dc: 30 Puff Sts.

Rnd 7: Ch 3, dc in BLO of next 10 dc, dc in next ch-1 sp, ch 1, skip next 15 Puff Sts and next 2 dc (Sleeve), dc in next ch-1 sp, dc in BLO of next 17 dc, dc in next ch-1 sp, ch 1, skip next 15 Puff Sts and next 2 dc (Sleeve), dc in next ch-1 sp, dc in BLO of last 6 dc; join with slip st to first dc, finish off: 38 dc.

SLEEVE TRIM

With **right** side facing, join thread with slip st in first ch-1 sp on Sleeve, sc in same sp, (sc, hdc, work Picot, sc) in each ch-2 sp across, sc in next ch-1 sp; finish off.

Repeat for second Sleeve.

COLLAR

Rnd 1: With **right** side facing, Head toward you and working in free loops on Rnd 1 of Bodice *(Fig. 21a, page 138)*, join thread with slip st at center back; ch 1, sc in same st, ch 3, skip next dc, (sc in next dc, ch 3, skip next dc) around; join with slip st to first sc: 16 ch-3 sps.

Rnd 2: Slip st in first ch-3 sp, ch 1, work Puff St in same sp, ch 3, (work Puff St in next ch-3 sp, ch 3) around; join with slip st to first Puff St: 16 Puff Sts.

Rnd 3: Slip st in first ch-3 sp, ch 1, (sc, hdc, work Picot, sc) in same sp and in each ch-3 sp around; join with slip st to first sc, finish off.

HAIR

Rnd 1: With top of Head toward you and working in free loops on Rnd 1, join thread with slip st in marked sc; ch 12, (slip st in next sc, ch 12) around; slip st in same st as joining.

Rnd 2: Ch 12, working in free loops on Rnd 3, slip st in sc above same sc, ch 12, (slip st in next sc, ch 12) around; slip st in same st as first slip st.

Rnd 3: Ch 12, working in free loops on Rnd 5, slip st in sc above same sc, ch 12, (slip st in next sc, ch 12) around; slip st in same st as first slip st.

Note: Begin working in rows.

Rows 1-5: Ch 12, turn; working in next rnd of free loops, slip st in first sc, (ch 12, slip st in next sc) across. Finish off.

BODY INSERT

Rnd 1 (Right side): Ch 4, 11 dc in fourth ch from hook; join with slip st to top of beginning ch: 12 sts.

Rnd 2: Ch 3, dc in same st, 2 dc in each dc around; join with slip st to first dc: 24 dc.

Rnd 3: Ch 3, dc in same st and in next dc, (2 dc in next dc, dc in next dc) around; join with slip st to first dc: 36 dc.

Rnd 4: Ch 3, working in BLO, dc in next dc and in each dc around; join with slip st to first dc.

Rnds 5-9: Ch 3, working in both loops, dc in next dc and in each dc around; join with slip st to first dc.

Rnd 10: Ch 2, working in BLO, dc in next 2 dc, (dc decrease, dc in next dc) around; skip beginning ch-2 and join with slip st to both loops of first dc: 24 dc. Stuff lightly.

Rnds 11 and 12: Ch 2, working in both loops, dc in next dc, dc decrease around; skip beginning ch-2 and join with slip st to first dc: 6 dc. Finish off leaving a long end for sewing.

HALO

Join thread with slip st around ring; ch 1, 100 sc in ring; join with slip st to first sc, finish off.

LEFT WING

Row 1 (Right side): Ch 2, 3 sc in second ch from hook. *Note:* Loop a short piece of thread around any stitch to mark last row as **right** side.

Row 2: Ch 1, turn; sc in first sc, (ch 3, sc in next sc) twice: 2 ch-3 sps.

Rows 3-15: Ch 1, turn; sc in first sc, ch 3, (sc in next ch-3 sp, ch 3) across, sc in last sc: 15 ch-3 sps.

Row 16: Ch 1, turn; sc in first sc, (ch 3, sc in next ch-3 sp) across to last ch-3 sp, ch 1, hdc in last ch-3 sp to form last sp.

Row 17: Ch 1, turn; sc in same sp, ch 3, (sc in next ch-3 sp, ch 3) across, sc in last sc; finish off.

RIGHT WING

Work same as First Wing, marking Row 2 as **right** side; do **not** finish off.

JOINING

Ch 1, turn; sc in first sc and in next ch-3 sp, (5 dc in next ch-3 sp, sc in next ch-3 sp) 7 times, sc in last sc, 3 sc in each of next 2 sps, with **right** side of Left Wing facing, 3 sc in first sp on Row 15 and in next sp, sc in first sc on Row 17 and in next ch-3 sp, (5 dc in next ch-3 sp, sc in next ch-3 sp) 7 times, sc in last sc; skip first row, [sc in end of each row across, 3 sc in free loop of beginning ch *(Fig. 21b, page 138)*] twice, sc in end of each row across to last row, skip last row; join with slip st to first sc, finish off.

FINISHING

For Wings only, see Starching and Blocking, page 142.

Thread needle with end from Body Insert and weave through remaining sts, gather tightly and secure.

Insert needle through center to opposite end of Insert and then back through, catching the beginning ch. Pull gently to flatten ends of Insert and secure thread end.

Place Body Insert inside Bodice and sew bottom seam. Tack Body Insert in place at sides, if necessary.

Tack Collar in place at center front and center back.

Sew Wings to back of Bodice.

Sew Halo to Head.

Add ribbon for hanger.

Quick FRILLY PHOTO RING

*Moms love to show off baby's photographs, and this lacy frame is pretty as
a picture! Worked in bedspread weight cotton thread around a metal ring, the
frame is embellished with satin ribbon woven through a dainty eyelet round.*

Finished Size: Approximately 5" in diameter

MATERIALS

Bedspread Weight Cotton Thread (size 10),
    approximately 40 yards
Steel crochet hook, size 6 (1.80 mm)
2" ring
1/8" Ribbon - 1/2 yard
Cardboard - 2 1/2" square
Glue

Note: Gauge is not important. Edging can be smaller or
    larger without changing the overall effect.

PATTERN STITCH
CLUSTER
(YO, insert hook in sp indicated, YO and pull up a loop, YO and
draw through 2 loops on hook) 3 times, YO and draw through
all 4 loops on hook *(Figs. 10a & b, page 134)*.

Rnd 1 (Right side): Join thread with slip st around ring; ch 3,
95 dc in ring; join with slip st to top of beginning ch-3: 96 sts.

Rnd 2 (Eyelet rnd): Ch 5, skip next dc, (dc in next dc, ch 2,
skip next dc) around; join with slip st to third ch of beginning
ch-5: 48 ch-2 sps.

Rnd 3: Slip st in first ch-2 sp, ch 3, 2 dc in same sp, 3 dc in
next ch-2 sp and in each ch-2 sp around; join with slip st to top
of beginning ch-3: 144 sts.

Rnd 4: Ch 1, sc in same st, ch 3, skip next 2 dc, (sc in next dc,
ch 3, skip next 2 dc) around; join with slip st to first sc: 48 sps.

Rnd 5: Ch 1, ★ sc in next ch-3 sp, ch 1, work Cluster in next
ch-3 sp, (ch 3, work Cluster) twice in same sp, ch 1; repeat
from ★ around; join with slip st to first sc: 24 scallops.

Rnd 6: Slip st in first ch-1 sp, ch 3, (slip st, ch 3) twice in each
of next 2 ch-3 sps, ★ (slip st in next ch-1 sp, ch 3) twice,
(slip st, ch 3) twice in each of next 2 ch-3 sps; repeat from ★
around to last ch-1 sp, slip st in last ch-1 sp, ch 3; join with
slip st to first st, finish off.

FINISHING

Weave ribbon through Eyelet rnd and tie in a bow.
Cut a circle out of cardboard, 1/4" larger than ring; glue to wrong
side of ring along bottom edge. Cut photo to fit and slip in place.

83

LACY LITTLE AFGHAN

As soft and cuddly as a newborn, this delicate afghan features lacy eyelet rows and puff stitches. Fashioned in baby sport weight yarn, it's worked from side to side in one piece. Scallops and ribbons add a fanciful flourish.

Finished Size: Approximately 31" x 42"

MATERIALS
Baby Sport Weight Yarn, approximately:
14 ounces, (400 grams, 1,415 yards)
Crochet hook, size F (3.75 mm) **or** size needed for gauge
3/8" Ribbon - 8 yards
Sewing needle and thread

GAUGE: In pattern, 8 ch-2 sps = 4"
and 10 rows = 3 3/4"

Note: Afghan is worked from side to side.

PATTERN STITCH
PUFF STITCH
★ YO, insert hook in st or sp indicated, YO and pull up a loop even with loop on hook; repeat from ★ 3 times **more** (9 loops on hook) *(Fig. 12, page 134)*, YO and draw through 8 loops on hook, YO and draw through remaining 2 loops on hook.

BODY
Ch 230 **loosely**.
Row 1 (Eyelet row)**:** Work Puff St in eighth ch from hook, ch 2, (skip next 2 chs, work Puff St in next ch, ch 2) across to last 3 chs, skip next 2 chs, dc in last ch: 74 Puff Sts.
Row 2 (Right side)**:** Ch 5 **(counts as first dc plus ch 2, now and throughout)**, turn; (dc in next Puff St, ch 2) across to beginning ch, skip next 2 chs, dc in next ch: 76 dc.
Note: Loop a short piece of yarn around any stitch to mark last row as **right** side.
Row 3: Ch 5, turn; sc in first ch-2 sp, ch 2, dc in next dc, (ch 2, sc in next ch-2 sp, ch 2, dc in next dc) across: 76 dc.
Row 4: Ch 5, turn; work Puff St in third ch from hook, dc in next dc, (ch 2, work Puff St in last dc made, dc in next dc) across: 75 Puff Sts.
Row 5: Ch 5, turn; dc in next dc, (ch 2, dc in next dc) across.
Rows 6-9: Repeat Rows 3-5 once, then repeat Row 3 once **more**.
Row 10: Ch 5, turn; dc in next dc, (ch 2, dc in next dc) across: 76 dc.

Row 11 (Eyelet row)**:** Ch 5, turn; (work Puff St in next dc, ch 2) across to last dc, dc in last dc: 74 Puff Sts.
Rows 12-81: Repeat Rows 2-11, 7 times.
Finish off.

SCALLOP EDGING
FIRST SCALLOP
Row 1: With **wrong** side of Body facing, skip first 5 rows and join yarn with slip st around first dc on next row; ch 1, (sc, ch 3, sc) in same sp.
Row 2: Ch 3, slip st in end of next row, turn; (ch 1, dc) 9 times in ch-3 sp, slip st in end of next 2 rows.
Row 3: Turn; work Puff St in first ch-1 sp, (ch 2, work Puff St in next ch-1 sp) across, slip st in end of next 2 rows: 9 Puff Sts.
Row 4: Ch 3, turn; (sc in next ch-2 sp, ch 3) across, slip st in end of next row: 9 ch-3 sps.
Row 5: Ch 3, turn; sc in first ch-3 sp, ch 3, ★ (sc, ch 3) twice in next ch-3 sp, sc in next ch-3 sp, ch 3; repeat from ★ across, slip st in end of same row as Row 4 and in next row: 14 ch-3 sps.
Row 6: Turn; work Puff St in first ch-3 sp, (ch 2, work Puff St in next ch-3 sp) across, slip st in end of next row; finish off.

LAST 7 SCALLOPS
Row 1: With **wrong** side of Body facing, skip next 5 rows to **left** of previous Scallop and join yarn with slip st around first dc on next row; ch 1, (sc, ch 3, sc) in same sp.
Rows 2-6: Work same as First Scallop.
Repeat for second end; at end of Row 6 on last Scallop, do **not** finish off.

TRIM
With **right** side facing, slip st in end of next row on Body, ch 3, working across Scallops, slip st in first ch-2 sp on next Scallop, (slip st, ch 4, dc, slip st) in next 11 ch-2 sps, slip st in last ch-2 sp, ★ † dc in end of next row on Body, slip st in first ch-2 sp on next Scallop, (slip st, ch 4, dc, slip st) in next 11 ch-2 sps, slip st in last ch-2 sp †, repeat from † to † across, ch 1; slip st in end of next row and in first dc on Body, ch 4,

(dc, slip st) in first ch-2 sp, (slip st, ch 4, dc, slip st) in each ch-2 sp across to last ch-2 sp, (slip st, ch 4, dc) in last ch-2 sp, slip st in last dc and in end of first row, ch 1, slip st in first ch-2 sp on next Scallop, (slip st, ch 4, dc, slip st) in next 11 ch-2 sps, slip st in last ch-2 sp; repeat from ★ once **more**; join with slip st to top of beginning ch-3, finish off.

FINISHING

Using photo as a guide for placement, weave ribbon through Eyelet row on each outer edge and every other Eyelet Row on Body; secure ends.

Make 6 bows, using a 16" length of ribbon for each.

Tack bows to each end of center ribbons.

CUDDLE BUNNY

This cuddly bunny makes a sweet playmate for baby. With floppy ears and soft ruffles, the huggable doll has ribbon for her eyes and nose, so she's safe for little ones.

Finished Size: Approximately 17" tall

MATERIALS

Worsted Weight Yarn, approximately:
    MC (Pink) - 2$\frac{1}{2}$ ounces, (70 grams, 165 yards)
Worsted Weight Brushed Acrylic Yarn, approximately:
    CC (White) - 2$\frac{1}{4}$ ounces, (65 grams, 145 yards)
Crochet hook, size H (5.00 mm) **or** size needed for gauge
$\frac{5}{8}$" Ribbon, approximately:
    Pink - 3 yards
    Blue - small amount
Yarn needle
Polyester stuffing

GAUGE: 14 hdc = 4"

PATTERN STITCH

DECREASE (uses next 2 hdc)
(YO, insert hook in **next** hdc, YO and pull up a loop) twice, YO and draw through all 5 loops on hook **(counts as one hdc)**.

HEAD

Rnd 1 (Right side): With CC, ch 3, 8 hdc in third ch from hook; do **not** join, place marker *(see Markers, page 138)*.
Rnd 2: Skip beginning ch, 2 hdc in each hdc around: 16 hdc.
Rnd 3: (Hdc in next 3 hdc, 2 hdc in next hdc) around: 20 hdc.
Rnd 4: 2 Hdc in next hdc, hdc in next 2 hdc, place marker around last hdc made to mark center top of nose, hdc in next hdc, 2 hdc in next hdc, hdc in each hdc around: 22 hdc.
Rnd 5: Hdc in next hdc, 2 hdc in next hdc, hdc in next 3 hdc, 2 hdc in next hdc, hdc in each hdc around: 24 hdc.
Rnd 6: Hdc in next 2 hdc, 2 hdc in next hdc, hdc in next 3 hdc, 2 hdc in next hdc, hdc in each hdc around: 26 hdc.
Rnd 7: Hdc in next 3 hdc, 2 hdc in next hdc, hdc in next 3 hdc, 2 hdc in next hdc, hdc in each hdc around: 28 hdc.
Rnd 8: Hdc in next 4 hdc, 2 hdc in next hdc, hdc in next 3 hdc, 2 hdc in next hdc, hdc in each hdc around: 30 hdc.
Rnd 9: Hdc in next 5 hdc, 2 hdc in next hdc, hdc in next 3 hdc, 2 hdc in next hdc, hdc in next 10 hdc, decrease, hdc in next hdc, decrease, hdc in last 5 hdc: 30 hdc.
Rnd 10: Hdc in next 6 hdc, 2 hdc in next hdc, hdc in next 3 hdc, 2 hdc in next hdc, hdc in next 10 hdc, decrease, hdc in next hdc, decrease, hdc in last 4 hdc.
Rnd 11: (Hdc in next 3 hdc, decrease) around: 24 hdc.
Rnd 12: Decrease around: 12 hdc.

Rnd 13: Hdc in each hdc around; slip st in next hdc, finish off leaving a long end for sewing.

BODY

With MC, ch 24 **loosely**; being careful not to twist ch, join with slip st to form a ring.
Rnd 1 (Right side): Ch 2 **(counts as first hdc, now and throughout)**, hdc in next ch and in each ch around; join with slip st to Front Loop Only of first hdc *(Fig. 20, page 138)*: 24 hdc.
Rnd 2 (Ruffle): Ch 1, working in Front Loops Only, sc in same st, ch 4, hdc in fourth ch from hook, (sc in next hdc, ch 4, hdc in fourth ch from hook) around; join with slip st to first sc.
Rnd 3: Ch 1, working **behind** Ruffle and in free loops on Rnd 1 *(Fig. 21a, page 138)*, slip st in first st; hdc in same st, 2 hdc in next hdc, (hdc in next hdc, 2 hdc in next hdc) around; do **not** join, place marker: 36 hdc.
Rnd 4: Working in both loops, (hdc in next 2 hdc, 2 hdc in next hdc) around: 48 hdc.
Rnd 5: (Hdc in next 3 hdc, 2 hdc in next hdc) around: 60 hdc.
Rnd 6: (Hdc in next 4 hdc, 2 hdc in next hdc) around: 72 hdc.
Rnd 7: (Hdc in next 11 hdc, 2 hdc in next hdc) around: 78 hdc.
Rnd 8: Hdc in next 11 hdc, skip next 18 hdc (armhole), hdc in next 21 hdc, skip next 18 hdc (armhole), hdc in next 10 hdc: 42 hdc.
Rnds 9-19: Hdc in each hdc around.
Rnd 20: (Hdc in next 5 hdc, decrease) around; do **not** finish off: 36 hdc.

LEFT LEG

Rnd 1 (Dividing rnd): Hdc in next 9 hdc, skip next 18 hdc (Right Leg), hdc in next 9 hdc: 18 hdc.
Rnds 2-7: Hdc in each hdc around.
Rnd 8: Hdc in each hdc around; slip st in Front Loop Only of next hdc.
Rnd 9 (Ruffle): Work same as Body Rnd 2.
Rnd 10: Ch 1, working **behind** Ruffle and in free loops on Rnd 8, slip st in first st; ch 1, sc in same st and in each hdc around; join with slip st to first sc, finish off: 18 sc.

FOOT

Rnd 1: With **right** side facing, skip first 11 sc and join CC with slip st in next sc; hdc in same st and in each sc around; do **not** join, place marker: 18 hdc.

Rnd 2: Hdc in next 7 hdc, 2 hdc in each of next 4 hdc, hdc in each hdc around: 22 hdc.

Rnd 3: Hdc in next 10 hdc, 2 hdc in each of next 2 hdc, hdc in each hdc around: 24 hdc.

Rnds 4 and 5: Hdc in each hdc around.

Rnd 6: Decrease around; slip st in next hdc, finish off leaving a long end for sewing: 12 hdc.

RIGHT LEG

Rnd 1: With Left Leg to your right, join MC with slip st in first skipped hdc; ch 2, hdc in next hdc and in each hdc around; do **not** join, place marker: 18 hdc.
Complete same as Left Leg.

ARM (Make 2)

Rnd 1: With **right** side facing, join MC with slip st in first skipped hdc of armhole; hdc in same st and in each hdc around; do **not** join, place marker: 18 hdc.

Rnds 2-7: Hdc in each hdc around.

Rnd 8: Hdc in each hdc around; slip st in Front Loop Only of next hdc.

Rnd 9 (Ruffle): Ch 1, working in Front Loops Only, sc in same st, ch 4, hdc in fourth ch from hook, (sc in next hdc, ch 4, hdc in fourth ch from hook) around; join with slip st to first sc.

Rnd 10: Working **behind** Ruffle and in free loops on Rnd 8, slip st in first st; ch 1, sc in same st and in each hdc around; join with slip st to first sc, finish off: 18 sc.

HAND

Rnd 1: With **right** side facing, join CC with slip st in any sc; hdc in same st and in each sc around; do **not** join, place marker: 18 hdc.

Rnds 2 and 3: Hdc in each hdc around.

Rnd 4: Decrease around; slip st in next hdc, finish off leaving a long end for sewing: 9 hdc.

EAR (Make 2)

With CC, ch 8 **loosely**.

Rnd 1: 2 Hdc in third ch from hook, hdc in next 4 chs, 4 hdc in last ch; working in free loops of beginning ch *(Fig. 21b, page 138)*, hdc in next 4 chs, 2 hdc in next ch; do **not** join, place marker: 16 hdc.

Rnd 2: 2 Hdc in next hdc, hdc in next 6 hdc, 2 hdc in each of next 2 hdc, hdc in next 6 hdc, 2 hdc in next hdc: 20 hdc.

Rnds 3-10: Hdc in each hdc around.

Rnd 11: Hdc in next 5 hdc, decrease, hdc in next 8 hdc, decrease, hdc in next 3 hdc: 18 hdc.

Rnd 12: Hdc in each hdc around.

Rnd 13: Hdc in next 5 hdc, decrease, hdc in next 7 hdc, decrease, hdc in next 2 hdc: 16 hdc.

Rnd 14: Hdc in each hdc around.

Rnd 15: Hdc in next 5 hdc, decrease, hdc in next 6 hdc, decrease, hdc in next hdc: 14 hdc.

Rnd 16: Hdc in each hdc around.

Rnd 17: (Hdc in next 5 hdc, decrease) twice: 12 hdc.

Rnd 18: Hdc in each hdc around; slip st in next hdc, finish off leaving a long end for sewing.

FINISHING

Stuff Head. Thread needle with end and weave through remaining sts; gather tightly and secure.

Flatten top of each Ear and sew to Head.

Flatten bottom of each Foot and sew closed.

Thread needle with end on one Hand and weave through remaining sts; gather tightly and secure. Repeat for remaining Hand.

Stuff Hands and Feet only.

Thread needle with MC and weave through sts at top of Ruffle on one Arm; gather and secure. Repeat for Ruffles on remaining Arm and Legs.

Stuff Arms, Legs, and Body lightly.

Sew Head to Body.

Thread needle with MC and weave through sts at top of Ruffle on Body; gather and secure.

Using photo as guide for placement, add ribbons for eyes and nose.

Add bows to Ears.

SOFT LAYETTE SET

Our distinctive layette set is sized especially for newborns. Made with baby fingering weight yarn, the set includes an afghan, a sacque, a bonnet, and a pair of booties. The pieces are created with a unique textured stitch and edgings of single crochet.

Finished Size: Layette - Newborn
Afghan - approximately 34" x 37"

MATERIALS

Baby Fingering Weight Yarn, approximately:

Complete Set
MC (Blue) - 2 ounces, (60 grams, 285 yards)
CC (White) - 1 ounce, (30 grams, 145 yards)

Afghan
MC (Blue) - 15 ounces, (430 grams, 2,145 yards)
CC (White) - 5 ounces, (140 grams, 715 yards)

Sacque
MC (Blue) - 1¼ ounces, (40 grams, 180 yards)
CC (White) - ¾ ounce, (20 grams, 110 yards)

Bonnet
MC (Blue) - ½ ounce, (15 grams, 75 yards)
CC (White) - 20 yards

Booties
MC (Blue) - ¼ ounce, (10 grams, 40 yards)
CC (White) - 18 yards

Crochet Hook, sizes G (4.00 mm), H (5.00 mm) **and** I (5.50 mm) **or** sizes needed for gauge

Yarn needle

AFGHAN

Note: Entire Afghan is worked holding two strands of yarn together.

GAUGE: In pattern,
With medium size hook,
16 sc and 22 rows = 4"
With larger size hook,
15 sts and 11 rows = 4"

CENTER

With larger size hook and MC, ch 110 **loosely**.

Row 1: (Sc, 2 dc) in second ch from hook, ★ skip next 2 chs, (sc, 2 dc) in next ch; repeat from ★ across to last 3 chs, skip next 2 chs, sc in last ch: 37 sc.

Row 2 (Right side)**:** Ch 1, turn; (sc, 2 dc) in first sc, ★ skip next 2 dc, (sc, 2 dc) in next sc; repeat from ★ across to last 3 sts, skip next 2 dc, sc in last sc.

Note: Loop a short piece of yarn around any stitch to mark last row as **right** side.

Rows 3-87: Repeat Row 2; do **not** finish off.

EDGING

Change to medium size hook.

Rnd 1: Ch 1, turn; 3 sc in first st, sc in each st across to last st, 3 sc in last st; sc evenly across end of rows; working in free loops of beginning ch *(Fig. 21b, page 138)*, 3 sc in first ch, sc in each ch across to last ch, 3 sc in last ch; sc evenly across end of rows; join with slip st to first sc, finish off.

Note: Work in Back Loops Only throughout *(Fig. 20, page 138)*.

Rnd 2: With **right** side facing, join CC with slip st in any sc; ch 1, sc in each sc around working 3 sc in center sc of each corner 3-sc group; join with slip st to first sc.

Rnd 3: Ch 1, turn; sc in each sc around working 3 sc in center sc of each corner 3-sc group; join with slip st to first sc, finish off.

Rnds 4 and 5: Using MC, repeat Rnds 2 and 3.

Rnds 6-15: Repeat Rnds 2-5 twice, then repeat Rnds 2 and 3 once **more**.

BONNET

GAUGE: With smaller size hook,
   10 sc and 10 rows = 2"
   With medium size hook,
   in pattern, 10 sts and 7 rows = 2"

BACK

With smaller size hook and MC, ch 12 **loosely**.

Row 1: Sc in second ch from hook and in each ch across to last ch, 3 sc in last ch; working in free loops of beginning ch *(Fig. 21b, page 138)*, sc in next 10 chs changing to CC in last sc *(Fig. 22a, page 138)*; do **not** cut yarn unless otherwise specified: 23 sc.

Note: Work in Back Loops Only throughout Back *(Fig. 20, page 138)*.

Row 2 (Right side)**:** Ch 1, turn; sc in first 10 sc, 2 sc in next sc, sc in next sc, 2 sc in next sc, sc in each sc across: 25 sc.

Note: Loop a short piece of yarn around any stitch to mark last row as **right** side.

Row 3: Ch 1, turn; sc in first 10 sc, 2 sc in next sc, (sc in next sc, 2 sc in next sc) twice, sc in each sc across changing to MC in last sc: 28 sc.

Row 4: Ch 1, turn; sc in first 12 sc, 2 sc in next sc, sc in next 2 sc, 2 sc in next sc, sc in each sc across: 30 sc.

Row 5: Ch 1, turn; sc in first 12 sc, 2 sc in next sc, sc in next 4 sc, 2 sc in next sc, sc in each sc across changing to CC in last sc: 32 sc.

Row 6: Ch 1, turn; sc in first 13 sc, 2 sc in next sc, (sc in next 2 sc, 2 sc in next sc) twice, sc in each sc across: 35 sc.

Row 7: Ch 1, turn; sc in first 12 sc, 2 sc in next sc, (sc in next 2 sc, 2 sc in next sc, sc in next sc, 2 sc in next sc) twice, sc in each sc across changing to MC in last sc: 40 sc.

Row 8: Ch 1, turn; sc in first 13 sc, 2 sc in next sc, (sc in next 5 sc, 2 sc in next sc) twice, sc in each sc across: 43 sc.

Row 9: Ch 1, turn; sc in first 15 sc, 2 sc in next sc, (sc in next 6 sc, 2 sc in next sc) twice, sc in each sc across changing to CC in last sc: 46 sc.

Row 10: Ch 1, turn; sc in first 14 sc, 2 sc in next sc, (sc in next 7 sc, 2 sc in next sc) twice, sc in each sc across: 49 sc.

Row 11: Ch 1, turn; sc in first 16 sc, 2 sc in next sc, (sc in next 8 sc, 2 sc in next sc) twice, sc in each sc across changing to MC in last sc; cut CC: 52 sc.

Row 12: Ch 1, turn; sc in first 15 sc, 2 sc in next sc, (sc in next 9 sc, 2 sc in next sc) twice, sc in each sc across; do **not** finish off: 55 sc.

CROWN

Change to medium size hook.

Rows 1-14: Ch 1, turn; working in both loops, (sc, 2 dc) in first sc, ★ skip next 2 sts, (sc, 2 dc) in next sc; repeat from ★ across to last 3 sts, skip next 2 sts, sc in last sc: 19 sc.
Finish off.

FINISHING
EDGING

With **wrong** side facing and smaller size hook, join CC with slip st in first sc; ch 1, sc in first 4 sts, ch 3, slip st in last sc made, ★ skip next dc, sc in next 2 sts, ch 3, slip st in last sc made; repeat from ★ across to last 3 sts, skip next dc, sc in last 2 sts; finish off.

The precious sacque, bonnet, and booties are perfect for baby's first outing.

NECK BAND
Turn Edging and last 2 rows of Crown to **right** side.
Row 1: With **right** side facing and smaller size hook, join MC with slip st in right corner of Crown; ch 1, working across end of rows and through **both** pieces of Crown and folded Edging, work 49 sc evenly spaced across.
Row 2: Ch 1, turn; sc in first sc, ★ ch 1, skip next sc, sc in next sc; repeat from ★ across: 24 ch-1 sps.

Row 3: Ch 1, turn; sc in first sc, 2 sc in each ch-1 sp across to last sc, sc in last sc; finish off: 50 sc.

TIE
Using smaller size hook and MC, ch 130; finish off.
Weave Tie through ch-1 sps on Row 2 of Neck Band.

SACQUE

PATTERN STITCHES

INCREASE
3 Sc in next sc.

DECREASE
Pull up a loop in next 2 sts, YO and draw through all 3 loops on hook **(counts as one sc)**.

GAUGE: With smaller size hook,
10 sc and 10 rows = 2"
With medium size hook,
in pattern, 10 sts and 7 rows = 2"

YOKE

With smaller size hook and MC, ch 49 **loosely**.

Row 1 (Right side)**:** Sc in second ch from hook and in next 5 chs, 3 sc in next ch, sc in next 10 chs, 3 sc in next ch, sc in next 12 chs, 3 sc in next ch, sc in next 10 chs, 3 sc in next ch, sc in last 6 chs: 56 sc.

Note #1: Loop a short piece of yarn around any stitch to mark last row as **right** side.

Note #2: Work in Back Loops Only throughout Yoke *(Fig. 20, page 138)*.

Row 2: Ch 1, turn; sc in first 7 sc, increase, sc in next 12 sc, increase, sc in next 14 sc, increase, sc in next 12 sc, increase, sc in last 7 sc changing to CC in last sc *(Fig. 22a, page 138)*; do **not** cut yarn unless otherwise specified: 64 sc.

Row 3: Ch 1, turn; sc in first 8 sc, increase, sc in next 14 sc, increase, sc in next 16 sc, increase, sc in next 14 sc, increase, sc in last 8 sc: 72 sc.

Row 4: Ch 1, turn; sc in first 9 sc, increase, sc in next 16 sc, increase, sc in next 18 sc, increase, sc in next 16 sc, increase, sc in last 9 sc changing to MC in last sc: 80 sc.

Row 5: Ch 1, turn; sc in first 10 sc, increase, sc in next 18 sc, increase, sc in next 20 sc, increase, sc in next 18 sc, increase, sc in last 10 sc: 88 sc.

Row 6: Ch 1, turn; sc in first 11 sc, increase, sc in next 20 sc, increase, sc in next 22 sc, increase, sc in next 20 sc, increase, sc in last 11 sc changing to CC in last sc: 96 sc.

Row 7: Sc in first 12 sc, increase, sc in next 22 sc, increase, sc in next 24 sc, increase, sc in next 22 sc, increase, sc in last 12 sc: 104 sc.

Row 8: Ch 1, turn; sc in first 13 sc, increase, sc in next 24 sc, increase, sc in next 26 sc, increase, sc in next 24 sc, increase, sc in last 13 sc changing to MC in last sc: 112 sc.

Row 9: Ch 1, turn; sc in first 14 sc, increase, sc in next 26 sc, increase, sc in next 28 sc, increase, sc in next 26 sc, increase, sc in last 14 sc: 120 sc.

Row 10: Ch 1, turn; sc in first 15 sc, increase, sc in next 28 sc, increase, sc in next 30 sc, increase, sc in next 28 sc, increase, sc in last 15 sc changing to CC in last sc: 128 sc.

Row 11: Ch 1, turn; sc in first 16 sc, increase, sc in next 30 sc, increase, sc in next 32 sc, increase, sc in next 30 sc, increase, sc in last 16 sc: 136 sc.

Row 12: Ch 1, turn; sc in first 17 sc, increase, sc in next 32 sc, increase, sc in next 34 sc, increase, sc in next 32 sc, increase, sc in last 17 sc changing to MC in last sc; cut CC, do **not** finish off: 144 sc.

BODY

Row 1 (Dividing row)**:** Ch 1, turn; working in Back Loops Only, sc in first 19 sc, ch 7 **loosely**, skip next 34 sc (armhole), sc in next 18 sc, 2 sc in next sc, sc in next 19 sc, ch 7 **loosely**, skip next 34 sc (armhole), sc in last 19 sc: 77 sc.
Change to medium size hook.

Row 2: Ch 1, turn; working in both loops, (sc, 2 dc) in first st, ★ skip next 2 sts, (sc, 2 dc) in next st; repeat from ★ across to last 3 sts, skip next 2 sts, sc in last st: 31 sc.

Rows 3-23: Repeat Row 2; do **not** finish off.

EDGING

Change to smaller size hook.

Row 1: Ch 1, work 35 sc evenly spaced across end of rows; working in free loops of beginning ch *(Fig. 21b, page 138)*, 3 sc in first ch, sc in next 5 chs, skip next ch, sc in next 10 chs, skip next ch, sc in next 5 chs, decrease, sc in next 5 chs, skip next ch, sc in next 10 chs, skip next ch, sc in next 5 chs, 3 sc in next ch; work 35 sc evenly spaced across end of rows: 117 sc.

Row 2: Ch 1, turn; working in Back Loops Only, sc in first 36 sc, increase, ch 1, skip next sc, (sc in next sc, ch 1, skip next sc) 21 times, increase, sc in each sc across.

Row 3: Ch 1, turn; sc in Back Loop Only of first 37 sc, increase, 2 sc in each ch-1 sp across; working in Back Loops Only, increase, sc in each sc across; finish off.

SLEEVE

Rnd 1: With **right** side facing, smaller size hook and working in free loops of ch-7 and in Back Loops Only of unworked sc of armhole, join MC with slip st in center ch; ch 1, work 33 sc evenly spaced around; join with slip st to first sc.
Change to medium size hook.

Rnd 2: Ch 1, turn; (sc, 2 dc) in first sc, skip next 2 sc, ★ (sc, 2 dc) in next sc, skip next 2 sc; repeat from ★ around; join with slip st to first sc: 11 sc.

Rnds 3-17: Ch 1, turn; (sc, 2 dc) in same st, ★ skip next 2 dc, (sc, 2 dc) in next sc; repeat from ★ around; join with slip st to first sc.

Change to smaller size hook.

Rnd 18: Ch 1, do **not** turn; sc in same st, ★ decrease, sc in next 2 sc, (decrease, sc in next sc) 4 times; repeat from ★ once **more**; join with slip st to Back Loop Only of first sc: 23 sc.

Rnd 19: Ch 1, do **not** turn; sc in Back Loop Only of each sc around; join with slip st to first sc, finish off.

Repeat for second Sleeve.

FINISHING
NECK TIE

With smaller size hook and using MC, ch 90; finish off.
Weave Tie through ch-1 sps on Row 2 of Edging.
Make 2 tassels *(Figs. 26a & b, page 140)*, and attach to each end of Tie.

FRONT TIE (Make 2)

With smaller size hook and using MC, ch 21; finish off leaving a 6" length for sewing.
Using photo as guide for placement, sew Ties to Front.

BOOTIES
PATTERN STITCH
DECREASE

Pull up a loop in next 2 sts, YO and draw through all 3 loops on hook **(counts as one sc)**.

GAUGE: With smaller size hook,
      10 sc and 10 rows = 2"
      With medium size hook,
      in pattern, 10 sts and 7 rows = 2"

SOLE AND SIDES

With smaller size hook and MC, ch 13 **loosely**.

Rnd 1: Sc in second ch from hook and in each ch across to last ch, 3 sc in last ch; working in free loops of beginning ch *(Fig. 21b, page 138)*, sc in next 11 chs; join with slip st to first sc changing to CC *(Fig. 22b, page 138)*; do **not** cut yarn unless otherwise specified: 25 sc.
Note: Work in Back Loops Only throughout Sole and Sides *(Fig. 20, page 138)*.

Rnd 2 (Right side)**:** Ch 1, turn; sc in next 11 sc, 2 sc in each of next 3 sc, sc in each sc across; join with slip st to first sc: 28 sc.
Note: Loop a short piece of yarn around any stitch to mark last round as **right** side.

Rnd 3: Ch 1, turn; sc in next 11 sc, 2 sc in next sc, sc in next sc, 2 sc in each of next 2 sc, sc in next sc, 2 sc in next sc, sc in each sc across; join with slip st to first sc changing to MC: 32 sc.

Rnd 4: Ch 1, turn; sc in next 11 sc, 2 sc in next sc, (sc in next 2 sc, 2 sc in next sc) 3 times, sc in each sc across; join with slip st to first sc: 36 sc.

Rnd 5: Ch 1, turn; sc in next 12 sc, 2 sc in next sc, sc in next 4 sc, 2 sc in each of next 2 sc, sc in next 4 sc, 2 sc in next sc, sc in each sc across; join with slip st to first sc changing to CC: 40 sc.

Rnds 6 and 7: Ch 1, turn; sc in each sc around; join with slip st to first sc changing to MC at end of Row 7.

Rnd 8: Ch 1, turn; sc in next 14 sc, decrease, (sc in next 3 sc, decrease) twice, sc in each sc across; join with slip st to first sc: 37 sc.

Rnd 9: Ch 1, turn; sc in next 16 sc, decrease, sc in next sc, decrease, sc in each sc across; join with slip st to first sc changing to CC; cut MC: 35 sc.

Rnd 10: Ch 1, turn; sc in each sc around; join with slip st to first sc, finish off.

CUFF

Row 1: With **right** side facing and smaller size hook, skip first 25 sc and join MC with slip st in next sc, ch 1; working in both loops sc in same st and in next 8 sc, 2 sc in next sc, sc in next 10 sc, leave remaining sc unworked: 21 sc.

Row 2: Ch 1, turn; sc in first sc, (ch 1, skip next sc, sc in next sc) across: 10 ch-1 sps.

Row 3: Ch 1, turn; sc in first sc, 2 sc in each ch-1 sp across to last sc, sc in last sc: 22 sc.
Change to medium size hook.

Row 4: Ch 1, turn; (sc, 2 dc) in first sc, ★ skip next 2 sc, (sc, 2 dc) in next sc; repeat from ★ across to last 3 sc, skip next 2 sc, sc in last sc: 8 sc.

Row 5: Ch 1, turn; (sc, 2 dc) in first sc, ★ skip next 2 dc, (sc, 2 dc) in next sc; repeat from ★ across to last 3 sts, skip next 2 dc, sc in last sc; finish off.

FINISHING

Sew unworked sts on Rnd 10 of Sides together to form instep.

TIE

With smaller size hook and MC, ch 75; finish off.
Weave Tie through ch-1 sps on Row 2 of Cuff.

fashion corner

Crocheting delightful additions for your wardrobe is easier than ever with this creative collection! Whether you choose our bright sweater or delicate beaded collar, you'll find wonderful fashion accents for yourself and your children.

GRANNY SQUARE SWEATER

For a bold new look, top a favorite turtleneck with this updated Granny Square sweater. It's striking paired with slacks — or you can go casual with jeans. Worked in double crochet stitches, the sweater can be made to fit sizes small, medium, or large.

Size:	Small	Medium	Large
Finished Measurement:	40"	44"	48"

Size Note: Instructions are written for size Small with sizes Medium and Large in braces. Instructions will be easier to read if you circle all the numbers pertaining to your size.

MATERIALS

Worsted Weight Yarn, approximately:

    MC (Black) - 21{24-29} ounces,
        [600{680-820} grams, 1,325{1,510-1,830} yards]

    Color A (Purple) - 1½ ounces, [40 grams, 95 yards]

    Color B (Green) - 1½ ounces, [40 grams, 95 yards]

    Color C (Gold) - 1½ ounces, [40 grams, 95 yards]

    Color D (Blue) - 1{2-2} ounces,
        [30{60-60} grams, 65{125-125} yards]

    Color E (Red) - 1{2-2} ounces,
        [30{60-60} grams, 65{125-125} yards]

Crochet hooks, sizes D (3.25 mm) **and** F (3.75 mm) **or** sizes needed for gauge

Yarn needle

GAUGE: Rnds 1-4 of Square = 4"
      In pattern, 6 3-dc groups and 12 rows = 5"

GRANNY SQUARE (Make 2)

With Color A and larger size hook, ch 4; join with slip st to form a ring.

Rnd 1 (Right side): Ch 3 **(counts as first dc, now and throughout)**, 2 dc in ring, ch 1, (3 dc in ring, ch 1) 3 times; join with slip st to first dc, finish off: 4 ch-1 sps.

Note: Loop a short piece of yarn around any stitch to mark last round as **right** side.

Rnd 2: With **right** side facing, join Color B with slip st in any ch-1 sp; ch 3, (2 dc, ch 1, 3 dc) in same sp, (3 dc, ch 1, 3 dc) in each of next 3 ch-1 sps; join with slip st to first dc, finish off: 8 3-dc groups.

Rnd 3: With **right** side facing, join Color C with slip st in any corner ch-1 sp; ch 3, (2 dc, ch 1, 3 dc) in same sp, 3 dc in sp **between** 3-dc groups, ★ (3 dc, ch 1, 3 dc) in next corner ch-1 sp, 3 dc in sp **between** 3-dc groups; repeat from ★ around; join with slip st to first dc, finish off: 12 3-dc groups.

Rnd 4: With **right** side facing, join Color D with slip st in any corner ch-1 sp; ch 3, (2 dc, ch 1, 3 dc) in same sp, 3 dc in each sp **between** 3-dc groups across to next corner ch-1 sp, ★ (3 dc, ch 1, 3 dc) in corner ch-1 sp, 3 dc in each sp **between** 3-dc groups across to next corner ch-1 sp; repeat from ★ around; join with slip st to first dc, finish off: 16 3-dc groups.

Rnd 5: Repeat Rnd 4 with Color E: 20 3-dc groups.

Rnd 6: Repeat Rnd 4 with MC; do **not** finish off: 24 3-dc groups.

Rnd 7: Slip st in next 2 dc and in next corner ch-1 sp, ch 3, (2 dc, ch 1, 3 dc) in same sp, 3 dc in each sp **between** 3-dc groups across to next corner ch-1 sp, ★ (3 dc, ch 1, 3 dc) in corner ch-1 sp, 3 dc in each sp **between** 3-dc groups across to next corner ch-1 sp; repeat from ★ around; join with slip st to first dc, finish off: 28 3-dc groups.

Rnds 8-12: Repeat Rnd 4, 5 times in the following Color Sequence: 1 Rnd **each** Color A, Color B, Color C, Color D, Color E: 48 3-dc groups.

Rnds 13 and 14: Repeat Rnds 6 and 7: 56 3-dc groups.

Rnds 15-17: Repeat Rnd 4, 3 times in the following Color Sequence: 1 Rnd **each** Color A, Color B, Color C: 68 3-dc groups.

Medium and Large Sizes Only

Rnd 18: Repeat Rnd 4 with Color D: 72 3-dc groups.

Rnd 19: Repeat Rnd 4 with Color E: 76 3-dc groups.

Large Size Only

Rnd 20: Repeat Rnd 4 with MC; do **not** finish off: 80 3-dc groups.

Rnd 21: Repeat Rnd 7: 84 3-dc groups.

CORNER

Row 1: With **right** side of Granny Square facing and larger size hook, join MC with slip st in any corner ch-1 sp; ch 3, 3 dc in each sp **between** 3-dc groups across to next corner ch-1 sp, dc in corner ch-1 sp: 16{18-20} 3-dc groups.

Row 2: Ch 3, turn; 3 dc in each sp **between** 3-dc groups across to last dc, dc in last dc: 15{17-19} 3-dc groups.

Repeat Row 2 for a **total** of 15{17-19} rows: 2 3-dc groups.

Last Row: Ch 3, turn; 3 dc in sp **between** 3-dc groups, dc in last dc; finish off.

Repeat on each side of each Granny Square.

SLEEVE (Make 2)

RIBBING

With MC and smaller size hook, ch 13 **loosely**.

Row 1: Sc in back ridge of second ch from hook and in each ch across *(Fig. 2a, page 133)*: 12 sc.

Row 2: Ch 1, turn; sc in Back Loop Only of each sc across *(Fig. 20, page 138)*.

Repeat Row 2 until 17{18-20} ribs [34{36-40} rows] are complete; do **not** finish off.

BODY

Change to larger size hook.

Row 1 (Right side): Ch 1, working in end of rows, work 1{2-1} sc in end of first row, sc in each row across: 34{37-40} sc.

Note: Mark last row as **right** side.

Row 2: Ch 3, turn; (skip next 2 sc, 3 dc in next sc) across to last 3 sc, skip next 2 sc, dc in last sc: 10{11-12} 3-dc groups.

Row 3 (Increase row): Ch 3, turn; 3 dc in sp **before** first 3-dc group, 3 dc in each sp **between** 3-dc groups across, 3 dc in sp **before** last dc, dc in last dc: 11{12-13} 3-dc groups.

Rows 4 and 5: Ch 3, turn; 3 dc in each sp **between** 3-dc groups across, 3 dc in sp **before** last dc, dc in last dc: 11{12-13} 3-dc groups.

Repeat Rows 3-5, 11{13-13} times: 22{25-26} 3-dc groups.

Repeat Row 4 until Sleeve measure approximately 20{22-22}" from bottom edge, finish off.

FINISHING

TOP RIBBING

Foundation Row: With **right** side facing and larger size hook, join MC with slip st in center dc of last row of Corner on Back; ch 1, work 91{103-111} sc evenly spaced across to center dc of last row of next Corner; finish off.

Repeat for Front; do **not** finish off.

Continued on page 98.

LACY PEARL COLLAR

Adding charm to a plain dress or sweater is easy with this lacy collar, designed especially for little girls. Pearl beads accent its pretty scalloped pattern, which is worked using bedspread weight cotton thread. The dainty accessory is simple and inexpensive to make, and it's sure to please a young miss!

Finished Size: Fits neck opening approximately 12" around

MATERIALS

Bedspread Weight Cotton Thread (size 10), approximately 95 yards

Steel crochet hook, size 7 (1.65 mm) **or** size needed for gauge

3/8" Button

5 mm Pearls - 26

Sewing needle and thread

GAUGE: 18 sc = 2"

Ch 110 **loosely**.

Row 1 (Right side): Sc in second ch from hook and in each ch across: 109 sc.

Note: Loop a short piece of thread around any stitch to mark last row as **right** side.

Row 2: Ch 9 **(counts as first dc plus ch 6)**, turn; skip next 3 sc, dc in next sc, (ch 6, skip next 3 sc, dc in next sc) across: 27 loops.

Row 3: Turn; slip st in first dc, ★ (sc, hdc, 6 dc, hdc, sc) in next loop, slip st in next dc; repeat from ★ across: 27 scallops.

Row 4: Ch 10 **(counts as first dc plus ch 7)**, turn; skip first scallop, dc in next slip st, (ch 7, skip next scallop, dc in next slip st) across.

Row 5: Turn; slip st in first dc, ★ (sc, hdc, 7 dc, hdc, sc) in next loop, slip st in next dc; repeat from ★ across.

Row 6: Ch 11 **(counts as first dc plus ch 8)**, turn; dc in next slip st, (ch 8, dc in next slip st) across.

Row 7: Turn; slip st in first dc, ★ (sc, hdc, 8 dc, hdc, sc) in next loop, slip st in next dc; repeat from ★ across.

Row 8: Ch 12 **(counts as first dc plus ch 9)**, turn; dc in next slip st, (ch 9, dc in next slip st) across.

Edging: Ch 6, turn; sc in center ch of first loop, ch 6, ★ sc in next dc, (ch 4, slip st in last sc made) 3 times, ch 6, sc in center ch of next loop, ch 6; repeat from ★ across to last dc, slip st in last dc, ch 6; working in end of rows, skip first row, slip st in next row, (ch 6, skip next row, slip st in next row) 3 times, ch 10, slip st in tenth ch from hook (button loop);

working in free loops of beginning ch *(Fig. 21b, page 138)*, [(sc, dc) in next ch, ch 2, skip next 2 chs, slip st in next ch] across to last ch, sc in last ch, ch 6; working in end of rows, skip first 2 rows, slip st in next row, ch 6, (skip next row, slip st in next row, ch 6) across to last row, skip last row; join with slip st to first st, finish off.

See Washing and Blocking, page 140.
Sew button on side opposite loop.
Using photo as a guide for placement, sew pearls along Edging.

GRANNY SQUARE SWEATER

Continued from page 96.

RIGHT SHOULDER

Row 1: Using smaller size hook, ch 16 **loosely**; with **right** side of Back facing, slip st in first 2 sc on Foundation Row, turn; skip first 2 slip sts, sc in back ridge of each ch across, slip st in next 2 sc on Front Foundation Row: 16 sc.

Row 2: Turn; skip first 2 slip sts, sc in Back Loop Only of each sc across, slip st in next 2 sc on Foundation Row: 16 sc.
Repeat Row 2 for a total of 19{25-29} rows.

FRONT

Row 1: Turn; skip first 2 slip sts, sc in Back Loop Only of first 8 sc, leave remaining 8 sc unworked: 8 sc.

Row 2: Ch 1, turn; sc in Back Loop Only of each sc across, slip st in next 2 sc on Foundation Row: 8 sc.

Row 3: Turn; skip first 2 slip sts, sc in Back Loop Only of each sc across: 8 sc.

Rows 4-51: Repeat Rows 2 and 3, 24 times.
Finish off.

BACK

Row 1: With **right** side facing and working in Back Loops Only, join MC with slip st in first sc on last row of Right Shoulder; ch 1, sc in each sc across, slip st in next 2 sc on Foundation Row: 8 sc.

Row 2: Turn; skip first 2 slip sts, sc in Back Loop Only of each sc across: 8 sc.

Row 3: Ch 1, turn; sc in Back Loop Only of each sc across, slip st in next 2 sc on Foundation Row: 8 sc.

Rows 4-51: Repeat Rows 2 and 3, 24 times; do **not** finish off.

LEFT SHOULDER

Row 1: Turn; skip first 2 slip sts, sc in Back Loop Only of each sc across Back **and** Front Ribbings, slip st in next 2 sc on Foundation Row: 16 sc.

Row 2: Turn; skip first 2 slip sts, sc in Back Loop Only of each sc across, slip st in next 2 sc on Foundation Row: 16 sc.
Repeat Row 2, 17{23-27} times.

Last Row: Turn; skip first 2 slip sts, sc in Back Loop Only of each sc across, slip st in last sc on Foundation Row; finish off.

Sew Sleeves in place, matching center of Sleeve to center of Top Ribbing and beginning 9{10½-11}" down.
Sew underarm and side in one continuous seam.

BOTTOM RIBBING

Foundation Rnd: With **right** side facing and larger size hook, join MC with slip st at side seam; ch 1, work 148{172-192} sc evenly spaced around bottom edge; join with slip st to first sc. Change to smaller size hook.
Ch 13 **loosely**.

Row 1: Sc in back ridge of second ch from hook and in each ch across, with **right** side facing, slip st in first 2 sc on Foundation Rnd: 14 sts.

Row 2: Turn; skip first 2 slip sts, sc in Back Loop Only of each sc across: 12 sc.

Row 3: Ch 1, turn; sc in Back Loop Only of each sc across, slip st in next 2 sc on Foundation Rnd: 14 sts.
Repeat Rows 2 and 3 around, ending by working Row 2; finish off leaving a long end for sewing.

Sew seam.

SOPHISTICATED RUFFLE

A fancy jabot will give any blouse an air of sophistication. Fashioned using fine cotton crochet thread, the Victorian-inspired ruffle features clusters and pretty picot shells. A satin bow and a golden charm lend a feminine touch.

Finished Size: Approximately 3½" high

MATERIALS

Cotton Crochet Thread (size 20), approximately 70 yards
Steel crochet hook, size 12 (1.00 mm)
1" Wire edge ribbon - 12"
Rose embellishment
Backing pin
Tapestry needle
Sewing needle and thread
Glue gun

Note: Gauge is not important. Ruffle can be smaller or larger without changing the overall effect.

PATTERN STITCHES
CLUSTER

★ YO twice, insert hook in st or sp indicated, YO and pull up a loop, (YO and draw through 2 loops on hook) twice; repeat from ★ 2 times **more**, YO and draw through all 4 loops on hook *(Figs. 10a & b, page 134)*.

SHELL
Work (Cluster, ch 2, Cluster) in st or sp indicated.

PICOT
Ch 7, sc in fourth ch from hook.

PICOT SHELL
Work (Cluster, ch 4, sc in fourth ch from hook, Cluster) in sp indicated.

Leaving a long end for sewing, ch 61 **loosely**.

Row 1 (Right side): Work Shell in fifth ch from hook, ★ skip next 3 chs, (tr, ch 3, tr) in next ch, skip next 3 chs, work Shell in next ch; repeat from ★ across: 8 Shells.

Row 2: Ch 4, turn; work Shell in first Shell (ch-2 sp), ★ ch 3, (dtr, ch 5, dtr) in next ch-3 sp, ch 3, work Shell in next Shell; repeat from ★ across.

Row 3: Ch 4, turn; work Shell in first Shell, ★ ch 3, skip next ch-3 sp, tr in next loop, (ch 1, tr) 5 times in same loop, ch 3, work Shell in next Shell; repeat from ★ across.

Row 4: Ch 4, turn; work Shell in first Shell, ★ ch 3, skip next ch-3 sp, (sc in next ch-1 sp, ch 3) 5 times, work Shell in next Shell; repeat from ★ across.

Row 5: Ch 4, turn; work (Cluster, ch 2, Shell) in first Shell, ★ ch 3, skip next ch-3 sp, (sc in next ch-3 sp, ch 3) 4 times, work (Cluster, ch 2, Shell) in next Shell; repeat from ★ across.

Row 6: Ch 4, turn; work Shell in first Shell, work Picot twice, ch 3, work Shell in next ch-2 sp, ★ ch 3, skip next ch-3 sp, (sc in next ch-3 sp, ch 3) 3 times, skip next ch-3 sp, work Shell in next Shell, work Picot twice, ch 3, work Shell in next ch-2 sp; repeat from ★ across.

Row 7: Ch 4, turn; work Shell in first Shell, work Picot twice, ch 3, sc in sp **between** next 2 Picots, work Picot twice, ch 3, work Shell in next Shell, ★ ch 3, skip next ch-3 sp, (sc in next ch-3 sp, ch 3) twice, work Shell in next Shell, work Picot twice, ch 3, sc in sp **between** next 2 Picots, work Picot twice, ch 3, work Shell in next Shell; repeat from ★ across.

Row 8: Ch 4, turn; work Picot Shell in first Shell, work Picot twice, ch 3, (sc in sp **between** next 2 Picots, work Picot twice, ch 3) twice, ★ work Picot Shell in each of next 2 Shells, work Picot twice, ch 3, (sc in sp **between** next 2 Picots, work Picot twice, ch 3) twice; repeat from ★ across to last Shell, work Picot Shell in last Shell.

Edging: Ch 9, turn; sc in fourth ch from hook, ch 5, skip first Picot Shell, (sc in sp **between** next 2 Picots, ch 9, sc in fourth ch from hook, ch 5) 3 times, ★ skip next 2 Picot Shells, (sc in sp **between** next 2 Picots, ch 9, sc in fourth ch from hook, ch 5) 3 times; repeat from ★ across, skip last Picot Shell, sc in top of turning ch, ch 5; working across end of rows, (sc **between** next 2 rows, ch 5) across to last row; working in free loops of beginning ch *(Fig. 21b, page 138)* and in ch-sps, sc in first ch, (ch 2, sc in next ch-sp, ch 2, sc in next ch) across, ch 5; working across end of rows, (sc **between** next 2 rows, ch 5) across, sc in first ch of beginning ch-9; finish off.

Thread tapestry needle with beginning end and weave through ch-2 sps on bottom of Edging; gather tightly and secure. Tie wire edge ribbon in a bow and shape as desired. Using photo as a guide for placement, sew bow in place. Glue rose embellishment to center front of bow and backing pin to center back of bow.

VIBRANT VEST

This dazzling vest gets its unique fluffy look from loop stitches. Crocheted using two types of worsted weight yarn, it's perfect for adding a splash of color to your neutral fashions! The vest is extra cozy, so it's just right for those chilly autumn afternoons.

Size:	Small	Medium	Large
Finished Measurement:	40"	44"	48"

Size Note: Instructions are written for size Small with sizes Medium and Large in braces. Instructions will be easier to read if you circle all the numbers pertaining to your size.

MATERIALS
Worsted Weight Brushed Acrylic Yarn, approximately:
   MC (Variegated) - 30{33-36} ounces,
      [850{940-1,020} grams, 1,380{1,520-1,655} yards]
Worsted Weight Yarn, approximately:
   CC (Purple) - 5{5-6} ounces,
      [140{140-170} grams, 230{230-275} yards]
Crochet hooks, sizes E (3.50 mm) **and** F (3.75 mm) **or**
   sizes needed for gauge
3/4" Buttons - 6
Yarn needle

GAUGE: With larger size hook, 16 sc and 16 rows = 4"

PATTERN STITCH
DECREASE
Pull up a loop in next 2 sts, YO and draw through all 3 loops on hook (**counts as one sc**).

BACK
RIBBING
With CC and smaller size hook, ch 13 **loosely**.
Row 1: Sc in back ridge of second ch from hook and in each ch across (***Fig. 2a, page 133***): 12 sc.
Row 2: Ch 1, turn; sc in in Back Loop Only of each sc across (***Fig. 20, page 138***).
Repeat Row 2 until 40{44-48} ribs [80{88-96} rows] are complete; do **not** finish off.

BODY
Change to larger size hook.
Row 1 (Right side)**:** Ch 1, sc in end of each row across changing to MC in last st (***Fig. 22a, page 138***): 80{88-96} sc.
Row 2: Ch 1, turn; work Loop St in each sc across (***Figs. 17a-c, page 136***).
Row 3: Ch 1, turn; sc in each Loop St across.

Rows 4-80: Repeat Rows 2 and 3, 38 times, then repeat Row 2 once **more**.
Finish off.

FRONT (Make 2)
RIBBING
With CC and smaller size hook, ch 13 **loosely**.
Row 1: Sc in back ridge of second ch from hook and in each ch across: 12 sc.
Row 2: Ch 1, turn; sc in in Back Loop Only of each sc across.
Repeat Row 2 until 20{22-24} ribs [40{44-48} rows] are complete; do **not** finish off.

BODY
Change to larger size hook.
Row 1 (Right side)**:** Ch 1, sc in end of each row across, changing to MC in last st: 40{44-48} sc.
Row 2: Ch 1, turn; work Loop St in each sc across.
Row 3: Ch 1, turn; sc in each Loop St across.
Rows 4-80: Repeat Rows 2 and 3, 38 times, then repeat Row 2 once **more**.
Finish off.

FINISHING
Sew side seams, working from bottom edge through Row 40.
Sew shoulder seams, working across 22{26-30} sts **each** side.

ARMHOLE RIBBING
Foundation Rnd: With **right** side facing and smaller size hook, join CC with slip st at side seam; ch 1, work 60{64-68} sc evenly spaced around; join with slip st to first sc.
Ch 5 **loosely**.
Row 1: Sc in back ridge of second ch from hook and in next 3 chs, with **right** side facing, sc in next 2 sc on Foundation Rnd: 6 sc.
Row 2: Turn; skip first 2 sc, sc in Back Loop Only of each sc across: 4 sc.
Row 3: Ch 1, turn; sc in Back Loop Only of each sc across, sc in next 2 sc on Foundation Rnd: 6 sc.
Repeat Rows 2 and 3 around to last sc.
Joining Row: Turn; with **wrong** sides together, working in Back Loop Only of last row **and** in free loops of beginning ch (***Fig. 21b, page 138***), slip st in each sc across; finish off.
Repeat for second Armhole.

FRONT EDGE AND NECK BAND

Foundation Row: With **right** side facing and smaller size hook, join CC with slip st in corner of Right Front Ribbing; ch 1, sc in Back Loop Only of each st across Ribbing, sc in end of each row across Body to last row, 3 sc in last row; working along Neck edge, sc in next 17 sts, decrease, sc in next 34 sts, decrease, sc in each st across; working in end of rows, 3 sc in first row, sc in each row across Body, sc in Back Loop Only of each st across Ribbing; do **not** finish off: 258 sc.

Row 1: Ch 1, turn; sc in Back Loop Only of each sc across to next corner sc, sc in corner sc; working in **both** loops, (dc in next sc, slip st in next sc) across to next corner sc; working in Back Loops Only, sc in next 2 sc, ch 3, ★ skip next 3 sc (buttonhole), sc in next 14 sc, ch 3; repeat from ★ across to last 6 sc, skip next 3 sc (buttonhole), sc in last 3 sc: 6 buttonholes.

Row 2: Ch 1, turn; sc in Back Loop Only of each sc and in each ch across Right Front, leave remaining sts unworked; finish off.

Add buttons.

FUN FARM VEST

*P*erfect for a day in the country, this child-size vest depicts a colorful farm scene.
Kids will love the bright rainbow fastener, trusty wheelbarrow (it doubles as a pocket!),
bright sun, and rustic barn. The vest and motifs are worked mostly using single
crochet stitches, and we've given instructions for sizes 2 through 6.

Size:	2	4	6
Finished Measurement:	24"	25"	26"

Size Note: Instructions are written for size 2 with sizes 4 and 6 in braces. Instructions will be easier to read if you circle all the numbers pertaining to your size.

MATERIALS

Sport Weight Yarn, approximately:
    Light Blue - 1½{1¾-2} ounces,
        [40{50-60} grams, 150{175-200} yards]
    Green - ¾{1-1¼} ounces,
        [20{30-35} grams, 75{100-125} yards]
    Red - ½ ounce, (20 grams, 50 yards)
    Brown - 7 yards
    Yellow - 10 yards
    Dark Blue - 5 yards
    White - 7 yards
Crochet hook, size H (5.00 mm) **or** size needed for gauge
Bobbins - 2
Embroidery needle
Sewing needle and thread
⅝" Buttons - 2

GAUGE: 16 sc and 18 rows = 4"

BOBBINS

Wind a small amount of Green and Light Blue onto separate bobbins. Work each side of the Barn with separate yarn. Always keep the bobbins on the wrong side of the garment.

PATTERN STITCH

DECREASE

Pull up a loop in next 2 sts, YO and draw through all 3 loops on hook **(counts as one sc)**.

BODY

With ball of Green, ch 93{97-101} **loosely**.
Row 1 (Right side)**:** Sc in second ch from hook and in each ch across: 92{96-100} sc.
Note: Loop a short piece of yarn around any stitch to mark last row as **right** side.
Row 2: Ch 1, turn; sc in each sc across.
Repeat Row 2 for a total of 6{8-14} rows.

Next 4 Rows: Ch 1, turn; sc in first 37{39-41} sc changing to Red in last sc worked *(Fig. 22a, page 138)*, sc in next 18 sc changing to Green in last sc worked, sc in each sc across. Finish off, cut second Green.
Next Row: With **right** side facing and working in Back Loops Only *(Fig. 20, page 138)*, join ball of Light Blue with slip st in first sc; ch 1, sc in first 37{39-41} sc changing to Red in last sc worked, sc in **both** loops of next 18 sc changing to Light Blue in last sc worked, sc in Back Loop Only of each sc across.
Next 13 Rows: Ch 1, turn; working in both loops, sc in first 37{39-41} sc changing to Red in last sc worked, sc in next 18 sc changing to Light Blue in last sc worked, sc in each sc across; do **not** cut Red or Blue.

RIGHT FRONT

Row 1: Ch 1, turn; sc in first 20{21-22} sc, leave remaining sc unworked.
Rows 2 and 3: Ch 1, turn; decrease, sc in each sc across to last 2 sc, decrease: 16{17-18} sc.
Row 4: Ch 1, turn; sc in each sc across to last 2 sc, decrease: 15{16-17} sc.
Row 5: Ch 1, turn; decrease, sc in each sc across: 14{15-16} sc.
Repeat Rows 4 and 5, 2{2-3} times: 10{11-10} sc.
Size 4 Only: Repeat Row 4: 10 sc.
Next 12{13-14} Rows: Ch 1, turn; sc in each sc across.
Last Row: Turn; slip st in first 5 sc, sc in last 5 sc; finish off.

BACK

Row 1: With **right** side facing, skip 4 sc from Right Front and join ball of Light Blue with slip st in next sc; ch 1, sc in same st and in next 13{14-15} sc changing to Red in last sc worked, sc in next 16 sc changing to Light Blue in last sc worked, sc in next 14{15-16} sc, leave remaining sts unworked: 44{46-48} sc.
Row 2: Ch 1, turn; decrease, sc in next 13{14-15} sc changing to Red in last sc worked, sc in next 14 sc changing to Light Blue in last sc worked, sc in each sc across to last 2 sc, decrease: 42{44-46} sc.
Row 3: Ch 1, turn; decrease, sc in next 13{14-15} sc changing to Red in last sc worked, sc in next 12 sc changing to Light Blue in last sc worked, sc in each sc across to last 2 sc, decrease: 40{42-44} sc.

Row 4: Ch 1, turn; sc in first 15{16-17} sc changing to Red in last sc worked, sc in next 10 sc changing to Light Blue in last sc worked, sc in each sc across.

Row 5: Ch 1, turn; sc in first 16{17-18} sc changing to Red in last sc worked, sc in next 8 sc changing to Light Blue in last sc worked, sc in each sc across.

Row 6: Ch 1, turn; sc in first 17{18-19} sc changing to Red in last sc worked, sc in next 6 sc changing to Light Blue in last sc worked, sc in each sc across.

Row 7: Ch 1, turn; sc in first 18{19-20} sc changing to Red in last sc worked, sc in next 4 sc changing to Light Blue in last sc worked, sc in each sc across.

Row 8: Ch 1, turn; sc in first 19{20-21} sc changing to Red in last sc worked, sc in next 2 sc changing to Light Blue in last sc worked, sc in each sc across; cut Red and Light Blue on bobbin.

Rows 9-18{20-22}: Ch 1, turn; sc in each sc across.

RIGHT SHOULDER

Row 1: Ch 1, turn; sc in first 10 sc, leave remaining sc unworked.

Rows 2 and 3: Ch 1, turn; sc in each sc across.

Row 4: Ch 1, turn; sc in first 5 sc, slip st in last 5 sc; finish off.

LEFT SHOULDER

Row 1: With **right** side facing, skip 20{22-24} sc from Right Shoulder and join Light Blue with slip st in next sc; ch 1, sc in same st and in each sc across: 10 sc.

Rows 2 and 3: Ch 1, turn; sc in each sc across.

Row 4: Turn; slip st in first 5 sc, sc in last 5 sc; finish off.

LEFT FRONT

Row 1: With **right** side facing, skip 4 sc from Back and join Light Blue with slip st in next sc; ch 1, sc in same st and in each sc across: 20{21-22} sc.

Rows 2 and 3: Ch 1, turn; decrease, sc in each sc across to last 2 sc, decrease: 16{17-18} sc.
Row 4: Ch 1, turn; decrease, sc in each sc across: 15{16-17} sc.
Row 5: Ch 1, turn; sc in each sc across to last 2 sc, decrease: 14{15-16} sc.
Repeat Rows 4 and 5, 2{2-3} times: 10{11-10} sc.
Size 4 Only: Repeat Row 4: 10 sc.
Next 12{13-14} Rows: Ch 1, turn; sc in each sc across.
Last Row: Ch 1, turn; sc in first 5 sc, slip st in last 5 sc; finish off.

Sew shoulder seams.

GRASS

With **right** side facing, bottom edge toward you and working in free loops on last Green row of Body *(Fig. 21a, page 138)*, join Green with slip st in first sc; ★ † dc around post of sc on third Light Blue row *(Fig. 13, page 135)*, slip st in next sc, sc around post of sc on second Light Blue row, slip st in next sc †, tr around post of sc on fourth Light Blue row, slip st in next sc, sc around post of sc on second Light Blue row, slip st in next sc; repeat from ★ 8{8-9} times **more**, then repeat from † to † 0{1-0} time; finish off.
Repeat for second side, beginning in sc next to Barn.

BARN ROOF

With White, ch 30 **loosely**.
Row 1 (Right side): Sc in second ch from hook and in next 13 chs, 3 sc in next ch, sc in last 14 chs: 31 sc.
Row 2: Ch 1, turn; sc in first 15 sc, 3 sc in next sc, sc in last 15 sc; finish off leaving a long end for sewing: 33 sc.

SUN

Rnd 1 (Right side): With Yellow, ch 2, 6 sc in second ch from hook; do **not** join, place marker *(see Markers, page 138)*.
Rnd 2: 2 Sc in each sc around: 12 sc.
Rnd 3: (Sc in next sc, 2 sc in next sc) around: 18 sc.
Rnd 4: (Sc in next 2 sc, 2 sc in next sc) around: 24 sc.
Rnd 5: (Sc in next 3 sc, 2 sc in next sc) around; slip st in next sc, finish off leaving a long end for sewing: 30 sc.

WHEELBARROW POCKET

With Brown, ch 28 **loosely**.
Row 1 (Right side): Sc in sixth ch from hook and in each ch across changing to Red in last st worked: 23 sc.
Row 2: Ch 1, turn; sc in first 11 sc, leave remaining 12 sc unworked.
Rows 3-9: Ch 1, turn; sc in each sc across; at end of Row 9, finish off leaving a long end for sewing.

WHEEL

Rnd 1 (Right side): With Brown, ch 6, dc in sixth ch from hook, ch 2, (dc in same ch, ch 2) 4 times; join with slip st to fourth ch of beginning ch-6: 6 ch-2 sps.
Rnd 2: Ch 1, sc in same st, 3 sc in next ch-2 sp, (sc in next dc, 3 sc in next ch-2 sp) around; join with slip st to first sc, finish off leaving a long end for sewing: 24 sc.

RAINBOW
BOTTOM HALF

With Red and leaving a long end for sewing, ch 19{21-23} **loosely**.
Row 1: Sc in second ch from hook and in each ch across changing to Yellow in last sc worked: 18{20-22} sc.
Row 2: Ch 1, turn; sc in each sc across changing to Green in last sc worked.
Row 3: Ch 1, turn; sc in each sc across changing to Dark Blue in last sc worked.
Row 4 (Right side): Ch 1, turn; sc in each sc across; finish off leaving a long end for sewing.
Note: Mark last row as **right** side.

TOP HALF

With Red and leaving a long end for sewing, ch 30{32-34} **loosely**.
Row 1: Sc in second ch from hook and in each ch across changing to Yellow in last sc worked: 29{31-33} sc.
Row 2 (Buttonhole row): Ch 1, turn; sc in each sc across to last 4 sc, ch 2, skip next 2 sc, sc in last 2 sc changing to Green in last sc worked.
Row 3: Ch 1, turn; sc in each sc and in each ch across changing to Dark Blue in last sc worked.
Row 4 (Right side): Ch 1, turn; sc in each sc across; finish off leaving a long end for sewing.
Note: Mark last row as **right** side.

FINISHING

Using photo as a guide for placement, sew Roof to Barn. With White, embroider door and window outlines using straight stitches.
Sew Sun to left Back shoulder and add sun rays with Yellow slip sts.
Leaving top edge free, sew Wheelbarrow Pocket to Right Front. Sew Wheel to Wheelbarrow.
Leaving 2" at buttonhole end free, sew Top Half of Rainbow on Right Front.
Sew Bottom Half of Rainbow on Left Front, lining up as a continuation of Top Half.
With Yellow, embroider flowers at Rainbow's end, using Lazy Daisy Stitch *(Fig. 32, page 142)*.
Add buttons.

SWEATER BOUQUET

Ready-made sweaters become personalized treasures when you embellish them with pretty crocheted designs like this one. Made using bedspread weight cotton thread, the flowers, leaves, and stems are worked separately and then attached to the sweater with thread and pearl bead accents. You can arrange the designs as you please to create your own beautiful bouquet!

MATERIALS

Bedspread Weight Cotton Thread (size 10), approximately:
- Small Flower (Pink) - 1 yard **each**
- Large Center (Yellow) - 1½ yards **each**
- Large Petals (Blue) - 2½ yards **each**
- Leaf (Green) - 2 yards **each**

Note: Allow extra yardage for Stems.

Steel crochet hook, size 6 (1.80 mm)
Assorted beads
Cotton knit pullover
Sewing needle and thread

Note: Gauge is not important. Pieces can be smaller or larger without changing the overall effect.

PATTERN STITCH

LOVE KNOT

Ch 1, pull up loop on hook to measure ½", YO and draw through (loose ch made), sc in back ridge only *(Fig. 1a)* of loose ch just made *(Fig. 1b)*.

Fig. 1a	Fig. 1b

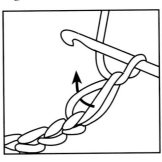
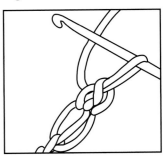

SMALL FLOWER

Ch 4; join with slip st to form a ring.
Rnd 1 (Right side)**:** Ch 1, (sc in ring, work 2 Love Knots) 6 times; join with slip st to first sc, finish off: 6 petals.

LARGE FLOWER

With Yellow, ch 6; join with slip st to form a ring.

Rnd 1 (Right side): Ch 3, 19 dc in ring; join with slip st to top of beginning ch-3, finish off: 20 sts.

Rnd 2: With **right** side facing, join Blue with sc in same st as joining *(see Joining With Sc, page 138)*, ch 3, ★ sc in Front Loop Only of next dc *(Fig. 20, page 138)*, ch 3; repeat from ★ around; join with slip st to both loops of first sc: 20 ch-3 sps.

Rnd 3: Slip st in first ch-3-sp, ch 1, sc in same sp, ch 3, (sc in next ch-3 sp, ch 3) around; join with slip st to first sc, finish off.

LEAF

Row 1: Ch 2, 3 sc in second ch from hook.

Row 2: Ch 1, turn; 2 sc in first sc, sc in next sc, 2 sc in last sc: 5 sc.

Rows 3 and 4: Ch 1, turn; 2 sc in first sc, sc in each sc across to last sc, 2 sc in last sc: 9 sc.

Rows 5-7: Ch 1, turn; pull up a loop in first 2 sts, YO and draw through all 3 loops on hook, sc in each st across to last 2 sts, pull up a loop in last 2 sts, YO and draw through all 3 loops on hook: 3 sts.

Row 8: Ch 1, turn; pull up a loop in each st across, YO and draw through all 4 loops on hook: one st.

Edging (Right side): Ch 1, do **not** turn; working in end of rows, sc evenly around working 3 sc in each end of Row 4; join with slip st to first sc, finish off.

STEM

Make chain desired length; finish off.

FINISHING

Make desired amount of Flowers, Leaves, and Stems and arrange on pullover.

Sew pieces in place, stitching Leaves at one end only to allow tips to fold forward.

Add beads as desired.

QUICK COZY MITTENS

It's easy to dress your kids in cozy fashion during the chilly months when you color-coordinate their mittens with their winter wear. Worked in solids or stripes using sport weight yarn, these warm mittens can be made in three sizes, so you can find just the right look and fit.

Size:	Small	Medium	Large
Palm Width:	3"	3½"	3½"
Hand Length:	3½"	5"	6¼"

Size Note: Instructions are written for size Small with sizes Medium and Large in braces. Instructions will be easier to read if you circle all the numbers pertaining to your size.

MATERIALS

Sport Weight Yarn, approximately:

Solid - 1{1¼-1½} ounces,
[30{35-40} grams, 100{125-125} yards]

Striped

MC (Blue) - ¾{¾-1} ounce,
[20{20-30} grams, 75{75-100} yards]

CC (Yellow) - ¼{½-½} ounce,
[10{15-15} grams, 25{50-50} yards]

Size Small - crochet hook, size F (3.75 mm) **or** size needed for gauge

Sizes Medium and Large - crochet hook, size G (4.00 mm) **or** size needed for gauge

Yarn needle

GAUGE: Size Small - 10 sc and 10 rows = 2"

Sizes Medium and Large - 9 sc and 9 rows = 2"

PATTERN STITCHES

FRONT POST DOUBLE CROCHET (abbreviated FPdc)

YO, insert hook from **front** to **back** around post of sc indicated in rnd **below** previous rnd *(Fig. 13, page 135)*, YO and pull up a loop even with loop on hook, (YO and draw through 2 loops on hook) twice. Skip st behind FPdc.

DECREASE

Pull up a loop in next 2 sts, YO and draw through all 3 loops on hook **(counts as one sc)**.

HAND

Note: For Striped Mittens, work Rnds 1-4 in MC, complete Hand alternating 2 rnds each CC and MC and carrying unused yarn **loosely** along the seam on the wrong side *(Fig. 22a, page 138)*.

Rnd 1 (Right side): Ch 2, 8 sc in second ch from hook; do **not** join, place marker *(see Markers, page 138)*.

Note: Loop a short piece of yarn around any stitch to mark last round as **right** side.

Rnd 2: 2 Sc in each sc around: 16 sc.

Rnd 3: (Sc in next sc, 2 sc in next sc) around: 24 sc.

Rnd 4: (Sc in next 7 sc, 2 sc in next sc) around: 27 sc.

Rnd 5: (Sc in next 2 sc, work FPdc around sc in rnd **below** next sc) around: 9 FPdc.
Rnd 6: Sc in each st around.
Rnd 7: (Sc in next 2 sc, work FPdc around sc before next FPdc) around.
Repeat Rnds 6 and 7, 4{5-7} times.
RIGHT MITTEN ONLY: Sc in first 4 sts, ch 4 **loosely**, skip next 4 sts (Thumb opening), sc in last 19 sts.
Next Rnd: Sc in next 2 sc, work FPdc around sc before next FPdc, sc in next sc and in next 4 chs, work FPdc around sc before next FPdc, (sc in next 2 sc, work FPdc around sc before next FPdc) around.
LEFT MITTEN ONLY: Sc in first 19 sts, ch 4 **loosely**, skip next 4 sts (Thumb opening), sc in last 4 sc.
Next Rnd: (Sc in next 2 sc, work FPdc around sc before next FPdc) 6 times, sc in next sc and in next 4 chs, work FPdc around sc before next FPdc, sc in next 2 sc, work FPdc around sc before next FPdc.
BOTH MITTENS: Sc in each st around.
SIZES MEDIUM AND LARGE ONLY: Repeat Rnds 5 and 6, {1-2} times; do **not** finish off.

CUFF

Note: For Striped Mittens, work in MC.
Foundation Rnd: Decrease, (sc in next 4 sc, decrease) 4 times, sc in next sc: 22 sc.

Ch 11 **loosely**.
Row 1: Sc in back ridge of second ch from hook and in each ch across *(Fig. 2a, page 133)*, sc in first 2 sts on Foundation Rnd: 12 sc.
Row 2: Turn; skip first 2 sc, sc in Back Loop Only of each sc across *(Fig. 20, page 138)*: 10 sc.
Row 3: Ch 1, turn; sc in Back Loop Only of each sc across, sc in next 2 sts on Foundation Rnd: 12 sc.
Repeat Rows 2 and 3, ending by working Row 2.
Joining Row: Turn; with **wrong** sides together, working in Back Loop Only of last row **and** in free loops of beginning ch *(Fig. 21b, page 138)*, slip st in each sc across; finish off.

THUMB

Note: For Striped Mittens, work in MC.
Rnd 1: With **right** side facing and working in unworked sts on Hand **and** in free loops of ch-4, join yarn with sc in first ch *(see Joining With Sc, page 138)*; sc in next 2 chs, 2 sc in next ch, sc in next 3 sc, 2 sc in next sc; do **not** join, place marker: 10 sc.
Rnds 2-4: Sc in each sc around.
Rnd 5: (Sc in next 3 sc, decrease) twice: 8 sc.
Repeat Rnd 2 until Thumb measures approximately 1¾{2-2¼}" **or** to desired length; finish off leaving a long end for sewing.

Thread yarn needle with end and weave through sts of last rnd; gather tightly and secure.

hooked on holidays

Decorating your home for special days is easy with the projects in this festive collection. You'll discover accents and gifts to help you celebrate six favorite holidays — from a heartwarming pillow for Valentine's Day to a collection of Christmas decorations that will bring cheer to every room. It's never been more fun to crochet your way through the seasons!

VALENTINE'S DAY

Embellished with a ring of filet crochet hearts, a purchased pillow becomes a thoughtful gift for Valentine's Day. The delicate creation will forever serve as a reminder of your affection.

SWEETHEART PILLOW

Finished Size: Approximately 12¹/₂" square

MATERIALS
Bedspread Weight Cotton Thread (size 10),
   approximately 235 yards
Steel crochet hook, size 7 (1.65 mm) **or** size needed
   for gauge
Purchased pillow
Sewing needle and thread

GAUGE: 15 Spaces and 15 rows = 4"

SQUARE
Ch 140 **loosely**.
Row 1 (Right side): Dc in eighth ch from hook, (ch 2, skip next 2 chs, dc in next ch) across: 45 Spaces.
Note: Loop a short piece of thread around any stitch to mark last row as **right** side.

Row 2: Work Beginning Space (**see Pattern Stitches, page 110)**, work Space Over Space across to last Space, skip next 2 chs, dc in next ch.
Rows 3-17: Follow Chart, page 110.
Row 18: Work Beginning Space, work 6 Spaces, work Left Increase, work 3 Blocks, 2 dc in same dc as last dc made, skip next 2 dc, dc in next dc, work 21 Spaces, skip next 2 dc, 3 dc in next dc, work 3 Blocks, work Right Increase, work 7 Spaces.
Rows 19-28: Follow Chart.
Row 29: Work Beginning Space, work 7 Spaces, skip next 2 dc, 3 dc in next dc, work 8 Blocks, work 11 Spaces, work 8 Blocks, 2 dc in same dc as last dc made, skip next 2 dc, dc in next dc, work 8 Spaces.
Rows 30-45: Follow Chart; do **not** finish off.

PATTERN STITCHES

BEGINNING SPACE

Ch 5 (**counts as first dc plus ch 2**), turn; dc in next dc.

SPACE OVER SPACE

Ch 2, dc in next dc.

SPACE OVER BLOCK

Ch 2, skip next 2 dc, dc in next dc.

BLOCK OVER SPACE

2 Dc in next ch-2 sp, dc in next dc.

BLOCK OVER BLOCK

Dc in next 3 dc.

RIGHT INCREASE

2 Dc in same dc as last dc made, dc in next dc.

LEFT INCREASE

3 Dc in next dc.

LEFT DECREASE SPACE (uses next 3 dc)

Ch 2, ★ YO, insert hook in **next** dc, YO and pull up a loop, YO and draw through 2 loops on hook; repeat from ★ 2 times **more**, YO and draw through all 4 loops on hook (**counts as ch 2 plus one dc**).

RIGHT DECREASE SPACE

Work last dc of previous Block until 2 loops remain on hook, ★ YO, insert hook in **next** dc, YO and pull up a loop, YO and draw through 2 loops on hook; repeat from ★ once **more**, YO and draw through all 4 loops on hook (**counts as one dc**), ch 2, dc in next dc.

DC CLUSTER (uses next 5 dc)

Ch 2, ★ YO, insert hook in **next** dc, YO and pull up a loop, YO and draw through 2 loops on hook; repeat from ★ 4 times **more**, YO and draw through all 6 loops on hook (**counts as one dc**), ch 2, dc in next dc.

EDGING

Rnd 1: Ch 1, work 126 sc evenly spaced across end of rows; working in free loops **and** in ch-2 sps of beginning ch *(Fig. 21b, page 138)*, 3 sc in first ch, 2 sc in each ch-2 sp and sc in each ch across to last ch, 3 sc in last ch; work 126 sc evenly spaced across end of rows; 3 sc in first dc, 2 sc in each ch-2 sp and sc in each dc across to last dc, 3 sc in last dc; join with slip st to first sc: 532 sc.

Rnd 2: Ch 2, skip next sc, (slip st in next sc, ch 2, skip next sc) around; join with slip st to joining, finish off.

FINISHING

See Washing and Blocking, page 140.

Sew Square to pillow.

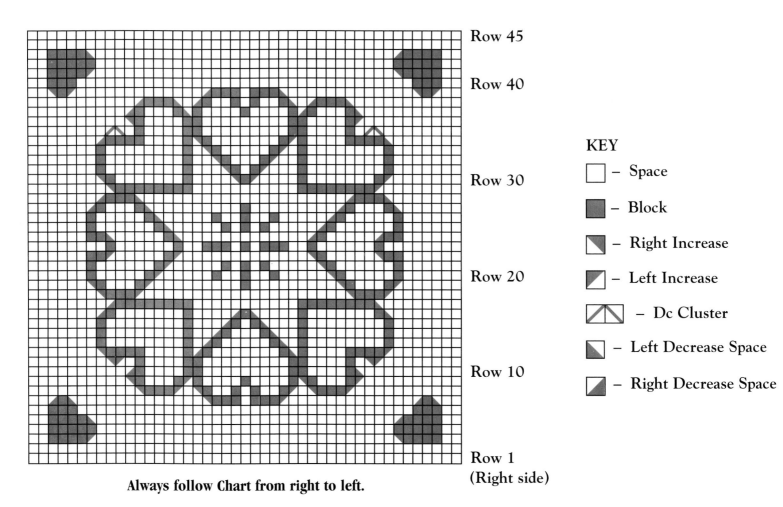

Row 45

Row 40

Row 30

Row 20

Row 10

Row 1
(Right side)

KEY

☐ – Space

■ – Block

◪ – Right Increase

◪ – Left Increase

◪ – Dc Cluster

◪ – Left Decrease Space

◪ – Right Decrease Space

Always follow Chart from right to left.

EASTER

Make your Easter bright and gay with this adorable rabbit! Crocheted using fabric strips, he makes an "egg-cellent" gift or centerpiece. With his bright eyes, quilting thread "whiskers," and jaunty bow tie, this little cottontail is all set for the celebration.

RAG RABBIT

Finished Size: Approximately 17" tall

MATERIALS

100% Cotton Fabric, 44/45" wide, approximately:
  MC - 6¹/₂ yards
  CC - 2 yards
Crochet hook, size J (6.00 mm) **or** size needed for gauge
18 mm Eyes - 2
18 mm Nose - 1

Heavy Duty Quilting thread - Black
Polyester stuffing
Yarn needle
Sewing needle and thread

Prepare fabric and cut into 1" strips leaving a 3" x 27" piece of CC for Tie **(see Preparing Fabric Strips and Joining Fabric Strips, page 139)**.

GAUGE: 7 sc and 8 rows = 4"

111

PATTERN STITCH
DECREASE
Pull up a loop in next 2 sts, YO and draw through all 3 loops on hook (counts as one sc).

HEAD AND TORSO
Rnd 1 (Right side): With MC, ch 2, 6 sc in second ch from hook; do **not** join, place fabric marker (see Markers, page 138).
Rnds 2 and 3: 2 Sc in each sc around: 24 sc.
Rnds 4-8: Sc in each sc around.
Rnd 9: Sc in next 12 sc, 2 sc in next sc, (sc in next sc, 2 sc in next sc) twice, sc in next 2 sc, 2 sc in next sc, (sc in next sc, 2 sc in next sc) twice: 30 sc.
Rnd 10: Sc in each sc around.
Rnd 11: Decrease, sc in next 7 sc, decrease, sc in next 4 sc, 3 sc in next sc, sc in next 3 sc, pull up a loop in next 3 sc, YO and draw through all 4 loops on hook, sc in next 3 sc, 3 sc in next sc, sc in next 4 sc: 30 sc.
Rnd 12: (Sc in next sc, decrease) 6 times, sc in next sc, 3 sc in next sc, (sc in next sc, decrease) 3 times, sc in next sc: 23 sc.
Rnd 13: Decrease 7 times, sc in next sc, decrease around: 12 sc.
Rnds 14-16: Sc in each sc around.
Rnd 17: 2 Sc in each sc around: 24 sc.
Rnd 18: (Sc in next 2 sc, 2 sc in next sc) around: 32 sc.
Rnds 19 and 20: Sc in each sc around.
Note: Begin working in rows.
Row 1: Sc in next 23 sc, leave remaining 9 sc unworked: 23 sc.
Row 2: Ch 1, turn; sc in first 26 sc, leave remaining sc unworked: 26 sc.
Rows 3-9: Ch 1, turn; sc in each sc across.
Note: Begin working in rounds.
Rnd 1: Ch 1, turn; sc in each sc across, ch 2; join with slip st to first sc.
Rnd 2: Ch 1, turn; sc in same st and in each ch and each sc around; do **not** join, place marker: 28 sc.
Rnd 3: (Sc in next 2 sc, decrease) around: 21 sc.
Rnd 4: (Sc in next sc, decrease) around: 14 sc.
Rnd 5: Decrease around; slip st in next sc, finish off leaving long end for sewing: 7 sc.
Thread yarn needle with end and weave through remaining sts; gather tightly and secure.

TUMMY
With CC, ch 7 **loosely**.
Row 1: Sc in second ch from hook and in each ch across: 6 sc.
Rows 2-10: Ch 1, turn; sc in each sc across; finish off.
Stuff Head and Torso **firmly**.
Sew Tummy to Torso.

ARM (Make 2)
Rnd 1 (Right side): With CC, ch 2, 6 sc in second ch from hook; do **not** join, place marker.
Rnd 2: 2 Sc in each sc around, changing to MC in last sc (Fig. 22a, page 138): 12 sc.
Rnd 3: Sc in Back Loop Only of each sc around (Fig. 20, page 138).
Rnds 4-9: Sc in both loops of each sc around.
Note: Begin working in rows.
Row 1: Sc in next sc, hdc in next 8 sc, sc in next sc, leave remaining 2 sts unworked: 10 sts.
Row 2: Ch 1, turn; decrease, sc in next 6 hdc, decrease; finish off leaving a long end for sewing: 8 sts.

LEG (Make 2)
Rnd 1 (Right side): With MC, ch 2, 6 sc in second ch from hook; do **not** join, place marker.
Rnds 2 and 3: 2 Sc in each sc around: 24 sc.
Rnd 4: (Sc in next 3 sc, 2 sc in next sc) around: 30 sc.
Rnds 5-7: Sc in each sc around.
Rnd 8: (Sc in next 3 sc, decrease) around; finish off leaving a long end for sewing: 24 sc.

FOOT (Make 2)
With CC, ch 10 **loosely**.
Rnd 1 (Right side): Sc in second ch from hook and in next 7 chs, 3 sc in last ch; working in free loops of beginning ch (Fig. 21b, page 138), sc in next 7 chs, 3 sc in next ch; join with slip st to first sc: 21 sc.
Rnd 2: Ch 2, hdc in same st, hdc in next sc, sc in next 7 sc, 3 sc in next sc, sc in next 7 sc, hdc in next sc, 2 hdc in next sc, 3 hdc in each of last 2 sc; join with slip st to top of beginning ch-2 changing to MC (Fig. 22b, page 138): 29 sts.
Rnd 3: Ch 1, sc in Back Loop Only of each st around; join with slip st to first sc.
Rnd 4: Ch 1, working in both loops, decrease, sc in next 19 sc, decrease 4 times; join with slip st to first sc: 24 sc.
Rnd 5: Ch 1, decrease, sc in next 6 sc, decrease, sc in next sc, decrease, sc in next 6 sc, decrease, pull up a loop in each of next 3 sc, YO and draw through all 4 loops on hook; join with slip st to first sc, finish off leaving a long end for sewing: 18 sts.

TAIL
Rnd 1 (Right side): With CC, ch 2, 6 sc in second ch from hook; do **not** join, place marker.
Rnd 2: 2 Sc in each sc around: 12 sc.
Rnds 3 and 4: Sc in each sc around.
Rnd 5: Decrease around; slip st in next sc, finish off leaving a long end for sewing: 6 sc.

Continued on page 115.

INDENDENCE DAY

Stars and stripes abound on this all-American afghan. Its field of stars is assembled using blue and white motifs; then the stripes are worked in groups of double crochet stitches. Perfect for taking along on your Fourth of July picnic, this spirited throw will draw a rousing cheer!

STARS AND STRIPES AFGHAN

Finished Size: Approximately 45" x 70"

MATERIALS
Worsted Weight Yarn, approximately:
   Red - 17 ounces, (480 grams, 1,070 yards)
   Sea Oats - 18 ounces, (510 grams, 1,135 yards)
   Blue - 8 ounces, (230 grams, 505 yards)
Crochet hook, size J (6.00 mm) **or** size needed for gauge
Yarn needle

GAUGE: One Motif = 4" (straight edge to straight edge)
   and 4¹/₂" (point to point)
   In pattern, (3 dc, ch 1) 4 times = 4¹/₄"
   and 7 rows = 4"

STAR FIELD

MOTIF (Make 46)
With Sea Oats, ch 3; join with slip st to form a ring.
Rnd 1 (Right side): Ch 1, 12 sc in ring; join with slip st to first sc.

Note: Loop a short piece of yarn around any stitch to mark last round as **right** side.

Rnd 2: Ch 2, (YO, insert hook in **next** sc, YO and pull up a loop, YO and draw through 2 loops on hook) twice, YO and draw through all 3 loops on hook, ★ ch 4, YO, insert hook in **same** sc, YO and pull up a loop, YO and draw through 2 loops on hook, (YO, insert hook in **next** sc, YO and pull up a loop, YO and draw through 2 loops on hook) twice, YO and draw through all 4 loops on hook; repeat from ★ 4 times **more** working last st in same sc as beginning ch-2, ch 4; join with slip st to first st, finish off: 6 ch-4 sps.

Rnd 3: With **right** side facing, join Blue with slip st in any ch-4 sp; ch 1, 6 sc in same sp and in each ch-4 sp around; join with slip st to first sc: 36 sc.

Rnd 4: Ch 3 **(counts as first dc, now and throughout)**, dc in next 2 sc, ch 2, (dc in next 6 sc, ch 2) 5 times, dc in last 3 sc; join with slip st to first dc, finish off: 6 dc **each** side.

HALF MOTIF (Make 6)

Row 1 (Right side)**:** With Blue, ch 4, 8 dc in fourth ch from hook: 9 sts.

Note: Mark last row as **right** side.

Row 2: Ch 1, turn; sc in first dc, (2 sc in next st, sc in next st) across: 13 sc.

Row 3: Ch 3, turn; dc in same st and in next sc, 2 dc in next sc, dc in next sc, ★ (dc, ch 2, dc) in next sc, dc in next sc, 2 dc in next sc, dc in next sc; repeat from ★ once **more**, (dc, ch 3, slip st) in last sc; finish off.

ASSEMBLY

Following Placement Diagram, whipstitch Motifs together *(Fig. 27a, page 140)*.

PLACEMENT DIAGRAM

EDGING

With **right** side facing, join Blue with slip st in ch-2 sp at point A *(see Placement Diagram)*; † ch 4, tr in next dc, YO twice, insert hook in next dc, YO and pull up a loop, (YO and draw through 2 loops on hook) twice, YO, insert hook in next dc, YO and pull up a loop, YO and draw through 2 loops on hook, YO and draw through all 3 loops on hook, dc in next dc, hdc in next 2 dc, sc in next ch-2 sp, hdc in next 2 dc, dc in next dc, YO, insert hook in next dc, YO and pull up a loop, YO and draw through 2 loops on hook, YO twice, insert hook in next dc, YO and pull up a loop, (YO and draw through 2 loops on hook) twice, YO and draw through all 3 loops on hook, ★ tr in next dc, YO 3 times, insert hook in next ch-sp, YO and pull up a loop, (YO and draw through 2 loops on hook) 3 times, YO 3 times, insert hook in joining, YO and pull up a loop, (YO and draw through 2 loops on hook) 3 times, YO 3 times, insert hook in next ch-sp, YO and pull up a loop, (YO and draw through 2 loops on hook) 3 times, YO and draw through all 4 loops on hook, tr in next dc, YO twice, insert hook in next dc, YO and pull up a loop, (YO and draw through 2 loops on hook) twice, YO, insert hook in next dc, YO and pull up a loop, YO and draw through 2 loops on hook, YO and draw through all 3 loops on hook, dc in next dc, hdc in next 2 dc, sc in next ch-2 sp, hdc in next 2 dc, dc in next dc, YO, insert hook in next dc, YO and pull up a loop, YO and draw through 2 loops on hook, YO twice, insert hook in next dc, YO and pull up a loop, (YO and draw through 2 loops on hook) twice, YO and draw through all 3 loops on hook; repeat from ★ 5 times **more**, tr in next dc and in next ch-2 sp; 3 sc around tr just made, sc in same ch-2 sp as tr and in next 6 dc, sc in next ch-sp, (2 sc around next dc, sc around next sc, 2 sc around next dc, sc in next ch, 2 sc around next dc, sc around next sc, 2 sc around next dc, sc in next ch-sp and in next 6 dc, sc in next ch-sp) 3 times †, slip st in same ch-sp; repeat from † to † once, 3 sc around beginning ch-4; join with slip st to top of ch-4, finish off.

STRIPES

With Red, ch 265 **loosely**.

Row 1 (Right side)**:** Dc in fourth ch from hook and in next ch **(3 skipped chs count as first dc)**, ★ ch 1, skip next ch, dc in next 3 chs; repeat from ★ across: 66 3-dc groups.

Note: Mark last row as **right** side.

Row 2: Ch 5 **(counts as first dc plus ch 2, now and throughout)**, turn; 3 dc in next ch-1 sp, (ch 1, 3 dc in next ch-1 sp) across, ch 2, skip next 2 dc, dc in last dc: 65 3-dc groups.

Row 3: Ch 3, turn; 2 dc in first ch-2 sp, (ch 1, 3 dc in next ch-1 sp) across to last ch-2 sp, ch 1, 2 dc in last sp, dc in last dc: 66 3-dc groups.

Row 4: Ch 5, turn; 3 dc in next ch-1 sp, (ch 1, 3 dc in next ch-1 sp) across, ch 2, skip next 2 dc, dc in last dc: 65 3-dc groups.

Rows 5 and 6: Repeat Rows 3 and 4, changing to Sea Oats at end of Row 6 *(Fig. 22a, page 138)*.

Rows 7-12: Repeat Rows 3 and 4, 3 times, changing to Red at end of Row 12.

Rows 13-18: Repeat Rows 3 and 4, 3 times, changing to Sea Oats at end of Row 18.

Rows 19-36: Repeat Rows 7-18 once, then repeat Rows 7-12 once **more**.

Row 37: Ch 3, turn; 2 dc in first ch-2 sp, (ch 1, 3 dc in next ch-1 sp) 39 times, leave remaining sts unworked: 40 3-dc groups.

Rows 38-42: Repeat Rows 2-6: 39 3-dc groups.

Rows 43-78: Repeat Rows 7-18, 3 times; at end of Row 78, do **not** change colors and do **not** finish off.

EDGING

With Red, ch 1, turn; using corresponding color, sc evenly around entire piece working 3 sc in each corner and decreasing at inner corner; join with slip st to first sc, finish off.

Whipstitch Star Field into upper left hand corner of Stripes.

RAG RABBIT

Continued from page 112.

EAR (Make 2)
INNER
With CC, ch 4 **loosely**.

Row 1 (Right side): Sc in second ch from hook and in each ch across: 3 sc.

Note: Loop a short piece of fabric around any stitch to mark last row as **right** side.

Rows 2 and 3: Ch 1, turn; sc in each sc across.

Row 4: Ch 1, turn; sc in first sc, 2 sc in next sc, sc in last sc: 4 sc.

Row 5: Ch 1, turn; sc in each sc across.

Row 6: Ch 1, turn; 2 sc in first sc, sc in next 2 sc, 2 sc in last sc: 6 sc.

Rows 7 and 8: Ch 1, turn; sc in each sc across.

Row 9: Ch 1, turn; decrease, sc in next 2 sc, decrease: 4 sc.

Row 10: Ch 1, turn; sc in each sc across.

Row 11: Ch 1, turn; decrease twice: 2 sc.

Row 12: Ch 1, turn; sc in first 2 sc.

Row 13: Ch 1, turn; decrease; finish off.

OUTER
With MC, work same as Inner Ear.

EDGING
Holding **wrong** sides of Inner and Outer Ears together with Inner Ear facing, and working through **both** pieces, join MC with slip st in end of Row 1; ch 1, 2 sc in same row, † working in end of rows, sc in next 4 rows, 2 sc in next row, sc in next row, 2 sc in next row, sc in next 4 rows †, 3 sc in next sc, repeat from † to † once, 2 sc in last row; finish off leaving a long end for sewing.

CHEEKS
RIGHT SIDE
Row 1 (Right side): With CC, ch 2, 3 sc in second ch from hook.

Note: Mark last row as **right** side.

Row 2: Ch 1, turn; 2 sc in first sc, 2 hdc in next sc, 2 sc in last sc: 6 sts.

Row 3: Ch 1, turn; decrease, hdc in next 2 hdc, decrease; finish off leaving a long end for sewing: 4 sts.

LEFT SIDE
Row 1: With **right** side facing, join CC with slip st in free loop of beginning ch on Right Side; ch 2, 3 sc in second ch from hook.

Rows 2 and 3: Work same as Right Side.

FINISHING
Using photo as a guide for placement:
Stuff Arms, Legs, Feet, and Tail.
Sew Arms, Legs, and Tail to Torso.
Sew Feet to Legs.
Sew Ears and Cheeks to Head.
Add eyes, nose, and quilting thread whiskers.
Tie 3" x 27" piece of CC fabric in a bow around neck.

HALLOWEEN

Halloween is a haunting good time to show off your crochet skills. Our doll on page 119 makes a bewitching accent, and these plump pumpkins will bring the fiery hues of autumn into your home. Worked in assorted sizes, they'll make a delightful display all through the harvest season.

PUMPKIN PATCH

Finished Size: Small - approximately 2½" tall
Medium - approximately 3½" tall
Large - approximately 4½" tall

MATERIALS
Worsted Weight Yarn, approximately:
Small Pumpkin (Orange) - 45 yards
Medium Pumpkin (Orange) - 70 yards
Large Pumpkin (Orange) - 75 yards
Stem (Green) - 3 yards **each**
Crochet hook, size F (3.75 mm) **or** size needed for gauge
Yarn needle
Polyester stuffing

GAUGE: 18 sc and 18 rows = 4"

SMALL PUMPKIN
With Orange, ch 21 **loosely**.
Row 1 (Right side): Sc in second ch from hook and in each ch across: 20 sc.
Note: Loop a short piece of yarn around any stitch to mark last row as **right** side.
Row 2: Ch 1, turn; sc in each sc across.
Row 3: Turn; slip st in Front Loop Only of each sc across *(Fig. 20, page 138)*.
Row 4: Ch 1, turn; sc in Back Loop Only of each st across.
Row 5: Ch 1, turn; sc in both loops of each sc across.
Rows 6-37: Repeat Rows 2-5, 8 times.
Finish off leaving a long end for sewing.

MEDIUM PUMPKIN
With Orange, ch 26 **loosely**.
Row 1 (Right side): Sc in second ch from hook and in each ch across: 25 sc.
Note: Loop a short piece of yarn around any stitch to mark last row as **right** side.
Row 2: Ch 1, turn; sc in each sc across.
Row 3: Turn; slip st in Front Loop Only of each sc across *(Fig. 20, page 138)*.
Row 4: Ch 1, turn; sc in Back Loop Only of each st across.
Row 5: Ch 1, turn; sc in both loops of each sc across.
Rows 6-53: Repeat Rows 2-5, 12 times.
Finish off leaving a long end for sewing.

LARGE PUMPKIN
With Orange, ch 32 **loosely**.
Row 1 (Right side): Sc in second ch from hook and in each ch across: 31 sc.

Note: Loop a short piece of yarn around any stitch to mark last row as **right** side.
Row 2: Ch 1, turn; sc in each sc across.
Row 3: Turn; slip st in Front Loop Only of each sc across *(Fig. 20, page 138)*.
Row 4: Ch 1, turn; sc in Back Loop Only of each st across.
Row 5: Ch 1, turn; sc in both loops of each sc across.
Rows 6-45: Repeat Rows 2-5, 10 times.
Finish off leaving a long end for sewing.

STEM
With Green, ch 7 **loosely**.
Row 1: Slip st in second ch from hook and in each ch across: 6 sts.
Rows 2 and 3: Turn; work 6 slip sts evenly spaced down center of Stem *(Fig. 1)*.

Fig. 1

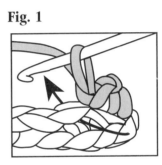

Note: Begin working in rounds.
Rnd 1: Slip st in end of rows, ch 1, work 8 sc evenly spaced around base of stem; join with slip st to first sc, finish off leaving a long end for sewing.

FINISHING
With **right** side of Pumpkin to inside, sew last row to first row forming a tube.
Thread yarn needle with a double strand of Orange and weave through end of rows at one end of tube; gather tightly and secure.
Turn **right** side out and stuff.
Thread yarn needle with a double strand of Orange and weave through end of rows at open end of tube; gather tightly and secure, do **not** finish off.
Pull yarn through Pumpkin from one gathered end through the other gathered end and then back again. Pull yarn tightly to indent both ends and secure.
Sew Stem to Pumpkin.

TRICKSIE THE WITCH

Finished Size: Approximately 39" tall

MATERIALS

Worsted Weight Yarn, approximately:
Color A (Green) - 7 ounces, (200 grams, 410 yards)
Color B (Black) - 14 ounces, (400 grams, 815 yards)
Color C (Purple) - 5 ounces, (140 grams, 290 yards)
Color D (Orange) - 2 ounces, (60 grams, 115 yards)
Crochet hooks, sizes E (3.50 mm), G (4.00 mm) **and**
K (6.50 mm) **or** sizes needed for gauge
Polyester stuffing
Embroidery floss - Black
Yarn needle
Embroidery needle
⁵⁄₈" Buttons (Eyes) - 2
¹⁄₂" Buttons (Blouse) - 3
³⁄₈" Buttons (Boots) - 6
Finishing materials: Flower, ribbon, etc.

GAUGE: With medium size hook,
16 sc and 20 rows = 4"

PATTERN STITCH
DECREASE
Pull up a loop in next 2 sts, YO and draw through all 3 loops on
hook **(counts as one sc)**.

BODY
HEAD
With medium size hook and Color A, ch 23 **loosely**.

Rnd 1 (Right side): 3 Sc in second ch from hook, sc in next
20 chs, 3 sc in last ch; working in free loops of beginning ch
(Fig. 21b, page 138), sc in next 20 chs; join with slip st to
first sc: 46 sc.

Rnd 2: Ch 1, turn; (sc in next 20 sc, 2 sc in each of next 3 sc)
twice; join with slip st to first sc: 52 sc.

Rnd 3: Ch 1, turn; ★ 2 sc in next sc, (sc in next sc, 2 sc in
next sc) twice, sc in next 21 sc; repeat from ★ once **more**; join
with slip st to first sc: 58 sc.

Rnd 4: Ch 1, turn; sc in next 21 sc, 2 sc in next sc, (sc in next
2 sc, 2 sc in next sc) twice, sc in next 22 sc, 2 sc in next sc,
(sc in next 2 sc, 2 sc in next sc) twice, sc in last sc; join with
slip st to first sc: 64 sc.

Rnds 5-7: Ch 1, turn; sc in each sc around; join with slip st to
first sc.

Rnd 8: Ch 1, turn; sc in next 21 sc, decrease, (sc in next 2 sc,
decrease) twice, sc in next 22 sc, decrease, (sc in next 2 sc,
decrease) twice, sc in last sc; join with slip st to first sc: 58 sc.

Rnds 9 and 10: Ch 1, turn; sc in each sc around; join with
slip st to first sc.

Rnd 11: Ch 1, turn; ★ decrease, (sc in next sc, decrease)
twice, sc in next 21 sc; repeat from ★ once **more**; join with
slip st to first st: 52 sc.

Rnds 12 and 13: Ch 1, turn; sc in each sc around; join with
slip st to first sc.

Rnd 14: Ch 1, turn; (sc in next 20 sc, decrease 3 times) twice;
join with slip st to first sc: 46 sc.

Rnds 15-27: Ch 1, turn; sc in each sc around; join with slip st
to first sc.

Rnd 28: Ch 1, turn; (sc in next 21 sc, decrease) twice; join
with slip st to first sc: 44 sc.

Rnd 29: Ch 1, turn; sc in next sc, decrease, sc in next 20 sc,
decrease, sc in each sc around; join with slip st to first sc:
42 sc.

Rnd 30: Ch 1, turn; (sc in next 19 sc, decrease) twice; join
with slip st to first sc: 40 sc.

Rnd 31: Ch 1, turn; sc in next sc, decrease, sc in next 18 sc,
decrease, sc in each sc around; join with slip st to first sc:
38 sc.

Rnd 32: Ch 1, turn; (sc in next 17 sc, decrease) twice; join
with slip st to first sc: 36 sc.

Rnd 33: Ch 1, turn; sc in next sc, decrease, sc in next 16 sc,
decrease, sc in each sc around; join with slip st to first sc:
34 sc.

Rnds 34-38: Ch 1, turn; sc in each sc around; join with slip st
to first sc, finish off leaving a long end for sewing.
Stuff and shape Head.
Thread yarn needle with end and weave through remaining sts;
gather tightly and secure.

TORSO

Rnd 1 (Right side): With medium size hook and Color A, ch 2,
6 sc in second ch from hook; do **not** join, place marker
(see Markers, page 138).

Rnd 2: 2 Sc in each sc around: 12 sc.

Rnd 3: (Sc in next sc, 2 sc in next sc) around: 18 sc.

Rnd 4: (Sc in next 2 sc, 2 sc in next sc) around: 24 sc.

Rnd 5: (Sc in next 3 sc, 2 sc in next sc) around: 30 sc.

Rnd 6: (Sc in next 4 sc, 2 sc in next sc) around: 36 sc.

Rnd 7: Sc in each sc around.

Rnd 8: (Sc in next 5 sc, 2 sc in next sc) around: 42 sc.

Rnds 9 and 10: Sc in each sc around.

Rnd 11: (Sc in next 13 sc, 2 sc in next sc) around: 45 sc.

Rnd 12: Sc in next 7 sc, 2 sc in next sc, (sc in next 14 sc, 2 sc
in next sc) twice, sc in next 7 sc: 48 sc.

Rnd 13: (Sc in next 15 sc, 2 sc in next sc) around: 51 sc.

Rnd 14: Sc in next 8 sc, 2 sc in next sc, (sc in next 16 sc, 2 sc
in next sc) twice, sc in next 8 sc: 54 sc.

Enchant trick-or-treaters with this whimsical witch! Her friendly smile will keep little goblins spellbound.

Rnd 15: (Sc in next 17 sc, 2 sc in next sc) around: 57 sc.

Rnd 16: Sc in next 9 sc, 2 sc in next sc, (sc in next 18 sc, 2 sc in next sc) twice, sc in next 9 sc: 60 sc.

Rnd 17: (Sc in next 19 sc, 2 sc in next sc) around: 63 sc.

Rnd 18: Sc in next 10 sc, 2 sc in next sc, (sc in next 20 sc, 2 sc in next sc) twice, sc in next 10 sc: 66 sc.

Rnd 19: (Sc in next 21 sc, 2 sc in next sc) around: 69 sc.

Rnd 20: Sc in next 11 sc, 2 sc in next sc, (sc in next 22 sc, 2 sc in next sc) twice, sc in next 11 sc: 72 sc.

Rnds 21-23: Sc in each sc around.

Rnd 24: (Sc in next 10 sc, decrease) around: 66 sc.

Rnd 25: (Sc in next 9 sc, decrease) around: 60 sc.

Rnd 26: (Sc in next 8 sc, decrease) around: 54 sc.

Rnds 27-36: Sc in each sc around.

Rnd 37: (Sc in next 17 sc, 2 sc in next sc) around: 57 sc.

Rnds 38 and 39: Sc in each sc around.

Rnd 40: Sc in next 9 sc, 2 sc in next sc, (sc in next 18 sc, 2 sc in next sc) twice, sc in next 9 sc: 60 sc.

Rnds 41 and 42: Sc in each sc around.

Rnd 43: (Sc in next 19 sc, 2 sc in next sc) around: 63 sc.

Rnds 44-47: Sc in each sc around.

Rnd 48: (Sc in next 19, decrease) around: 60 sc.

Rnd 49: (Sc in next 8 sc, decrease) around: 54 sc.

Rnd 50: Sc in each sc around.

Rnd 51: (Sc in next 7 sc, decrease) around: 48 sc.

Rnd 52: Sc in each sc around.

Rnd 53: (Sc in next 6 sc, decrease) around: 42 sc.

Rnd 54: (Sc in next 5 sc, decrease) around: 36 sc.

Rnd 55: (Sc in next 4 sc, decrease) around: 30 sc.

Stuff **firmly** and shape Torso.

Rnd 56: (Sc in next 3 sc, decrease) around: 24 sc.

Rnd 57: (Sc in next 2 sc, decrease) around: 18 sc.

Rnd 58: (Sc in next sc, decrease) around: 12 sc.

Rnds 59-61: Sc in each sc around; at end of Rnd 61, slip st in next st, finish off leaving a long end for sewing.

Stuff remaining Torso **firmly**.

LEFT ARM

Rnd 1 (Right side)**:** With medium size hook, Color A and leaving a long end for sewing, ch 2, 6 sc in second ch from hook; do **not** join, place marker.

Rnd 2: 2 Sc in each sc around: 12 sc.

Rnd 3: (2 Sc in next sc, sc in next 2 sc) around: 16 sc.

Rnd 4: 2 Sc in next sc, sc in next 3 sc, (2 sc in next sc, sc in next 2 sc) around: 21 sc.

Rnds 5-31: Sc in each sc around.

Rnd 32: Sc in next 3 sc, decrease, (sc in next 2 sc, decrease) around: 16 sc.

Stuff and shape.

Rnd 33: (Sc in next 2 sc, decrease) around: 12 sts.

Rnd 34: (Sc next 3 sc, 2 sc in next sc) around: 15 sc.

Rnds 35-54: Sc in each sc around.

Rnd 55: (Sc in next sc, decrease) around: 10 sc.

Rnd 56: Sc in each sc around.

Stuff and shape.

Rnd 57: ★ 2 Sc in next sc, sc in next 2 sc, 2 sc in next sc, sc in next sc; repeat from ★ once **more**: 14 sc.

Rnds 58-62: Sc in each sc around.

Rnd 63: Sc in next sc, ch 2, (sc, hdc, sc) in back ridge of second ch from hook *(Fig. 2a, page 133)* (thumb), slip st in next sc, ★ ch 10, slip st in back ridge of ninth ch from hook, slip st in same st on Arm and in next sc; repeat from ★ 2 times **more**, ch 7, sc in back ridge of sixth ch from hook, slip st in same st on Arm and in each sc around; slip st in next sc, finish off leaving a long end for sewing.

Add additional stuffing, if necessary, and sew opening closed.

RIGHT ARM

Rnds 1-62: Work same as Left Arm.

Rnd 63: Sc in next sc, ch 7, sc in back ridge of sixth ch from hook, slip st in same st on Arm and in next sc, ★ ch 10, slip st in back ridge of ninth ch from hook, slip st in same st on Arm and in next sc; repeat from ★ 2 times **more**, ch 2, (sc, hdc, sc) in back ridge of second ch from hook (thumb), slip st in same st as Arm and in each sc around; slip st in next sc, finish off leaving a long end for sewing.

Add additional stuffing, if necessary, and sew opening closed.

BOOT AND LEG (Make 2)

Rnd 1 (Right side)**:** With medium size hook and Color B, ch 4, 3 dc in fourth ch from hook; join with slip st to top of beginning ch: 4 sts.

Note: Loop a short piece of yarn around any stitch to mark last round as **right** side.

Rnd 2: Ch 3, dc in same st, 2 dc in each of next 2 dc, loop a short piece of yarn around last dc made to mark beginning point for Rnd 3, 2 dc in last dc; join with slip st to top of beginning ch-3, ch 8 **loosely**, finish off.

Rnd 3: With **right** side facing, join Color B with slip st in marked dc; ch 1, sc in same st and in next 2 dc, sc in top of beginning ch-3 and in next 7 chs, 3 sc in last ch; working in free loops of ch, sc in next 7 chs, sc in next 3 dc, 2 sc in last dc; do **not** join, place marker: 26 sc.

Rnd 4: 2 Sc in next sc, sc in next 10 sc, 2 sc in each of next 3 sc, sc in next 10 sc, 2 sc in each of next 2 sc: 32 sc.

Rnd 5: Sc in next sc, 2 sc in next sc, sc in next 11 sc, 2 sc in next sc, (sc in next sc, 2 sc in next sc) twice, sc in next 11 sc, 2 sc in next sc, sc in next sc, 2 sc in next sc: 38 sc.

Rnd 6: Sc in next 16 sc, decrease twice, sc in each sc around: 36 sc.

Rnd 7: Sc in next 16 sc, decrease, sc in each sc around: 35 sc.

Rnd 8: Sc in next 12 sc, decrease 5 times, sc in next 13 sc: 30 sc.

Rnd 9: Sc in next 9 sc, decrease 6 times, sc in next 9 sc: 24 sc.

Rnd 10: Sc in next 2 sc, decrease, (sc in next 4 sc, decrease) 3 times, sc in next 2 sc: 20 sc.

Rnds 11-16: Sc in each sc around changing to Color D in last sc on Rnd 16 *(Fig. 22a, page 138)*.

Stuff Boot **firmly** and shape.

Note: Work remaining Leg in the following stripe sequence: 3 Rnds Color D, (3 rnds Color C, 3 rnds Color D) throughout.

Rnds 17 and 18: Sc in each sc around.

Rnd 19: (Sc in next sc, 2 sc in next sc) around: 30 sc.

Rnds 20-33: Sc in each sc around.

Rnd 34: (Sc in next 3 sc, decrease) around: 24 sc.

Rnd 35: Sc in each sc around.

Rnd 36: (Sc in next 2 sc, decrease) around: 18 sc.

Rnds 37-39: Sc in each sc around.

Stuff **firmly**.

Rnd 40: (Sc in next 2 sc, 2 sc in next sc) around: 24 sc.

Rnd 41: Sc in each sc around.

Rnd 42: (Sc in next 3 sc, 2 sc in next sc) around: 30 sc.

Rnds 43-68: Sc in each sc around.

Rnd 69: (Sc in next 3 sc, decrease) around: 24 sc.

Rnd 70: Sc in each sc around.

Rnd 71: (Sc in next sc, decrease) around: 16 sc.

Stuff **firmly**.

Rnd 72: Sc in each sc around.

Rnd 73: Decrease around; slip st in next sc, finish off leaving a long end for sewing: 8 sc.

Add additional stuffing, if necessary, and sew opening closed. Sew Arms to sides and Legs to bottom of Torso.

NOSE

Rnd 1: With medium size hook and Color A, ch 2, 3 sc in second ch from hook; do **not** join, place marker.

Rnd 2: 2 Sc in each sc around: 6 sc.

Rnds 3-12: Sc in each sc around.

Rnd 13: (Sc in next sc, 2 sc in next sc) around: 9 sc.

Rnd 14: (Sc in next 2 sc, 2 sc in next sc) around: 12 sc.

Rnds 15 and 16: Sc in each sc around; at end of Rnd 16, slip st in next sc, finish off leaving a long end for sewing.

Stuff **lightly** and shape.

DRESS

BLOUSE FRONT

With smallest size hook and Color B, ch 31 **loosely**.

Row 1 (Right side): Sc in second ch from hook and in each ch across: 30 sc.

Note: Mark last row as **right** side.

Rows 2-28: Ch 1, turn; sc in each sc across.

Finish off.

BLOUSE BACK

Work Same as Blouse Front.

Sew side seams from beginning ch to Row 14.

Sew shoulder seams, leaving a 3" neck opening.

NECK EDGING

Rnd 1: With **right** side facing and medium size hook, join Color B with slip st at shoulder seam; ch 1, work 30 sc evenly spaced around neck opening; join with slip st to first sc.

Rnd 2: Ch 1, 2 sc in same st, 3 sc in next sc, (2 sc in next sc, 3 sc in next sc) around; join with slip st to first sc, finish off: 75 sc.

SLEEVE

Rnd 1: With **right** side facing and largest size hook, join Color B with slip st at underarm seam; ch 1, work 30 sc evenly spaced around armhole; do **not** join, place marker.

Rnds 2-23: Sc in each sc around.

Rnd 24: Decrease around: 15 sc.

Rnd 25: (Decrease, sc in next sc) around: 10 sc.

Rnd 26: Sc in each sc around; slip st in next sc.

Rnd 27 (Edging): Ch 1, 2 sc in same st, 3 sc in next sc, (2 sc in next sc, 3 sc in next sc) around; join with slip st to first sc, finish off: 25 sc.

Repeat for second Sleeve.

SKIRT

Rnd 1: With **right** side of Blouse Front facing and smallest size hook, join Color B with slip st at side seam; ch 1, working in free loops of beginning ch, sc in same st and in each ch around; join with slip st to first sc: 60 sc.

Rnds 2 and 3: Ch 1, sc in each sc around; join with slip st to first sc.

Change to largest size hook.

Rnd 4: Ch 3 **(counts as first dc, now and throughout)**, dc in same st, 2 dc in each of next 8 sc, 3 dc in next sc, (2 dc in each of next 9 sc, 3 dc in next sc) around; join with slip st to first dc: 126 dc.

Rnds 5-20: Ch 3, dc in next dc and in each dc around; join with slip st to first dc.

Finish off.

PANTALOONS

With smallest size hook and Color B, ch 60 **loosely**; being careful not to twist ch, join with slip st to form a ring.

Rnd 1 (Right side): Ch 1, sc in same ch and in each ch around; join with slip st to first sc: 60 sc.

Note: Mark last round as **right** side.

Rnd 2: Ch 1, sc in each sc around; join with slip st to first sc. Change to largest size hook.

Rnd 3: Ch 1, sc in first 2 sc, decrease, (sc in next 2 sc, decrease) around; join with slip to first sc: 45 sc.

Rnd 4: Ch 3, dc in next sc and in each sc around; join with slip st to first dc.

Rnds 5-8: Ch 3, dc in next dc and in each dc around; join with slip st to first dc, do **not** finish off.

LEFT LEG

Note: Loop a short piece of yarn through the 35th stitch on Rnd 8 to mark inner leg.

Rnd 1: Ch 3, dc in next 10 dc; work dc through **both** thicknesses of next dc **and** in marked dc; dc in last 10 dc; join with slip st to first dc: 22 dc.

Rnds 2-15: Ch 3, dc in next dc and in each dc around; join with slip st to first dc.

Rnd 16 (Edging): Ch 1, 2 sc in same st, 3 sc in next dc, (2 sc in next dc, 3 sc in next dc) around; join with slip st to first sc, finish off: 55 sc.

RIGHT LEG

Rnd 1: With **right** side facing and largest size hook, skip 11 dc from Left Leg, join Color B with slip st in next dc; ch 3, dc in next 9 dc, work dc through **both** thicknesses of next dc **and** in first skipped st, dc in last 11 dc; join with slip st to first dc: 22 dc.

Rnds 2-16: Work same as Left Leg.

HAT
CROWN

Rnd 1 (Right side): With medium size hook and Color B, ch 2, 3 sc in second ch from hook; do **not** join, place marker.

Note: Mark last round as **right** side.

Rnd 2: 2 Sc in each sc around: 6 sc.

Rnds 3-5: Sc in each sc around.

Rnd 6: (Sc in next sc, 2 sc in next sc) around: 9 sc.

Rnds 7 and 8: Sc in each sc around.

Rnd 9: (Sc in next 2 sc, 2 sc in next sc) around: 12 sc.

Rnds 10 and 11: Sc in each sc around.

Rnd 12: (Sc in next 2 sc, 2 sc in next sc) around: 16 sc.

Rnds 13 and 14: Sc in each sc around.

Rnd 15: (Sc in next 3 sc, 2 sc in next sc) around: 20 sc.

Rnd 16 and ALL EVEN NUMBERED RNDS THROUGH Rnd 24: Sc in each sc around.

Rnd 17: (Sc in next 4 sc, 2 sc in next sc) around: 24 sc.

Rnd 19: (Sc in next 5 sc, 2 sc in next sc) around: 28 sc.

Rnd 21: (Sc in next 6 sc, 2 sc in next sc) around: 32 sc.

Rnd 23: (Sc in next 7 sc, 2 sc in next sc) around: 36 sc.

Rnd 25: (Sc in next 5 sc, 2 sc in next sc) around: 42 sc.

Rnd 26: Sc in each sc around; slip st in Front Loop Only of next sc *(Fig. 20, page 138)*, do **not** finish off.

BRIM

Rnd 1: Ch 1, working in Front Loops Only, 2 sc in same st and in next sc, (sc in next sc, 2 sc in next sc) around; join with slip st to **both** loops of first sc: 64 sc.

Rnd 2: Ch 1, working in both loops, sc in same st and in next 2 sc, 2 sc in next sc, (sc in next 3 sc, 2 sc in next sc) around; join with slip st to first sc: 80 sc.

Rnd 3: Ch 1, sc in each sc around; join with slip st to first sc.

Rnd 4: Ch 1, sc in same st and in next 14 sc, 2 sc in next sc, (sc in next 15 sc, 2 sc in next sc) around; join with slip st to first sc: 85 sc.

Rnd 5: Ch 3, dc in next sc and in each sc around; join with slip st to first dc.

Rnd 6: Ch 4, tr in next dc and in each dc around; join with slip st to top of beginning ch-4, finish off.

HAIR

Add fringe in free loops on Rnd 26 of Hat *(Figs. 28a & b, page 141, and Fig. 21a, page 138)*, using five 23" strands of Color C for each fringe.

FINISHING

Put Pantaloons on Doll and stitch to Torso at waistline.

Weave a 10" piece of Color B through each Leg of Pantaloons above Edging rnd; gather and secure.

Sew buttons to front of Blouse and put Dress on Doll.

Weave ribbon through each Sleeve above Edging rnd; gather and tie in a bow.

Using photo as a guide for placement, sew Nose to face, add buttons for eyes, embroider mouth using Backstitch *(Fig. 30, page 142)*, and sew buttons to Boots.

Sew Hat to Head and add flower and ribbon as desired.

Trim Hair.

Sew Head to Torso.

Add ribbon around tops of Boots as desired.

THANKSGIVING

*W*hen friends and family gather around the table for Thanksgiving dinner, accent the occasion with this lovely linen table runner. The lacy edging is crocheted using cotton thread and features a pretty pattern of pineapples — traditional symbols of hospitality.

LOVELY TABLE RUNNER

Finished Size: Runner - approximately 14" x 56"
Edging - approximately 14" x 2½"

MATERIALS
Crochet Cotton Thread (size 20), approximately
110 yards

Steel crochet hook, size 9 (1.40 mm) **or** size needed
for gauge
Linen - 15" x 52"
Sewing needle and thread

GAUGE: 10 dc = 1"

PATTERN STITCHES

BEGINNING SHELL

Ch 3, (2 dc, ch 3, 3 dc) in same sp.

SHELL

(3 Dc, ch 3, 3 dc) in sp indicated.

EDGING (Make 2)

Ch 147 **loosely**.

Row 1 (Right side)**:** Sc in back ridge of second ch from hook and in each ch across *(Fig. 2a, page 133)*: 146 sc.

Note: Loop a short piece of thread around any stitch to mark last row as **right** side.

Row 2: Ch 1, turn; sc in first sc, ★ ch 6, skip next 4 sc, sc in next sc; repeat from ★ across: 29 loops.

Row 3: Turn; slip st in first loop, work beginning Shell, ★ ch 1, sc in next loop, ch 1, work Shell in next loop; repeat from ★ across: 15 Shells.

Row 4: Turn; slip st in first 3 dc and in next ch-3 sp, work beginning Shell, ch 2, 7 dc in next Shell (ch-3 sp), ch 2, ★ work Shell in each of next 2 Shells, ch 2, 7 dc in next Shell, ch 2; repeat from ★ across to last Shell, work Shell in last Shell: 10 Shells.

Row 5: Turn; slip st in first 3 dc and in next ch-3 sp, work beginning Shell, ch 2, skip next ch-2 sp, dc in next dc, (ch 1, dc in next dc) 6 times, ch 2, ★ work Shell in each of next 2 Shells, ch 2, skip next ch-2 sp, dc in next dc, (ch 1, dc in next dc) 6 times, ch 2; repeat from ★ across to last Shell, work Shell in last Shell.

Row 6: Turn; slip st in first 3 dc and in next ch-3 sp, work beginning Shell, ch 2, skip next ch-2 sp, sc in next ch-1 sp, (ch 4, sc in next ch-1 sp) 5 times, ch 2, ★ work Shell in each of next 2 Shells, ch 2, skip next ch-2 sp, sc in next ch-1 sp, (ch 4, sc in next ch-1 sp) 5 times, ch 2; repeat from ★ across to last Shell, work Shell in last Shell.

Row 7: Turn; slip st in first 3 dc and in next ch-3 sp, work beginning Shell, ch 2, skip next ch-2 sp, sc in next ch-4 sp, (ch 4, sc in next ch-4 sp) 4 times, ch 2, ★ work Shell in each of next 2 Shells, ch 2, skip next ch-2 sp, sc in next ch-4 sp, (ch 4, sc in next ch-4 sp) 4 times, ch 2; repeat from ★ across to last Shell, work Shell in last Shell.

Row 8: Turn; slip st in first 3 dc and in next ch-3 sp, work beginning Shell, ch 2, skip next ch-2 sp, sc in next ch-4 sp, (ch 4, sc in next ch-4 sp) 3 times, ch 2, ★ work Shell in each of next 2 Shells, ch 2, skip next ch-2 sp, sc in next ch-4 sp, (ch 4, sc in next ch-4 sp) 3 times, ch 2; repeat from ★ across to last Shell, work Shell in last Shell; do **not** finish off.

FIRST PINEAPPLE

Row 1: Turn; slip st in first 3 dc and in next ch-3 sp, work beginning Shell, ch 2, skip next ch-2 sp, sc in next ch-4 sp, (ch 4, sc in next ch-4 sp) twice, ch 2, work Shell in next Shell, leave remaining sts unworked: 2 Shells.

Row 2: Turn; slip st in first 3 dc and in next ch-3 sp, work beginning Shell, ch 2, skip next ch-2 sp, sc in next ch-4 sp, ch 4, sc in next ch-4 sp, ch 2, work Shell in last Shell.

Row 3: Turn; slip st in first 3 dc and in next ch-3 sp, work beginning Shell, ch 2, skip next ch-2 sp, sc in next ch-4 sp, ch 2, work Shell in last Shell.

Row 4: Turn; slip st in first 3 dc and in next ch-3 sp, slip st in next Shell; finish off.

REMAINING 4 PINEAPPLES

Row 1: With **right** side facing, join thread with slip st in next Shell on Row 8 to left of last completed Pineapple, work beginning Shell, ch 2, skip next ch-2 sp, sc in next ch-4 sp, (ch 4, sc in next ch-4 sp) twice, ch 2, work Shell in next Shell, leave remaining sts unworked: 2 Shells.

Rows 2-4: Work same as First Pineapple.

FINISHING

Press long edges of Linen ¼" to wrong side; press ¼" to wrong side again. Using thread to match Linen, machine stitch across each long edge ³/₁₆" from outer pressed edge.

Repeat on short edges of Linen.

Pin Edging along hem on **right** side of short edge. Hand sew to secure.

Repeat on opposite end.

CHRISTMAS

At Christmastime, festive decorations magically transform our surroundings into a winter wonderland. You can create a flurry of three-dimensional snowflakes for your tree, or choose from the delightful accents and trims shown on the following pages.

SNOW CRYSTAL

Finished Size: Approximately 8" in diameter

MATERIALS

Bedspread Weight Cotton Thread (size 10), approximately 55 yards
Steel crochet hook, size 7 (1.65 mm) **or** size needed for gauge
Glue gun
Translucent nylon thread
Starching materials: Commercial fabric stiffener, 2 pieces 5" x 14" heavy cardboard, transparent tape, plastic wrap, resealable plastic bag, terry towel, paper towels, and stainless steel pins

GAUGE: Rnds 1 and 2 = 1¹/₂"

(Make 2)

Ch 6; join with slip st to form a ring.

Rnd 1: Ch 4 **(counts as first tr, now and throughout)**, tr in ring, ch 5, (2 tr in ring, ch 5) 5 times; join with slip st to first tr: 6 loops.

Rnd 2: Slip st in next tr and in next loop, ch 4, (3 tr, ch 7, 4 tr) in same loop, (4 tr, ch 7, 4 tr) in next loop and in each loop around; join with slip st to first tr.

Rnd 3: Slip st in next 3 tr and in next 3 chs, ch 1, (sc, ch 15, sc) in same loop, ch 5, skip next 4 tr, sc in sp **before** next tr, ch 5, ★ (sc, ch 15, sc) in next loop, ch 5, skip next 4 tr, sc in sp **before** next tr, ch 5; repeat from ★ around; join with slip st to first sc: 18 loops.

Rnd 4: Slip st in first loop, ch 1, (3 sc, ch 3, 3 hdc, 3 dc, 3 tr) in same loop, ★ † (ch 7, slip st in fourth ch from hook) 5 times, (ch 4, slip st in fourth ch from hook) 4 times, slip st in next 3 chs of last ch-7 worked, ch 4, slip st in fourth ch from hook, (ch 7, slip st in fourth ch from hook) 3 times, ch 3, (3 tr, 3 dc, 3 hdc, ch 3, 3 sc) in same loop, (3 sc, ch 4, slip st in fourth ch from hook, 3 sc) in next loop, ch 7, slip st in fourth ch from hook, (ch 4, slip st in fourth ch from hook) 4 times, slip st in next 3 chs of last ch-7 worked, (3 sc, ch 4, slip st in fourth ch from hook, 3 sc) in next loop †, (3 sc, ch 3, 3 hdc, 3 dc, 3 tr) in next loop; repeat from ★ 4 times **more**, then repeat from † to † once; join with slip st to first sc, finish off.

FINISHING

See Starching and Blocking, page 142.
Using nylon thread, add hanger.

Worked with bright thread, a Christmas tree motif is trimmed with gold beads to lend holiday style to towels.

FESTIVE TOWEL TRIM

Finished Size: Approximately 3" tall

MATERIALS

Bedspread Weight Cotton Thread (size 10), approximately:
  Green - 10 yards **each**
  Tan - 1 yard **each**
  Gold - 1 yard **each**
Steel crochet hook, size 8 (1.50 mm) **or** size needed
  for gauge
Fingertip hand towel
4 mm Beads - 14 **each**
Sewing needle and thread

GAUGE: 20 dc and 10 rows = 2"

TREE

Row 1: With Green, ch 4, 3 dc in fourth ch from hook: 4 sts.
Row 2 (Right side)**:** Ch 3 **(counts as first dc, now and throughout),** turn; dc in same st and in next 2 dc, 2 dc in last st: 6 dc.
Note: Loop a short piece of thread around any stitch to mark last row as **right** side.
Rows 3-9: Ch 3, turn; dc in same st and in each dc across to last dc, 2 dc in last dc: 20 dc.
Row 10: Ch 3, turn; dc in next dc and in each dc across.

Edging: Ch 3, do **not** turn; working in end of rows, (dc, hdc) in first row, 2 sc in next row, [ch 3, (dc, hdc) in next row, 2 sc in next row] across; 3 sc in free loop of beginning ch *(Fig. 21b, page 138)*; working in end of rows, 2 sc in first row, (hdc, dc) in next row, ch 3, ★ 2 sc in next row, (hdc, dc) in next row, ch 3; repeat from ★ across; working across sts on last row, sc in first 9 dc, place marker around last sc worked for Trunk joining, sc in each dc across, slip st in next ch; finish off.

TRUNK

Row 1: With **right** side of Tree facing, join Tan with slip st in marked sc on Edging; ch 1, sc in same st and in next 3 sc, leave remaining sts unworked: 4 sc.
Rows 2-4: Ch 1, turn; sc in each sc across.
Finish off.

STAR

With Gold, ch 2, sc in second ch from hook, ch 3, (sc in same ch, ch 3) 5 times; join with slip st to first sc, finish off leaving a long end for sewing.

FINISHING

Using photo as a guide for placement, sew beads and Star to Tree.
Sew Tree to towel.

A jolly snowman fashioned with fabric strips lets you bring some wintertime fun indoors!

JOLLY SNOWMAN

Finished Size: Approximately 23" tall

MATERIALS
   100% Cotton Fabric, 44/45" wide, approximately:
      White - 5½ yards
      Black - 2 yards
      Red - 1 yard
   Crochet hook, size N (9.00 mm) **or** size needed for gauge
   Polyester stuffing
   ⁷/₁₆" Buttons (eyes) - 2

3" x 5" Orange felt (nose)
1" Buttons (body) - 2
Sticks (arms)
Trim for hat
Glue gun

Prepare fabric and tear into 1½" strips *(see Preparing Fabric Strips and Joining Fabric Strips, page 139)*.

GAUGE: 7 sc and 7 rows = 4"

PATTERN STITCHES
SC DECREASE
Pull up a loop in next 2 sts, YO and draw through all 3 loops on hook (counts as one sc).

DC DECREASE (uses next 2 sts)
★ YO, insert hook in **next** st, YO and pull up a loop, YO and draw through 2 loops on hook; repeat from ★ once **more**, YO and draw through all 3 loops on hook **(counts as one dc)**.

SNOWMAN
HEAD
Rnd 1 (Right side): With White, ch 2, 6 sc in second ch from hook; do **not** join, place fabric marker **(see Markers, page 138)**.

Rnds 2 and 3: 2 Sc in each sc around: 24 sc.

Rnd 4: Sc in each sc around.

Rnd 5: (2 Sc in next sc, sc in next 3 sc) around: 30 sc.

Rnd 6: Sc in each sc around.

Rnd 7: (2 Sc in next sc, sc in next 4 sc) around: 36 sc.

Rnds 8-10: Sc in each sc around.

Rnd 11: (Sc decrease, sc in next 4 sc) around: 30 sc.

Rnd 12: Sc in each sc around.

Rnd 13: (Sc decrease, sc in next 3 sc) around: 24 sc.

Rnd 14: (Sc decrease, sc in next 2 sc) around: 18 sc.

Rnd 15: Sc in each sc around; slip st in next sc, do **not** finish off.

UPPER BODY
Rnd 1: Ch 3 **(counts as first dc, now and throughout)**, dc in same st and in next sc, (2 dc in next sc, dc in next sc) around; join with slip st to first dc: 27 dc.

Rnd 2: Ch 3, dc in same st and in next 2 dc, (2 dc in next dc, dc in next 2 dc) around; join with slip st to first dc: 36 dc.

Rnds 3-5: Ch 3, dc in next dc and in each dc around; join with slip st to first dc.

Rnd 6: Ch 1, sc in first 4 dc, sc decrease, (sc in next 4 dc, sc decrease) around; join with slip st to first sc, do **not** finish off: 30 sc.

LOWER BODY
Rnd 1: Ch 3, dc in same st and in next 2 sc, (2 dc in next sc, dc in next 2 sc) around; join with slip st to first dc: 40 dc.

Rnd 2: Ch 3, dc in same st and in next 7 dc, (2 dc in next dc, dc in next 7 dc) around; join with slip st to first dc: 45 dc.

Rnds 3-5: Ch 3, dc in next dc and in each dc around; join with slip st to first dc.

Rnd 6: Ch 1, sc in first 7 dc, sc decrease, (sc in next 7 dc, sc decrease) around; join with slip st to first sc: 40 sc.

Rnd 7: Ch 1, sc in each sc around; join with slip st to Back Loop Only of first sc **(Fig. 20, page 138)**.

Rnd 8: Ch 1, sc in Back Loop Only of each sc around; join with slip st to both loops of first sc.

Stuff Head and Body **firmly**.

Rnd 9: Ch 3, working in both loops, dc in next sc, dc decrease, (dc in next 2 sc, dc decrease) around; join with slip st to first dc: 30 dc.

Rnd 10: Ch 3, dc decrease, (dc in next dc, dc decrease) around; join with slip st to first dc: 20 dc.

Rnd 11: Ch 1, sc in first 2 dc, (sc decrease, sc in next dc) around; join with slip st to first sc: 14 sc.

Rnd 12: Sc decrease around; join with slip st to first sc, finish off leaving a long end for sewing: 7 sc.

Add additional stuffing, if necessary.

Weave end through remaining sts; gather tightly and secure.

HAT
CROWN
Rnd 1 (Right side): With Black, ch 2, 6 sc in second ch from hook; do **not** join, place marker.

Rnds 2 and 3: 2 Sc in each sc around: 24 sc.

Rnd 4: (2 Sc in next sc, sc in next 3 sc) around; do **not** finish off: 30 sc.

SIDE
Rnd 1: Slip st in next sc, sc in Back Loop Only of same sc and in each sc around.

Rnds 2-8: Sc in both loops of each sc around; do **not** finish off.

BRIM
Rnd 1: Working in Front Loops Only, slip st in next sc, ch 1, 2 sc in same st, sc in next 2 sc, (2 sc in next sc, sc in next 2 sc) around; join with slip st to both loops of first sc: 40 sc.

Rnd 2: Ch 1, working in both loops, 2 sc in same st, sc in next 7 sc, (2 sc in next sc, sc in next 7 sc) around; join with slip st to first sc, finish off: 45 sc.

SCARF
With Red, ch 61 **loosely**.

Row 1 (Right side): Sc in second ch from hook and in each ch across: 60 sc.

Rows 2 and 3: Ch 1, turn; sc in Front Loop Only of each sc across.
Finish off.

FINISHING
Form cone shape with felt and glue sides together.

Using photo as a guide for placement, glue eyes and nose to face and glue buttons to Body.

Attach stick arms.

Add trim to Hat as desired.

Place Hat on Head.

Wrap Scarf around neck, overlapping ends to secure.

Our elegant beaded garland and lacy bell ornaments will add a frosty shimmer to your Christmas tree.

FROSTY BEADED GARLAND

MATERIALS
Bedspread Weight Cotton Thread (size 10),
   approximately 140 yards
Steel crochet hook, size 7 (1.65 mm)
Beaded garland - 3 yard length

Note #1: Gauge is not important. Ruffle can be smaller or
   larger without changing the overall effect.
Note #2: When working in space between beads, work around
   string.

Row 1: Join thread with slip st in sp between first and second beads; ch 1, sc in same sp, (ch 5, sc in sp between next 2 beads) across (must have an uneven number of ch-5 loops).
Row 2: Turn; (slip st, ch 1, sc) in first loop, ★ dc in next loop, (ch 2, dc) 4 times in same loop, sc in next loop; repeat from ★ across.
Row 3: Ch 1, turn; sc in first sc and in next ch-2 sp, (ch 3, sc in next ch-2 sp) across, sc in last sc.
Edging: Slip st in end of Row 1 and between first and second beads, ch 1, turn to work across opposite side of beads, sc in same sp, (ch 3, sc in sp between next 2 beads) across; finish off.

129

SILVER BELLS

Finished Size: Approximately 2¼"

MATERIALS

Bedspread Weight Cotton Thread (size 10), approximately:
    Bell #1- 15 yards **each**
    Bell #2 - 18 yards **each**
    Bell #3 - 20 yards **each**
Steel crochet hook, size 7 (1.65 mm) **or** size needed
    for gauge
Translucent nylon thread
Starching materials: Commercial fabric stiffener,
    blocking board, plastic wrap, resealable plastic bag,
    terry towel, paper towels, and stainless steel pins

GAUGE: 16 dc = 2"

BELL #1

Ch 3; join with slip st to form a ring.

Rnd 1 (Right side)**:** Ch 1, 6 sc in ring; join with slip st to first sc.

Rnd 2: Ch 3 **(counts as first dc, now and throughout)**, 2 dc in same st, ch 1, dc in next sc, ch 1, (3 dc in next sc, ch 1, dc in next sc, ch 1) twice; join with slip st to first dc: 12 dc.

Rnd 3: Ch 3, dc in next 2 dc and in next ch-1 sp, ch 3, dc in next ch-1 sp, (dc in next 3 dc and in next ch-1 sp, ch 3, dc in next ch-1 sp) twice; join with slip st to first dc: 15 dc.

Rnd 4: Ch 1, sc in same st, ch 5, skip next dc, sc in next dc, ch 5, sc in next ch-3 sp, ★ ch 5, (skip next dc, sc in next dc, ch 5) twice, sc in next ch-3 sp; repeat from ★ once **more**, ch 2, dc in first sc to form last loop: 9 loops.

Rnd 5: Ch 1, sc in same loop, (ch 5, sc in next loop) around, ch 2, dc in first sc to form last loop: 9 loops.

Rnd 6: Ch 4, tr in same sp, ch 2, (2 tr in next loop, ch 2) around; join with slip st to top of beginning ch-4.

Rnd 7: Ch 3, dc in next tr, 3 dc in next ch-2 sp, (dc in next 2 tr, 3 dc in next ch-2 sp) around; join with slip st to first dc: 45 dc.

Rnd 8: Ch 4, tr in same st, 2 tr in next dc, ch 2, skip next 3 dc, (2 tr in each of next 2 dc, ch 2, skip next 3 dc) around; join with slip st to top of beginning ch-4.

Rnd 9: Ch 1, sc in same st, (ch 3, sc in next tr) 3 times, 2 sc in next ch-2 sp, ★ sc in next tr, (ch 3, sc in next tr) 3 times, 2 sc in next ch-2 sp; repeat from ★ around; join with slip st to first sc, finish off.

BELL #2

Ch 3; join with slip st to form a ring.

Rnd 1: Ch 3, 2 dc in ring, ch 5, (3 dc in ring, ch 5) twice; join with slip st to top of beginning ch-3: 3 loops.

Rnd 2: (Ch 3, slip st in next dc) twice, 5 sc in next loop, ★ slip st in next dc, (ch 3, slip st in next dc) twice, 5 sc in next loop; repeat from ★ once **more**; join with slip st in same st as joining: 15 sc.

Rnd 3: ★ (Slip st, ch 2, 2 dc) in next ch-3 sp, ch 3, (2 dc, ch 2, slip st) in next ch-3 sp, sc in next 5 sc; repeat from ★ around; join with slip st to first slip st: 3 ch-3 sps.

Rnd 4: Slip st in first 2 chs, slip st in next 2 dc and in next ch-3 sp, ch 1, 3 sc in same sp, ch 3, skip next 2 sc, 3 tr in next sc, ch 3, ★ 3 sc in next ch-3 sp, ch 3, skip next 2 sc, 3 tr in next sc, ch 3; repeat from ★ once **more**; join with slip st to first sc: 6 ch-3 sps.

Rnd 5: Ch 1, sc in same st, ch 3, skip next sc, sc in next sc, 3 sc in next ch-3 sp, sc in next 3 tr, 3 sc in next ch-3 sp, ★ sc in next sc, ch 3, skip next sc, sc in next sc, 3 sc in next ch-3 sp, sc in next 3 tr, 3 sc in next ch-3 sp; repeat from ★ once **more**; join with slip st to first sc: 33 sc.

Rnd 6: (Slip st, ch 2, 2 dc, ch 3, 2 dc, ch 2, slip st) in first ch-3 sp, ch 3, skip next 4 sc, 2 dc in next sc, ch 1, dc in next sc, ch 1, 2 dc in next sc, ★ ch 3, skip next 4 sc, (slip st, ch 2, 2 dc, ch 3, 2 dc, ch 2, slip st) in next ch-3 sp, ch 3, skip next 4 sc, 2 dc in next sc, ch 1, dc in next sc, ch 1, 2 dc in next sc; repeat from ★ once **more**, ch 2, sc in first slip st to form last sp.

Rnd 7: Ch 1, sc in same sp, ch 3, 3 sc in next ch-3 sp, ch 3, sc in next ch-3 sp, 3 dc in each of next 2 ch-1 sps, ★ sc in next ch-3 sp, ch 3, 3 sc in next ch-3 sp, ch 3, sc in next ch-3 sp, 3 dc in each of next 2 ch-1 sps; repeat from ★ once **more**; join with slip st to first sc.

Rnd 8: Ch 1, sc in same st, sc in next ch-3 sp and in next sc, ch 5, skip next sc, sc in next sc and in next ch-3 sp, sc in next 4 sts, ch 5, ★ sc in next 4 sts, sc in next ch-3 sp and in next sc, ch 5, skip next sc, sc in next sc and in next ch-3 sp, sc in next 4 sts, ch 5; repeat from ★ once **more**, sc in last 3 dc; join with slip st to first sc: 6 loops.

Rnd 9: Slip st in next 2 sc and in first loop, ch 3, 6 dc in same loop, ch 1, (7 dc in next loop, ch 1) around; join with slip st to top of beginning ch-3.

Rnd 10: Ch 4, (dc in next dc, ch 1) 6 times, sc in next ch-1 sp, ch 1, ★ (dc in next dc, ch 1) 7 times, sc in next ch-1 sp, ch 1; repeat from ★ around; join with slip st to third ch of beginning ch-4: 48 ch-1 sps.

Rnd 11: ★ (Ch 1, slip st in next ch-1 sp) 7 times, slip st in next sc and in next ch-1 sp; repeat from ★ around, ch 1; join with slip st in same st as joining, finish off.

BELL #3

Ch 3; join with slip st to form a ring.

Rnd 1: Ch 3, 11 dc in ring; join with slip st to top of beginning ch-3: 12 sts.

Rnd 2: Ch 5, skip next dc, (slip st in next dc, ch 5, skip next dc) around; join with slip st in same st as joining: 6 loops.

Rnd 3: Slip st in first loop, ch 3, 4 dc in same loop, 5 dc in next loop and in each loop around; join with slip st to top of beginning ch-3: 30 sts.

Rnd 4: Ch 1, sc in same st, ch 3, skip next dc, sc in next dc, ch 3, ★ skip next dc, sc in next 2 dc, ch 3, skip next dc, sc in next dc, ch 3; repeat from ★ around to last 2 dc, skip next dc, sc in last dc; join with slip st to first sc: 12 ch-3 sps.

Rnd 5: Slip st in first ch-3 sp, ch 1, 3 sc in same sp and in next ch-3 sp, (ch 3, 3 sc in each of next 2 ch-3 sps) around, dc in first sc to form last sp: 36 sc.

Rnd 6: Ch 3, 5 dc in same sp, ch 1, (6 dc in next ch-3 sp, ch 1) around; join with slip st to top of beginning ch-3: 6 dc groups.

Rnd 7: Slip st in next dc, ch 4, dc in next dc, (ch 1, dc in next dc) twice, ch 3, sc in next ch-1 sp, ch 3, ★ skip next dc, dc in next dc, (ch 1, dc in next dc) 3 times, ch 3, sc in next ch-1 sp, ch 3; repeat from ★ around; join with slip st to third ch of beginning ch-4.

Rnd 8: Ch 1, slip st in first ch-1 sp, ch 1, (slip st, ch 3, slip st) in next ch-1 sp, (ch 1, slip st in next sp) twice, ★ ch 8, slip st in next ch-3 sp, ch 1, slip st in next ch-1 sp, ch 1, (slip st, ch 3, slip st) in next ch-1 sp, (ch 1, slip st in next sp) twice; repeat from ★ around, ch 4, tr in last ch-3 sp to form last loop: 6 loops.

Rnd 9: Ch 1, 2 sc in same loop, ch 5, (3 sc in next loop, ch 5) around, sc in same loop as first sc; join with slip st to first sc.

Rnd 10: Ch 1, sc in same st and in next sc, 6 sc in next loop, (sc in next 3 sc, 6 sc in next loop) around to last sc, sc in last sc; join with slip st to first sc: 54 sc.

Rnd 11: Ch 5, (tr in next sc, ch 1) around; join with slip st to fourth ch of beginning ch-5: 54 ch-1 sps.

Rnd 12: Slip st in first ch-1 sp, ch 1, sc in same sp and in next 3 ch-1 sps, (slip st, ch 4, slip st) in next ch-1 sp, ★ sc in next 8 ch-1 sps, (slip st, ch 4, slip st) in next ch-1 sp; repeat from ★ around to last 4 ch-1 sps, sc in last 4 ch-1 sps; join with slip st to first sc, finish off.

FINISHING

See Starching and Blocking, page 142.
Using nylon thread, add hanger.

general instructions

ABBREVIATIONS

BLO	Back Loop(s) Only
BPdc	Back Post double crochet(s)
CC	Contrasting Color
ch(s)	chain(s)
dc	double crochet(s)
dtr	double treble crochet(s)
FPdc	Front Post double crochet(s)
hdc	half double crochet(s)
MC	Main Color
mm	millimeters
Rnd(s)	Rounds(s)
sc	single crochet
sp(s)	space(s)
st(s)	stitch(es)
tr	treble crochet
YO	yarn over

★ — work instructions following ★ as many **more** times as indicated in addition to the first time.

† to † — work all instructions from first † to second † **as many** times as specified.

( ) or [ ] — work enclosed instructions **as many** times as specified by the number immediately following **or** work all enclosed instructions in the stitch or space indicated **or** contains explanatory remarks.

work even — work without increasing or decreasing in the established pattern.

GAUGE

Correct gauge is essential for proper size or fit. Hook sizes given in instructions are merely guides and should never be used without first making a sample swatch as indicated. Then measure it, counting your stitches and rows or rounds carefully. If your swatch is smaller than specified, try again with a larger size hook; if larger, try again with a smaller size. Keep trying until you find the size that will give you the specified gauge. DO NOT HESITATE TO CHANGE HOOK SIZE TO OBTAIN CORRECT GAUGE. On garments, once proper gauge is obtained, measure width of piece approximately every 3" to be sure gauge remains consistent.

basic stitch guide

CHAIN

When beginning a first row of crochet in a chain, always skip the first chain from the hook, and work into the second chain from hook (for single crochet) or third chain from hook (for half double crochet), etc. *(Fig. 1)*.

Fig. 1

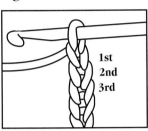

1st
2nd
3rd

WORKING INTO THE CHAIN

Method 1: Insert hook into back ridge of each chain indicated *(Fig. 2a)*.
Method 2: Insert hook under top two strands of each chain *(Fig. 2b)*.

Fig. 2a   Fig. 2b

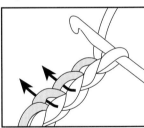
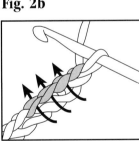

MAKING A BEGINNING RING

Chain amount indicated in instructions. Being careful not to twist chain, slip stitch in first chain to form a ring *(Fig. 3)*.

Fig. 3

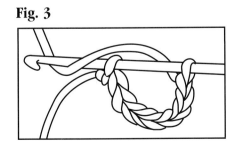

SINGLE CROCHET *(abbreviated sc)*

Insert hook in stitch or space indicated, YO and pull up a loop, YO and draw through both loops on hook *(Fig. 4)*.

Fig. 4

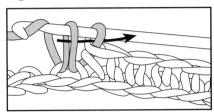

LONG SINGLE CROCHET
(abbreviated Long sc)

Insert hook in sc indicated *(Fig. 5a)*, YO and pull up a loop even with loop on hook, YO and draw through both loops on hook *(Fig. 5b)*(**counts as one sc**).

Fig. 5a   Fig. 5b

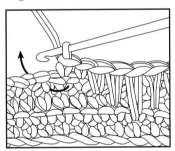
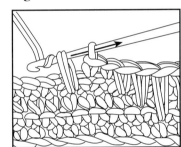

HALF DOUBLE CROCHET
(abbreviated hdc)

YO, insert hook in stitch or space indicated, YO and pull up a loop, YO and draw through all 3 loops on hook *(Fig. 6)*.

Fig. 6

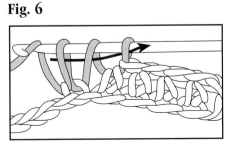

DOUBLE CROCHET *(abbreviated dc)*

YO, insert hook in stitch or space indicated, YO and pull up a loop, YO and draw through 2 loops on hook *(Fig. 7a)*, YO and draw through remaining 2 loops on hook *(Fig. 7b)*.

Fig. 7a   **Fig. 7b**

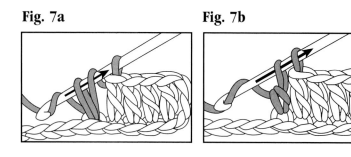

TREBLE CROCHET *(abbreviated tr)*

YO twice, insert hook in stitch or space indicated, YO and pull up a loop *(Fig. 8a)*, (YO and draw through 2 loops on hook) 3 times *(Fig. 8b)*.

Fig. 8a   **Fig. 8b**

DOUBLE TREBLE CROCHET
(abbreviated dtr)

YO three times, insert hook in stitch or space indicated, YO and pull up a loop *(Fig. 9a)*, (YO and draw through 2 loops on hook) 4 times *(Fig. 9b)*.

Fig. 9a   **Fig. 9b**

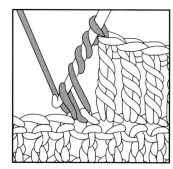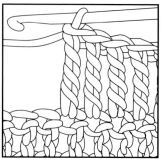

CLUSTER

A Cluster can be worked all in the same stitch or space *(Figs. 10a & b)*, **or** across several stitches *(Figs. 11a &b)*.

Fig. 10a   **Fig. 10b**

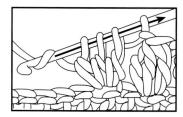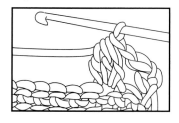

Fig. 11a   **Fig. 11b**

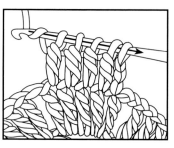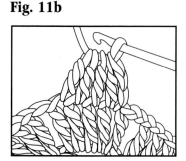

PUFF STITCH

★ YO, insert hook in st or sp indicated, YO and pull up a loop even with loop on hook; repeat from ★ 3 times **more** (9 loops on hook) *(Fig. 12)*; complete as instructed.

Fig. 12

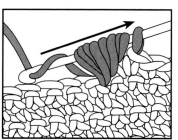

POST STITCH

Work around post of stitch indicated, inserting hook in direction of arrow *(Fig. 13)*.

Fig. 13

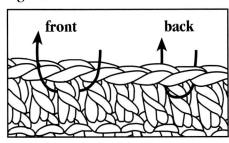

REVERSE SINGLE CROCHET
(abbreviated Reverse sc)

Working from **left** to **right**, insert hook in stitch to right of hook *(Fig. 14a)*, YO and draw through, under and to left of loop on hook (2 loops on hook) *(Fig. 14b)*, YO and draw through both loops on hook *(Fig. 14c)* **(Reverse sc made, Fig. 14d)**.

Fig. 14a

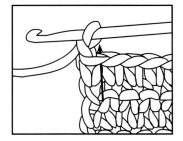

Fig. 14b

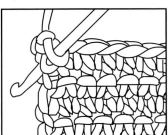

Fig. 14c

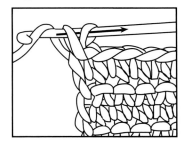

Fig. 14d

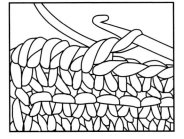

REVERSE HALF DOUBLE CROCHET
(abbreviated Reverse hdc)

Working from **left** to **right**, YO, insert hook in stitch indicated to right of hook *(Fig. 15a)*, YO and draw through, under and to left of loops on hook (3 loops on hook) *(Fig. 15b)*, YO and draw through all 3 loops on hook *(Fig. 15c)* **(Reverse hdc made, Fig. 15d)**.

Fig. 15a

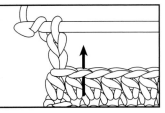

Fig. 15b

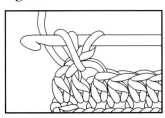

Fig. 15c

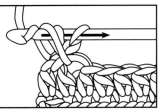

Fig. 15d

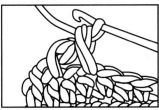

SLANT ST

YO, working **around** last 3-dc group, insert hook in same st as first dc of 3-dc group, YO and pull up a loop even with loop on hook *(Fig. 16)*, (YO and draw through 2 loops on hook) twice.

Fig. 16

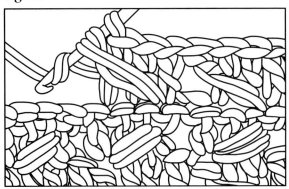

LOOP STITCH

Insert hook in next st, wrap yarn around index finger of left hand once **more**, insert hook through both loops on finger following direction indicated by arrow *(Fig. 17a)*, being careful to hook all loops *(Fig. 17b)*, draw through st pulling each loop to measure approximately 2", remove finger from loop, YO and draw through all 3 loops on hook **(Loop St made, *Fig. 17c*)**.

Fig. 17a

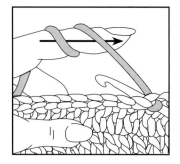

Fig. 17b

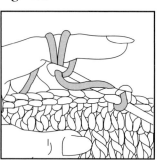

Fig. 17c

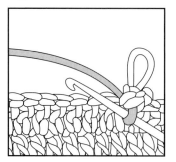

BLOCKS

Join second Block to first Block with slip st around beginning ch of previous Block *(Fig. 18a)*, ch 3, 3 dc in same sp *(Fig. 18b)*.

Fig. 18a   **Fig. 18b**

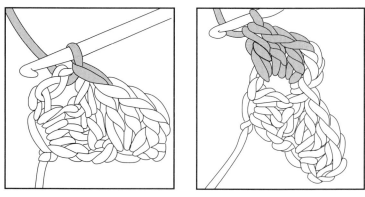

Symbol crochet chart illustrates Rows 1-5 of Dishcloth.

SYMBOL CROCHET KEY

∘ chain
● slip st
† double crochet

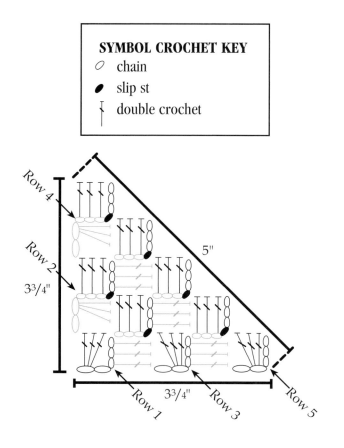

YARN

Yarn weight (type or size) is divided into four basic categories:
Fingering (baby clothes), **Sport** (light-weight sweaters and afghans), **Worsted** (sweaters, afghans, toys), and **Bulky** (heavy sweaters, potholders, and afghans).
Baby yarn may either be classified as Fingering or Sport - check the label for the recommended gauge.
These weights have absolutely nothing to do with the number of plies. Ply refers to the number of strands that have been twisted together to make the yarn. There are fingering weight yarns consisting of four plies - and there are bulky weight yarns made of a single ply.

SUBSTITUTING YARN

Once you know the **weight** of the yarn specified for a particular pattern, **any** brand of the **same** weight may be used for that pattern.
You may wish to purchase a single skein first, and crochet a gauge swatch. Compare the gauge (remember, it **must** match the gauge in the pattern) and then compare the way the new yarn looks to the photographed item to be sure that you'll be satisfied with the finished results.
How many skeins to buy depends on the **yardage**. Compare the labels and don't hesitate to ask the shop owner for assistance. Ounces and grams can vary from one brand of the same weight yarn to another, but the yardage required to make a garment or item, in the size and pattern you've chosen, will always remain the same provided gauge is met and maintained.

DYE LOTS

Yarn is dyed in "lots" and then numbered. Different lots of the same color will vary slightly in shade and will be noticeable if crocheted in the same piece.
When buying yarn, it is important to check labels for the dye lot number. You should purchase enough of one color, from the same lot, to finish the entire project. It is a good practice to purchase an extra skein to be sure that you have enough to complete your project.

HOOKS

Crochet hooks used for working with **yarn** are made from aluminum, plastic, bone, or wood. They are lettered in sizes ranging from size B (2.25 mm) to the largest size Q (15.00 mm) - **the higher the letter, the larger the hook size.**
Crochet hooks used for **thread** work are most commonly made of steel. They are numbered in sizes ranging from size 00 (3.50 mm) to a very small size 14 (.75 mm) and, unlike aluminum hooks, **the higher the number, the smaller the hook size.**

HOW TO DETERMINE THE RIGHT SIDE

Many designs are made with the **front** of the stitch as the **right** side. Two of the designs for the Versatile Veggies, page 22, are made with the **back** of the stitch as the **right** side. Notice that the **front** of the stitches are smooth *(Fig. 19a)* and the **back** of the stitches are bumpy *(Fig. 19b)*. The **back** or bumpy side of the stitches will be outside and the **right** side of your piece. For easy identification, it may be helpful to place a marker. When working in rounds this means that you will be working with the bulk of the piece in front of the hook.

Fig. 19a

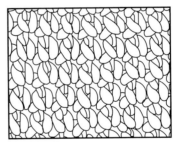

Fig. 19b

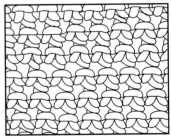

JOINING WITH SC

When instructed to join with sc, begin with a slip knot on hook. Insert hook in stitch or space indicated, YO and pull up a loop, yarn over and draw through both loops on hook.

MARKERS

Markers are used to help distinguish the beginning of each round being worked. Place a 2" scrap piece of yarn or fabric before the first stitch of each round, moving marker after each round is complete. Remove when no longer needed.

BACK OR FRONT LOOP ONLY

Work only in loop(s) indicated by arrow *(Fig. 20)*.

Fig. 20

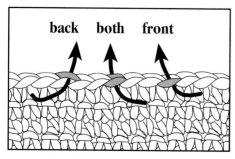

FREE LOOP

After working in Back or Front Loops Only on a row or round, there will be a ridge of unused loops. These are called the free loops. Later, when instructed to work in the free loops of the same row or round, work in these loops *(Fig. 21a)*. When instructed to work in a free loop of a beginning chain, work in loop indicated by arrow *(Fig. 21b)*.

Fig. 21a   **Fig. 21b**

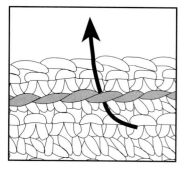
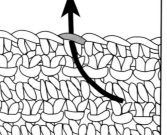

CHANGING COLORS

Work the last stitch to within one step of completion, hook new yarn *(Fig. 22a)* and draw through loops on hook. Cut old yarn and work over both ends unless otherwise specified. When working in rounds, join with slip stitch to first stitch changing to color indicated *(Fig. 22b)*.

Fig. 22a

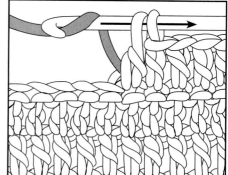

Fig. 22b

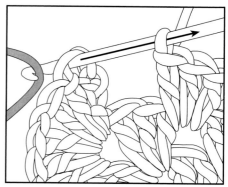

WORKING OVER WIRE

Place wire against round or row indicated. Work sts indicated over wire *(Fig. 23)*.

Fig. 23

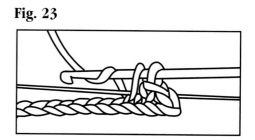

PREPARING FABRIC STRIPS

Fabric selected should be high quality, even weave 100% cotton, such as those sold for piecing quilts. Yardages given are based on fabrics 44/45" wide.

If the fabric is not pre-shrunk, it should be gently machine washed and dried. Straighten your fabric by pulling it across the bias. It may be necessary to lightly press the fabric.

To avoid joining strips often, we recommend that your strips be two yards or longer.

TEARING STRIPS

Tear off selvages, then tear into 1½" strips.

CUTTING STRIPS

1. Fold the fabric in half, short end to short end, as many times as possible, while still being able to cut through all thicknesses *(Fig. 24a)*.

Fig. 24a

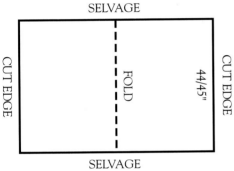

2. Cut fabric into 1" wide strips *(Fig. 24b)*. For quick results, a rotary cutter and mat may be used to cut several layers of fabric at one time.

Fig. 24b

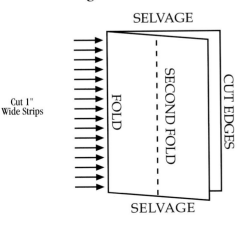

JOINING FABRIC STRIPS

The following is a technique for joining fabric strips without sewing strips together, and eliminates knots or ends to weave in later.

1. To join a new strip of fabric to working strip, cut a ½" slit, about ½" from ends of both fabric strips *(Fig. 25a)*.

Fig. 25a

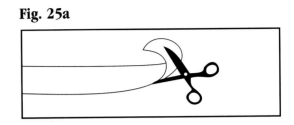

2. With **right** sides up, place end of new strip over end of working strip and match slits *(Fig. 25b)*.

Fig. 25b

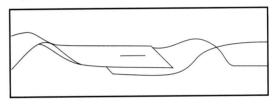

3. Pull free end of new strip through both slits from bottom to top *(Fig. 25c)*.

Fig. 25c

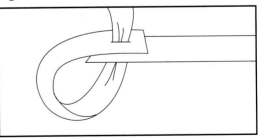

4. Pull new strip firmly to form a small knot *(Fig. 25d)*. Right sides of both strips should be facing up. Continue working with new strip.

Fig. 25d

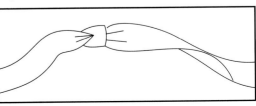

finishing

MAKING PILLOW FORM

Using crocheted piece for pattern, cut two pieces of fabric, allowing ¼" for seam allowance.

With **right** sides together, sew seam leaving a 2" opening for turning.

Clip corners; turn right side out.

Stuff firmly and sew opening closed.

WASHING AND BLOCKING

For a more professional look, thread projects should be washed and blocked. Using a mild detergent and warm water and being careful not to rub, twist, or wring, gently squeeze suds through the piece. Rinse several times in cool, clear water. Roll piece in a clean terry towel and gently press out the excess moisture. Lay piece on a flat surface and shape to proper size; where needed, pin in place using stainless steel pins. Allow to dry **completely**.

TASSEL

Cut a piece of cardboard 3" wide by the desired length of finished tassel. Wind a double strand of yarn around the cardboard approximately 20 times. Cut an 18" length of yarn and insert it under all of the strands at the top of the cardboard; pull up **tightly** and tie securely. Leave the yarn ends long enough to attach the tassel. Cut the yarn at the opposite end of the cardboard *(Fig. 26a)* and then remove it. Cut a 6" length of yarn and wrap it **tightly** around the tassel twice, ½" below the top *(Fig. 26b)*; tie securely. Trim the ends.

Fig. 26a

Fig. 26b

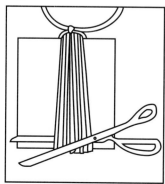

WHIPSTITCH

With **wrong** sides together, and beginning in corner stitch, sew through both pieces once to secure the beginning of the seam, leaving an ample yarn end to weave in later. Insert needle from **front** to **back** through both loops of **each** piece *(Fig. 27a)* or through inside loops *(Fig. 27b)*. Bring needle around and insert it from **front** to **back** through the next loops of **both** pieces. Continue in this manner across to corner, keeping the sewing yarn fairly loose.

Fig. 27a

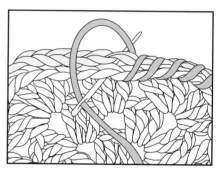

Fig. 27b

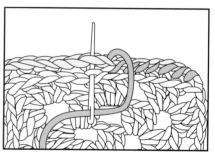

FRINGE

Cut a piece of cardboard 3" wide by ¹/₂" longer than the desired length of finished fringe. Wind the yarn **loosely** and **evenly** around the cardboard until the card is filled, then cut across one end; repeat as needed. Hold together half as many strands of yarn as needed for the finished fringe; fold in half. With **wrong** side facing and using a crochet hook, draw the folded end up through a row or stitch and pull the loose ends through the folded end *(Fig. 28a)*; draw the knot up **tightly** *(Fig. 28b)*. Repeat, spacing as desired. Lay flat on a hard surface and trim the ends.

Fig. 28a

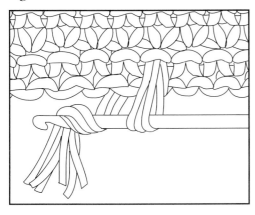

Fig. 28b

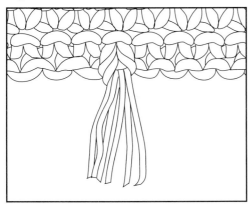

CROSS STITCH

The embroidery is worked by following the charts, page 69. Each square on the chart represents one complete cross stitch. Cross stitches are worked over the upright bar of the Afghan Stitch *(Fig. 29)*. If you find it difficult to see where to work the cross stitches, hold the Block at each side and pull slightly. Evenly spaced holes will be apparent on each side of the upright bars.

Fig. 29

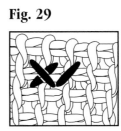

Thread a yarn needle with an 18" strand of yarn. Hold Block with **right** side facing and marked edge at top. Count to find the bar where you wish to begin. Bring needle up from back of Block through first hole, leaving a 3" end on back. Work over this end to secure. Bring needle down through hole diagonally across, pulling yarn flat against Block, but not so tight as to cause a pucker. You have now made one half of a cross stitch. You can either complete the stitch now, or work across an area in half crosses and then work back, crossing them as you go. Just be sure that the top half of every cross stitch is worked in the same direction.

Finish off by weaving end of yarn under several stitches; cut close to work.

141

BACKSTITCH

Working from right to left, come up at 1, go down at 2 and come up at 3 *(Fig. 30a)*. The second stitch is made by going down at 1 and coming up at 4 *(Fig. 30b)*. Continue in same manner.

Fig. 30a

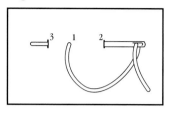

Fig. 30b

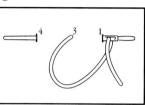

FRENCH KNOT

Bring needle up at 1. Wrap yarn desired number of times around needle and insert needle at 2, holding end of yarn with non-stitching fingers *(Fig. 31)*. Tighten knot; then pull needle through, holding yarn until it must be released.

Fig. 31

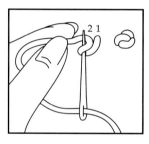

LAZY DAISY STITCH

Make all loops equal in length. Come up at 1 and make a counterclockwise loop with the yarn. Go down at 1 and come up at 2, keeping the yarn below the point of the needle *(Fig. 32)*. Secure loop by bringing thread over loop and down at 3. Repeat for the desired number of petals or leaves.

Fig. 32

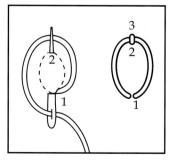

STARCHING & BLOCKING

TIPS

1. If using the same fabric stiffener for both white and colored items, starch the white items first, in case thread dye should bleed into the solution.
2. A good blocking board can make pinning easier. You can use heavy cardboard, an ironing board, ceiling board, etc.
3. Stainless steel pins with balls on the end will be easier to use and will help keep fingers from hurting. Fabric stiffener will permanently damage pins used for sewing. These can be set aside for all starching projects.
4. Fabric stiffener can be returned to the bottle after starching if it has not been contaminated with particles and dye. Clip one corner of the bag, then squeeze the bag, forcing the solution to flow into the bottle.
5. An acrylic spray can be used after starching to protect the piece from heat and humidity.

STARCHING

Each item requires a stiffening process to achieve the desired effect. Read the following instructions before beginning.

1. Wash item using a mild detergent and warm water. Rinse thoroughly. Roll each piece in a clean terry towel and gently press out the excess moisture. Lay piece flat and allow to dry **completely**.
2. Pour fabric stiffener in a resealable plastic bag. Do not dilute stiffener. ***Note:*** This method is permanent and will not wash out.
3. Immerse dry piece in fabric stiffener, remove air, and seal the bag. Work solution thoroughly into each piece. Let soak for several hours or overnight.

BLOCKING

Good blocking techniques make a big difference in the quality of the finished piece. When pinning piece be careful not to split the threads when inserting pins between the stitches. Make sure curved parts are smooth, straight parts are straight and symmetrical components are equal. It is often necessary to pin spaces and picots open, and use pins to create curves, points, and angles. Use photo as a guide and use a generous quantity of pins to hold all of the components in place until dry.

Refer to further instructions on page 143 for specific projects.

ANGEL WINGS

1. The blocking pattern given is designed to make accurate blocking easier. Trace the blocking pattern, page 142. Place pattern on blocking board and cover with plastic wrap.
2. Remove Wings from solution and squeeze gently to remove as much excess stiffener as possible. Blot with a paper towel several times to remove excess from holes.
3. With **right** side facing, spread Wing over the blocking pattern and pin at regular intervals.
4. Allow to dry **completely**.

SNOW CRYSTAL

1. The blocking pattern given is designed to make accurate blocking easier. Trace the blocking pattern as many times as necessary to obtain 2 patterns for each Crystal that you will be blocking at one time.
2. Make a triangular form by taping two pieces of 5" x 14" heavy cardboard together along one long edge, then pinning it to blocking board.
   For each Crystal, fold 2 of the blocking patterns along the dotted lines and place on triangular form. Cover all with plastic wrap.
3. Remove Crystals from solution and squeeze gently to remove as much excess stiffener as possible. Blot with a paper towel several times to remove excess from holes.

4. With **wrong** side facing, spread a Crystal over a blocking pattern and pin the tip of each main spoke to the long lines. Use the short lines to align components between the main spokes.
5. Allow to dry **completely**.
6. Glue both pieces together along fold. Allow to dry.

BELL

1. Remove Bell from solution and squeeze gently to remove as much excess stiffener as possible. Blot with a paper towel several times to remove excess from holes.
2. Lightly stuff Bell with plastic wrap and shape as desired, pinning the bottom edge to blocking board covered with plastic wrap.
3. Allow to dry **completely**.

POTPOURRI HOLDERS

1. Remove Holder from solution and squeeze gently to remove as much excess stiffener as possible. Blot with a paper towel several times to remove excess from holes.
2. Place Holder over an object, covered with plastic wrap, that is the same size and shape desired when finished. Pin at regular intervals, shaping as desired.
3. Allow to dry **completely**.

143

credits

We extend a warm *thank you* to the generous people who allowed us to photograph our projects at their homes:

- *The Living Room*: Shirley Held
- *For the Bath* and *For the Bedroom*: Dr. Dan and Sandra Cook
- *Wrapped Up in Afghans, Granny Square Sweater, Lacy Pearl Collar,* and *Fun Farm Vest*: Nancy Gunn Porter
- *Rag Rabbit, Stars and Stripes Afghan,* and *Sweetheart Pillow*: Carol and Frank Clawson

To Magna IV Color Imaging of Little Rock, Arkansas, we say thank you for the superb color reproduction and excellent pre-press preparation. We want to especially thank photographers Larry Pennington, Ken West, and Mark Mathews of Peerless Photography, Little Rock, Arkansas, and Jerry R. Davis of Jerry Davis Photography, Little Rock, Arkansas, for their time, patience, and excellent work.

A special word of thanks goes to the talented designers who created the lovely projects in this book:

Joan Beebe: *Red-Hot Pot Holder*, page 23; *Ice Cream Button Covers*, page 54; *Cheery Plant Pokes*, page 72; and *Sweetheart Pillow*, page 108

Carla Bentley: *TV Pillows*, page 60

Sherry Berry: *Guardian Angel*, page 80

Nancy Fuller: *Pumpkin Patch*, page 117

Sue Galucki: *Heirloom Rose Pillow*, page 14

Shobha Govindan: *Classic Diamonds*, page 32, and *Pretty Coasters*, page 58

Sarah J. Green: *Housewarming Set*, page 56

Cathy Hardy: *Beribboned Tissue Box Cover*, page 18; *Dolly Draft Dodger*, page 63; *Thirsty Baby Bibs*, page 78; and *Frilly Photo Ring*, page 83

Jan Hatfield: *Cozy Mile-A-Minute*, page 36

Sara Jenny: *Dainty Lampshade Cover,* page 8

Carol Jensen: *Soft Layette Set*, page 88

Terry Kimbrough: *Lacy Throw Rug*, page 15; *Elegant Towel Set*, page 18; *Soft Rag Rug and Wastebasket Cover*, page 19; *Apple Pillow*, page 44; *Bath Basket*, page 46; *Heartwarming Wrap*, page 76; *Lacy Little Afghan*, page 84; *Cuddle Bunny*, page 86; and *Sophisticated Ruffle*, page 98

Ann Kirtley: *Victorian Elegance*, page 38, and *Lacy Pearl Collar*, page 96

Jennine Korejko: *Charming Valance Edging*, page 23; *Log Cabin Comfort*, page 40; *Floral Sachets*, page 52; and *Silver Bells,* page 130

Tammy Kreimeyer: *Rag Rabbit*, page 111

Cynthia Lark: *Granny's Dogwood*, page 34

Jean Leffler: *Fun Farm Vest*, page 102, and *Cozy Mittens*, page 106

Linda Luder: *Simple Potpourri Holders*, page 13, and *Stars and Stripes Afghan*, page 113

Helen Milton: *Snow Crystal*, page 125

Sue Penrod: *Versatile Veggies*, page 22

Carolyn Pfeifer: *Jolly Snowman*, page 127

Lois Phillips: *Festive Towel Trim*, page 126

Sarah Anne Phillips: *Dresden Plate Favorite*, page 30

Carole Prior: *Slant Stitch Afghan*, page 26; *Long Stitch Afghan*, page 28; and *Rainbow Soft*, page 28

Mary Jane Protus: *Granny Square Sweater*, page 94

Delsie Rhoades: *Blooming Tea Set*, page 74, and *Frosty Beaded Garland*, page 129

Katherine Satterfield Robert: *Vibrant Vest*, page 100

Evie Rosen: *Doggie Wear*, page 70

Teri Sargent: *Tricksie the Witch*, page 118

C. Strohmeyer: *Delicate Dresser Scarf*, page 12

Lorraine White: *Ring Bearer's Pillow*, page 48, and *Lovely Table Runner*, page 123

Emma Willey: *Floral Doily Set*, page 8

We extend a sincere *thank you* to the people who assisted in making and testing the projects for this book: Janet Akins, Anitta Armstrong, Connie Balough, Pam Bland, JoAnn Bowling, Nair Carswell, Judy Crowder, MellaDeane Evans, Patricia Funk, Linda Graves, Raymelle Greening, Jean Hall, Kathleen Hardy, Lisa Hightower, Tammy Kreimeyer, Pat Little, Carol McElroy, Kay Meadors, Dale Potter, Emma Richardson, Hilda Rivero, Rondi Rowell, Donna Soellner, Faith Stewart, Bill Tanner, Carol Thompson, Leanne Tribett, and Sherry Williams.